HAMILTON A. TYLER

Illustrated by Lawrence Ormsby

PUEBLO BIRDS AND MYTHS

Northland Publishing

First softcover edition

ISBN 0-87358-519-4
Library of Congress Catalog Card Number   90-53588

Cataloging in Publication Data

Tyler, Hamilton A.
    Pueblo birds and myths.
    Bibliography
    Includes index.
    1. Pueblo Indians—Religion and mythology.   2. Indians of North America—
Southwest, New—Religion and mythology.   3. Folk-lore of birds.   4. Birds—
Southwest, New.   I. Title.   II. Series.
E99.P9T893   299'.7   90-53588
ISBN 0-87358-519-4

Designed by Carole Thickstun
Typography by Andresen Typographics
Manufactured in Hong Kong by Wing King Tong

CONTENTS

*great
horned owl*

Dedicated to the Memory of My Father

JOHN GRIPPER TYLER

Ornithologist
1883–1969

Florence Martin Bailey, in *Birds of New Mexico*, quotes under the blue grosbeak:

In California, where Mr. Tyler found the California Blue Grosbeak, he says that "while tramping around in the late spring among the rank weeds and grass along the ditches or at the edge of tule ponds, a bird lover in the San Joaquin Valley is often attracted by a sudden explosive spink *from a large-billed, blue-coated bird, and very often this call is answered in a more subdued* pink *by a brown-colored bird, otherwise quite similar in appearance to her mate.*

He was always a careful observer and a good listener.

PREFACE

Pueblo Indian thinking has a style of its own, which is usually just as recognizable as a style of house or of village architecture. These styles seem to carry across the linguistic distinctions that divide the Pueblos into the Hopis, Zuñis, Keres, Tewas, Tiwas, and Towas. Such a diversity of tongues indicates at the very least a variety of separate influences that have been drawn together in the common Pueblo culture, while it may point to differences in origin as well. When their pantheon was examined in *Pueblo Gods and Myths,* the gods were found to express this diversity, and it was only the style of relating to these divinities that showed a common religion.

When we turn from the gods to another aspect of the surrounding world—that of the role of animals, birds, snakes, and lesser creatures—the common style of Pueblo thinking draws closer together. In a second book, *Pueblo Animals and Myths,* the integration of major animals within Pueblo life was explored. Although the subject is too complex for simple formulas, it was evident that these animals provide a basic frame of reference in Pueblo ceremonialism. Birds, in contradistinction to animals, have an advantage for use as simpler signs, because even individual feathers can stand for the bird or for the thought to be expressed.

The Pueblos have been watching their birds for centuries and during that time have incorporated these creatures into every aspect of community life. Even such mundane tasks as building a room or planting a field require the presentation of feathers from particular

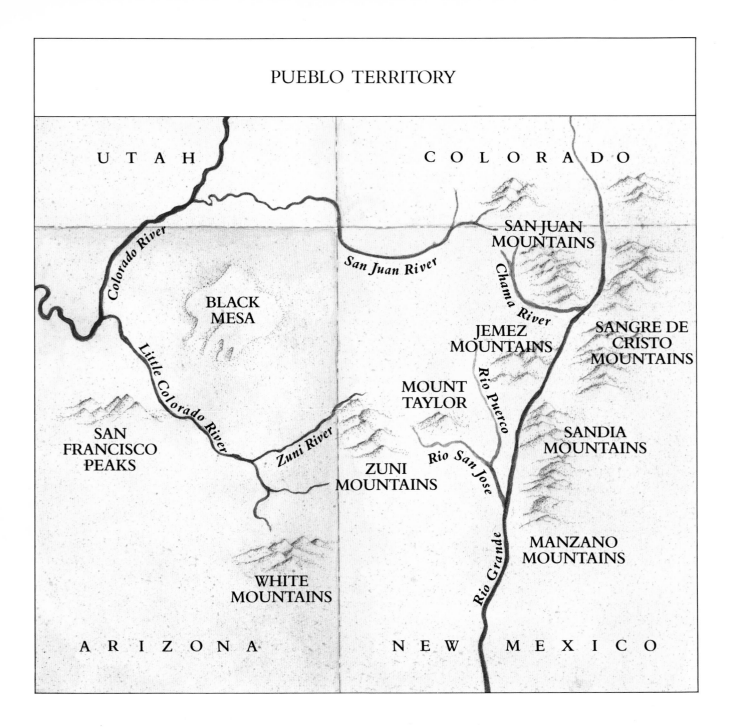

PUEBLO TERRITORY

U T A H

C O L O R A D O

Colorado River

SAN JUAN
MOUNTAINS

San Juan River

Chama River

BLACK
MESA

JEMEZ
MOUNTAINS

SANGRE DE
CRISTO
MOUNTAINS

Little Colorado River

MOUNT
TAYLOR

Rio Puerco

SAN
FRANCISCO
PEAKS

Zuni River

SANDIA
MOUNTAINS

ZUNI
MOUNTAINS

Rio San Jose

Rio Grande

MANZANO
MOUNTAINS

WHITE
MOUNTAINS

A R I Z O N A

N E W   M E X I C O

birds, while in the rituals that support religious ceremonialism birds and their feathers become counters that keep a complex symbol system in order. As signs, birds relate to gods, act as messengers between men and gods, or stand as signals between man and man. As a part of the surrounding world, birds relate to all manner of natural phenomena and to weather control.

When preparations were made for this book the native names, in various languages, for over 200 species of birds were uncovered, which is to say the names of a good percentage of the species present in the Southwest or Pueblo area. Out of this vast array of birds it seems that perhaps 100 kinds have an essential place in Pueblo ritual, ceremony, myth, or folklore, and it is the roles of these that this book will follow. With so many kinds to be distinguished, one from the other, and with exactness often a requirement, some kind of system for separating and relating different birds is a necessity. In our scientific system we relate birds to an objective order that represents the evolutionary steps from loons to finches. When the details for this volume were first gathered, they followed that order out of long habit. But that, of course, made no sense at all of the Pueblo material, which stems from a different premise.

To keep the symbols in order, Pueblo ornithology must study and relate the birds themselves, but the system is not primarily designed to make sense of an outer world, because the natural world is assumed to *be* the sense. The order and perfection of nature may therefore be drawn into less stable society, where it will impart meaning to transitory human affairs. In this light the information gathered was allowed to settle, birdlike, wherever it would, and habitat groups began to appear. These habitat groups seemed to be central themes tying varied kinds of birds together; these now form centers that become the separate chapters that follow. Whereas each theme would be recognized by a Pueblo reader, there is no implication that these Indians had a conscious system resembling the sequence of chapters in this book. The arrangement is simply what was seen while bird watching over the Pueblo's shoulder, so to speak, and quite different arrangements of the same material would no doubt be possible.

Beyond the complexities and symbols there is a simpler Pueblo view that shines out at every turn as a pervading feeling of reverence for all wildlife. Birds have many roles, but often they are simply spokesmen within a quiet cosmos, their voices an expression of processes that flow around mankind. A song from the pueblo of Acoma sets the notes of a swallow, as it flies along a stream, to native words:

> *Beni chi, beni chi, beni nu tsoutr,*
> Western river, western river, coming from the west,
> *So ya ta.*
> I sing of you.
> *Beni chi, beni chi, beni nu tsoutr,*
> Western river, western river, coming from the west,
> *So ya ta.*
> I sing of you.
> *Wa wi, wa wi, ha ha, ha ha!*

In the blending of bird notes with human voices there is always a harmony that all men can share.

Hamilton Tyler

Healdsburg, California

ACKNOWLEDGMENTS

I am greatly indebted to Timothy Pember of Rodmell, England, who gave his time to a careful reading of the entire manuscript. As always, my wife Mary offered her skills in English usage and, even more importantly, showed the constant faith in my projects, without which writing would be a task rather than the joy it is.

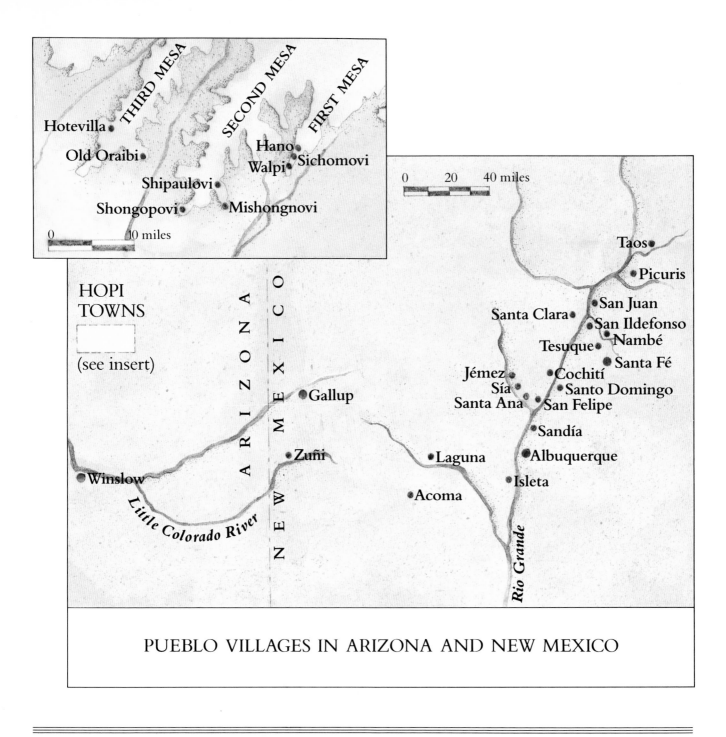

THIRD MESA

SECOND MESA

FIRST MESA

Hotevilla

Old Oraibi

Hano
Walpi
Sichomovi

Shipaulovi

Shongopovi

Mishongnovi

0   10 miles

0   20   40 miles

HOPI
TOWNS

(see insert)

Taos

Picuris

San Juan

Santa Clara

San Ildefonso

Nambé

Tesuque

Santa Fé

A R I Z O N A

N E W   M E X I C O

Gallup

Jémez

Cochití

Sía

Santo Domingo

Santa Ana

San Felipe

Sandía

Zuñi

Laguna

Albuquerque

Winslow

Isleta

Little Colorado River

Acoma

Rio Grande

PUEBLO VILLAGES IN ARIZONA AND NEW MEXICO

I PUEBLO ORNITHOLOGY

Some constants in the use of feathers may be mentioned here lest they mar the stories of individual birds later on. Feathers are signs that can be used in various ways to create a supplementary language, one which in turn involves the mechanics of presentation. When the spirits are addressed, prayer-sticks mounted with feathers are "planted" in fields or elsewhere to carry these messages. Or again, detached feathers may be offered, in which case they are tied to strings of native cotton or placed around a wooden altar. Less frequently loose feathers are offered by placing them under stones or by casting them into streams and lakes.

If feathers are used on altars, they may be stuck into the tops of each pole or tied to a cord that runs from one to the other. Sometimes they are placed on the floor around the altar, often to indicate the six directions that surround this religious center. Another ceremonial device is the fetish, and important ones are entirely wrapped in a variety of feather-sets from specified birds. Kachina masks are also important in religious ceremonies; these masks bear indicative feathers, as do the "dolls," which are carved to stand for the kachina dancers. A dancer, who becomes a spirit by putting on the mask, may also wear other feathers in his hair and on various parts of his dress as visible signs, or even conceal some within his moccasins to convey secret meanings.

Bird feathers are signs to men, as well as messages to gods and abstract spirit forces. When other men are being notified, the feather worn may indicate what ceremony is taking place, what religious society an individual belongs to, or what office the wearer holds. In all of these instances of feathered signs there is an actual bird feather or entire birdskin used to carry the message.

If one is telling a myth or a story, the names of certain birds will be mentioned. In folktales it may be only a "just-so" reference, telling how the woodpecker got his head bloodied and the like. But more often there is a serious note; the bird's name will signal to the listener one or more ideas for which that bird stands. Many times ritual poetry is recited by Pueblo priests as part of a ceremony, and when a bird's name occurs in the poem it conveys an important meaning reference.

Birds have valuable magical properties that can be put to human use—they are the extended kin of mankind and thus share common desires with men, so their powers are encouraged. Birds are a part of nature, but they are also agents; hence the flight or just the appearance of certain birds may control the fall of rain or snow, and the seasons, the sunshine, and the heat. All of these matters that make up Pueblo ornithology will unfold, but first we outline some notes on the mechanics of feather presentation.

prayer-sticks   When Pueblo Indians make a general offering to the spirit world, it is by casting cornmeal to each direction. Cornmeal is a basic foodstuff and is shared to show a relationship with spirits who control the cosmos. At times corn pollen is added to the ground grain, and bits of shell or turquoise are mixed in. Shells relate to water, and turquoise is a sky-blue gem dug from the earth; so, when these are combined with meal and the pollen that fertilizes corn plants, all the essentials of life are brought together.

For specific offerings feathered prayer-sticks are the most important vehicle. Ladd, a Zuñi Indian and a serious student of birds, estimates that each member of his tribe offers at present between sixteen and eighty prayer-sticks a year, the number depending on the religious roles of the individual who offers them. To make these Zuñi offerings, feathers from seventy-two species of birds are needed.★ Most of the feathers used for this and other purposes are specified, not only the kind of bird but also the type of feather—whether primary wing, tail, downy breast, or whatever.

Because one obviously needs a varied group of feathers, it is convenient for most male Indians to keep an assortment on hand. In the old days these were rolled in a skin bundle, but in modern times they may be kept in containers such as cigar boxes. On a few occasions it is mandatory for the man making the offering actually to kill the bird and to bring in its feathers. However, in general it is necessary only to *have* the specific feather, so those from any bird, whether found or killed, are brought to the older priests. One will begin to see that, although birds are valued as parts of a symbol system, they must also be studied and related to keep the symbols in order.

There is variety of form in the sticks to which feathers are attached; seventeen basic types have been noted for the pueblo of Acoma alone. The most common kinds of sticks are made from peeled willow branches. They vary in size from those shorter than a finger to others that are measured from one's elbow to the fingertips. Most of the prayer-sticks are painted, while various notches and grooves are added to make them specific; then signifying feathers are bound on, or in some other way fixed to the stick.

Both sticks and feathers must first fit the occasion, then the spirits addressed, and finally the religious role of those who plant them. A layman may not offer the same set as a member of the society to whom the particular rite or ceremony belongs, nor may he copy those on sticks made by an officiating priest. Taboos in this respect can be very strict, but there are also feathers whose use is general. Those from the Mountain Turkey, for example, are thought of as "clothes" for the stick, so they appear on almost all, and anyone can tie them on.

★My debt to *Zuñi Ethno-ornithology,* from which this information derives, is greater than the number of references might indicate. This valuable study by Edmund J. Ladd was submitted as a master's thesis in anthropology to the University of New Mexico in 1963, and it was the first clear proof to me that the Pueblo Indians actually do have a systematized interest in and knowledge of southwestern birds.

Because prayer-sticks relate to gods and spirits, all of the attached feathers are thought of as "breath-feathers." Breath is the spirit part of any living thing, so it must hold the meanings and intentions that flow back and forth between men and spirits. Birds are like the breath in that they travel through the air and become media for these breath messages. The Sun god oversees the planting of each prayer-stick and counts every offering as it is set out.

There are two breath rites for prayer-sticks and fetishes: One consists in a breathing *on* the feathered stick, and another in breathing *from* it. A Hopi will breathe from his offering, because as a fetish it has a power of its own. He then offers the prayer-stick to the Sun, who will likewise breathe from it. A Zuñi, on the other hand, breathes *on* the feathers while making the stick to be offered, just as he breathes on prayer meal before casting it. The Mother goddess of the Keres breathed *on* the first feathered corn-ear fetish, which was to stand for her power, so that the Indians could then breathe *from* it to gain her health.

corn-mother fetishes

The Keresan name for this important fetish, which stands for the goddess Iyatiku, is *iarriko.* It is made by first selecting an ear of corn that is perfect right down to the tip; in the village of Cochiti it must be an ear of blue corn. Feathers are then affixed to the ear, the short inner ones being held on splints and the longer ones wrapped outside of these. The ear base is hollowed out and a "heart" of flint inserted; then the hole is closed with native cotton. Next, the entire fetish is based with a woven basket and a wooden bottom so that the object will stand upright when placed before altars or set out for ceremonies.

At Zuñi similar fetishes are called *mi'li,* and Table 1 lists the feathers used on this and on the Keresan fetishes from different villages. The *mi'li* is a personal fetish representing its owner, but it is made by a society father and is presented to a new member on his initiation. Instead of a flint heart, this one is filled with all kinds of seeds. When the owner dies, these seeds are planted in the fields worked by fellow townsmen.

Table 1

FEATHERS USED ON FETISHES

<u>Zuñi *mi'li*</u>
(from Stevenson, *Zuñi,* 420)
4 long macaw feathers
6 white *o'wa* (dove) plumes
6 Steller's Jay feathers
3 Military Macaw feathers
12 male duck shoulder feathers
6 dove wing feathers
15 duck underwing feathers
20 small red parrot feathers
3 fluffy eagle plumes ("representing the feather
   adornment on the head of the Corn Mother")
14 small male turkey neck feathers

<u>Keresan *iarriko*</u>
("mother of all the Indians")
Sia (from White, *Sia,* 307)
eagle feathers at top
wren feathers especially
magpie feathers
roadrunner feathers
turkey feathers
duck or mockingbird feathers
Taboo are owl, crow, blackbird, and flicker feathers.
   Sia (from Stevenson, "Sia," 40, Pl. IX)
eagle feathers
parrot feathers

<u>Acoma (fetish called *honaní* here)</u>
(from Stirling, *Origin Myth of Acoma,* 31–32)
eagle feathers
duck feathers
roadrunner feathers
magpie feathers
"nowadays just pretty feathers"

<u>Santa Ana</u>
(from White, *Santa Ana,* 339)
2 parrot tail feathers
mass fluffy eagle feathers

<u>Cochiti</u>
(from Lange, *Cochiti,* 247, 259)
"various feathers"

<u>Cochiti</u>
(from Dumarest, *Notes on Cochiti,* 155)
eagle down
parrot feathers
turkey feathers

<u>Hopi *tiponi*</u>
(from Stephen, "Hopi Tales," 62)
eagle feathers
turkey feathers
(from Stephen, *Hopi Journal,* 1305)
"all sacred feathers"

According to Stevenson the *mi'li* represents not a corn mother but A'wonawil'ona, a god who is the breath of life and life itself.[1] When the name of this spirit is translated, it seems to mean something like "lightning flash being." Lightning is a fertilizing force; where it strikes a field, flint points are found, so there is a curious reversal from the Keresan fetish. One represents a corn mother but has a heart of flint, while the Zuñi fetish represents a god of lightning and is filled with seeds. Either way the symbols are divided, the related concepts are the same.

At Zuñi each society makes its own special kind of *mi'li* and the feathers listed in Table 1 apply only to the Mystery Medicine order of the Little Fire society. It is likely that some of the feathers, perhaps those from eagles, macaws, and ducks, are basic to all, because they stand for Sky, Sun, and Water. The Hopis continue a similar cluster of thoughts in a fetish called a *tiponi.*

The *tiponi* differs from the fetishes just described in that it is not a personal fetish held by each member of the group. This object pertains only to a chief and also differs in that there may be no corn ear at the center. The concept is similar however as the center is composed of cornmeal and "all seeds." These are wrapped first in corn husks and then in a deerskin, while around the outside are tied "all sacred feathers." Unfortunately the source does not name specific birds. This *tiponi* is variously said to represent the "Mother of All," the "Mother of Animals," and "Mother of the Clan." If it is the last, eagle and turkey feathers are attached to the top.[2]

birds of the six directions

The Pueblos, as well as many Indians to the south of them, give an important place in rituals and ceremonies to the six directions. These represent an enclosing and comforting sphere in which one's own pueblo stands at the center. The horizon directions differ from those of whites in that the Pueblo Indians point to corners: to the northeast sunrise and northwest sunset of the longest day, and to the southeast and southwest rising and setting of the shortest day. Sometimes this rectangle is divided by midpoints on each side, which are more like the usual cardinal directions. The Zenith and

Table 2

DIRECTIONAL BIRDS

(and colors associated with each direction)

ZUÑI

(from Stevenson, "Ethnobotany," 89)

North—Yellow-breasted Chat—yellow
West—Steller's Jay—blue
South—macaw—red
East—Rufous-sided Towhee *(ka'tetasha)*—white
Zenith—Purple Martin—all colors
Nadir—Painted Bunting—Black

TEWA

(from Harrington, "Ethnogeography," 43)

North—eagle *(tse)*—blue
West—(?)
South—Red-tailed Hawk *(qwaempi)*—red or
   macaw *(tansi)*—white
East—(?)
Zenith—"corn bird" *(k'untsire)*—all colors
Nadir—"leaf bird" (?) *(katsire)*—black

KERES

Sia (from Stevenson, "Sia," 70)

North—Western Tanager—yellow
West—*shasto* (?)—blue green
South—cardinal—red
East—magpie—white
Zenith—eagle—light yellow
Nadir—roadrunner—black

Sia (from White, *Sia*, 112)

North—Western Tanager
West—cardinal
South—unidentified
East—magpie
Zenith—unidentified
Nadir—night bird, like poorwill but larger

HOPI

Soyal ceremony (from Dorsey and Voth,
Oraibi Soyal Ceremony, 28)

North—flycatchers or warblers—yellow
West—bluebird—blue
South—parrot—red
East—magpie—white
Zenith—Hepatic Tanager—black
Nadir—blackbird (Yellow-headed?)—multicolor

Powamu ceremony (from Voth,
Oraibi Powamu Ceremony, 134)

North—oriole—yellow
West—bluebird—blue
South—parrot—red
East—magpie—white
Zenith—Hepatic Tanager—black
Nadir—roadrunner—multicolor

Table 2 (continued)

Niman Kachina ceremony (from Stephen, *Hopi Journal,* 517)
Northwest—oriole—yellow
Southwest—Arctic Bluebird—blue
Southeast—parakeet or macaw—red
Northeast—magpie—white
Zenith—Yellow-winged (Yellow-headed?)
    Blackbird or crow—black
Nadir—all sacred birds—multicolor

Wuwuchim ceremomy (from Stephen, *Hopi Journal,* 220)
Northwest—Yellow-winged (Yellow-headed?)
    Blackbird or warbler—yellow
Southwest—Mountain Jay or bluebird—blue
Southeast—redshaft, flicker, or robin—red
Northeast—magpie—white
Zenith—crow—black
Nadir—whippoorwill or Rock Wren—multicolor

Skins on Agave altar (from Stephen, *Hopi Journal,* 962)
Northwest—warbler *(tawa mana)*—yellow
Southwest—jay and bluebird—blue
Southeast—flicker or robin—red
Northeast—magpie and whippoorwill—white
North (Zenith)—crow, blackbird—black
South (Nadir)—White-winged Bluebird,
    Lark Bunting (?)—multicolor

Skins on Flute altar (from Stephen, *Hopi Journal,* 770)
Northwest—"yellowbird"—yellow
Southwest—jay and bluebird—blue
Southeast—2 flickers—red
Northeast—2 magpies—white
North (Zenith)—Yellow-winged (Yellow-headed?)
    Blackbird—black
South (Nadir)—whippoorwill and Hepatic
    Tanager—multicolor

Nadir are next added, and it is assumed that at each corner stand mountains where favorable spirits rule. About these mountains clusters of symbols gather, much as do visible clouds.

Each mountain is governed by a weather spirit, sometimes with a consort, and there are warriors and seed bearers for each direction and a set of representative animals, trees, snakes, butterflies, and, more nebulously, colored cloud spirits. There are also sets of birds whose feathers indicate the directions; some of these are given in Table 2. Color is important here, and the birds are not as fixed as parallel groups of animals. North is always represented by Mountain Lion; but a number of birds with yellow feathers will do for that direction. The most constant bird is Magpie for East, as the flashes of white against the gloss black suggest dawn.

The Zenith and Nadir have a confusing way of alternating as the world turns upside down with the seasons. Basically the Below is black and the Above "all colors," but when seasons change, the reverse is true. So we may find a crow at the Zenith and "all sacred birds," a multi-color, at the Nadir. There would be many more sets than those listed in the table if information on this subject had been studied carefully for the numerous ceremonies of each Pueblo group.

how Pueblos classify birds

It is unlikely that the Pueblos had a conscious aim of classifying birds in any way, since their interest in them was largely for the use of their feathers in a system of religious symbols. Still, it is easier to remember details of a system if the parts can somehow be related to one another. When the material for this book was literally re-sorted in a search for the Indian order, each bird was removed from its scientific niche. The birds then seemed to fall naturally into a number of groups and subgroups, each with a central theme and its divisions. These might be thought of as something like a taxonomic arrangement, but the whole plan is flexible, because most themes are interlaced.

For convenience the major themes can be grouped under either Nature or Culture. The themes from nature seem to be: Sun, Sky, Earth, Rain, Water, Day and Night, and the Seasons that tie all of these together. Themes relating to culture are: Speech, Hunting and War, Agriculture, Household Arts, Puberty and Death, Curing, and Purification. There is never a strict separation between themes of nature and culture. The woodpecker, for example, is tightly bound to the theme of war because of his persistent drumming. But the same drumming is also suggestive of thunder, which brings rain, so one is back again under the tent of the sky and its seasons.

One theme may gather up other themes, as the sky may include everything within its sphere, whether seasons, sun, days and nights, or storms with thunder and lightning bringing rains or snow. Nevertheless, most birds seem to relate principally to one of the major themes and secondarily to others. Distinctions have a logic based in myth. Rain and water may be joined, but they are not the same thing. Some water wells up from underground sources that are controlled by the Horned Water Serpent. These waters bubble out in springs or flow in streams to join lakes, which are sacred entrances into the underworld, or they may flow away in rivers that will carry one into another world.

The earth is a great receptacle containing all themes. It is the plane on which lightning strikes, rain falls, and the sun shines down in his various seasons. This earth is beneath a transparent crystal dome of sky and on its surface man lives, cultivates, hunts, weaves, builds, at times makes war, but more often performs his ceremonial dances. The Mountain Turkey represents both the earth to which it is bound and the dead who begin a new life beneath it, or above when they pass across the sky as clouds, sometimes bringing rain.

broad-tailed hummingbird

From the sky, eagles survey the entire world, so these birds or their abstractions become Beast gods of the Zenith. Eagles are the only birds elevated to a place among other deities, but other birds are the forms gods take when traveling, so the point is not always distinct. Between eagles soaring within the sky's dome and the earthly turkeys, there are all of the other feathered kinds that fly close to man. Some are related specifically to the sun, while others speak to the sun's seasons.

Hummingbirds have rainbow hues and suck nectar from flowers. Nectar is a quintessential liquid representing all the moist forces in growth and life. Macaws or parrots likewise exemplify the wedding of sun and rain, because they are multihued. Indian corn is not all yellow but grows in many colors that are sometimes mixed on a single ear. So these birds are associated with both the sun and the basic grain. In myths these themes are repeated in stories of the fleeing Corn Maidens.

Colorless doves signify the waterholes or springs to which they must return at dusk to drink. Their voice is an invocation to such water and an indication to men of where it may be found. The thirst of doves derives from a diet of seeds, which are the products of grasses or flowers; these in turn need rain to bring them into bloom and then to a seedbearing stage. Hence the voices of doves can become something of a rain song.

Migratory songbirds with their bright colors bring the summer. Many of these species are marked with yellow, which links them both to the sun and to the yellow flowers of summer. Against this bright picture there is also a dark one. Crows and ravens arrive with the black rain clouds of summer, but they also tend to thievery and may bring disaster. Rain as well as corn can be stolen, bringing drought, sickness, and evil.

Owls, too, are ambiguous; they may on the one hand drive away the little birds of summer, causing drought, or they may announce the onset of summer heat and storms that combine to produce good crops. Owl is also an omen bringer who speaks to chiefs—about war—but Owl is neutral, like the night favoring neither side.

Perhaps these first glimpses will give some idea of the themes that are woven into the Pueblo stories of their birds. How they are interwoven, changed with constant reweaving and new working, will be the story of this book. For this journey we are called up, first of all, toward the bright Sun.

2 BIRDS OF THE SUN
macaws, parrots, and parakeets

There is never a single theme for any bird, but macaws and their relatives are first of all for the Sun. As an undertone they come close to the rain birds, because they are found in close conjunction with a rain god and with Cloud Boys; they are also pets of Cloud. The distinction between sun and rain birds can be seen if members of the parrot family are set against the brightly colored hummingbirds, which are likewise associated with the rainbow. Macaws and others are similarly arrayed in bright hues, reminding Pueblos of the rain signs that appear in the sky. But in this case the clouds have parted to reveal the visible sun as the source behind a rainbow.

The multicolored plumage of macaws is also directly related to the many colors found on ears of Indian corn, represented by the Corn Maidens, who are brought back to the Pueblo world each summer. Then the sun reigns supreme from germination time until harvest, but with the approach of winter he returns to his home in the far southland. Macaws, parrots, and parakeets are birds which belong to the distant south but have been brought to the northland and are thus fellow travelers with the sun.

Because the ultimate importance of the sun lies in governing the corn cycle, it is not surprising that macaw/parrot feathers, as his symbol, crown the Corn Mother fetishes and also the Keresan poles or dance standards that represent Sun Youth. Summer, the Sun's product, is a time for salt-gathering expeditions, which also become rain-making ceremonies. The drying, and hence salt-producing, effect of the sun shining on small lakes links bird and sun and salt together. These birds represent the apex of a cycle that includes the bright sun and his rays, which are refracted through a shower of rain that falls to earth through a colored bow, and then the same sun draws the moisture skyward again through maturing corn plants.

Macaws, parrots, and parakeets are all exotic birds; none was found in the Pueblo area, although the Thick-billed Parrot touched southern Arizona and New Mexico. Nevertheless, there is abundant archaeological evidence that imported macaws and parrots were kept in the villages from at least 1100 A.D., possibly earlier, which indicates that their feathers were as important then as in modern ceremonialism where they rank with those from eagles and turkeys. Feathers from the parrot family are used on masks, on fetishes, on prayer-stick offerings; they are worn in the hair. With this great need, not all of the feathers could come from caged birds; loose feathers were also imported from the south. A detached feather is hard to attribute to a particular bird, so we will take note of the species known to be used and of two others that may have been used by the Pueblos.

First of all, there are two highly conspicuous macaws; both are large bodied and have very long, slender tails. The Military Macaw, which has a bright red forehead, lores, and tail base, has wing coverts of purplish blue and tail coverts of cerulean blue. It occupies the arid and semiarid parts of Mexico, including the border states of Sonora and Chihuahua. The Scarlet Macaw is a companion species inhabiting the humid lowlands of southern Mexico; its plumage is a dazzling array of red, scarlet, and crimson with wing feathers of chrome yellow and purplish blue. Quite naturally the Pueblos favored these brilliant macaws. Earlier archaeologists tabulated the bones of both species of macaws and the Thick-billed Parrot. But when Hargrave restudied all of these bones again for his 1970 publication, it turned out that of the 146 specimens from New Mexico and Arizona ruins, 101 belonged to the Scarlet Macaw, 44 were too fragmentary to determine, and only 1 was a Military Macaw.[1] That is clear evidence of a preference for the species with bright red feathers, which is consonant with the fact that red is the directional color for South, and that Scarlet Macaws, like the Sun, have a home in the far southland.

Unlike macaws, most Mexican parrots have short tails that are square or wedge-shaped and thus lack the magnificent tail plumes of their relatives. The Thick-billed Parrot is a bird of high pine forests, which once ranged as far north as the Verde Valley in Arizona. It does have a tail of moderate length, more like a macaw than a true parrot. However, the color of this smaller bird is a drab olive. Parakeets are like small macaws in shape, with predominantly green tail feathers. The English name "parakeet" appears in Hopi stories. Because there were three different native words indicating members of the parrot family, it is possible that one may indicate parakeets.[2] If so, both the Green and the Orange-fronted Parakeets are found not far south of the border in the wild and also where the people of Casas Grandes raised various members of the family for the feather trade.

Most Indian bird names are quite definite, but under the circumstances the macaw/parrot conjunction is not always clear, so a survey of Pueblo names may be of value. It is said that the Tewas greatly prize the feathers of a bird they call *tañi,* which is the same bird that the Mexicans call *guacamayo.*[3] Both macaws are called by this name, but it is especially for the Military Macaw, because that bird descends to the ground in May to eat poisonous *Ava* nuts. The same informants say that in former times both feathers and live birds were obtained from Mexico, and it is further said that the Tewas called parrots by borrowed names: *perico* or Polly. That linguistic distinction seems to indicate that the macaws were more important from ancient times.

The Keres were familiar with macaws; a caged one was kept at Santo Domingo in 1910, and in 1881 Bourke met a man from that town whose name was "Little Yellow Bird." "The Little Yellow Bird," he told me, "was the young Huacamayo Macaw."[4] Recently the Keresan name for "parrot" is given as *shawiti,* but no word for macaw is listed. That same *shawiti* turns up as a kiva name for a Zuñi child, who had a Mexican father, perhaps implying that the child, like the bird, came from the southland.[5] Probably there has been a recent tendency to make "parrot" an all-inclusive term, because at

Zuñi Ladd gives *mula* as the native word for both birds. In earlier days Hodge had listed *Mula* for the Macaw clan and *Pichi* for the Parrot clan, and the translation of *Mula* as macaw is also found in Stevenson. Yet a third name appears in a tale describing a "parrot dance," the word being *lapa,* "parrots."[6] The Isletan word for parrot, *te'ri,* sounds like it might be derived from the Spanish *perico.*[7]

At Hopi the distinctive names for the macaw and the parrot appear clearly enough, but they are complicated by the use of "parakeet" in translations. Edgar Mearns, in 1890, got the name *ke-ah-roo* for parrots, which corresponds with Stephen's *ka'ro* for the same bird.[8] After the turn of the century Voth notes the use of a red "karro" feather to indicate the south direction in the Soyal Sun ceremony.[9] A similar sounding word, *gya'zro,* is most often translated by Stephen as simply parakeet, for example, when he mentions that *gya'zro* is Cloud's pet, but sometimes he extends its meaning, as in describing a dancer who carried a tray on which was placed "a capital bright painted effigy of a macaw or parroquet."[10] On the other hand, when *gya'zro* is given as either a lineage of the Kachina clan or an alternate name for the clan, the word is translated as "parrot."[11] Colton lists a Parrot kachina with the alternative native names of "Gyarz or Kyaro or Kyash Kachina."[12] The last word, *Kyash,* names a Second Mesa clan, which Lowie translates as "parrot." But because he translates the name for Peregrine Falcon as "chicken hawk," not much weight can be given to the usage.[13]

Distance and exotic origin have troubled and perhaps mixed these names, but it was the same factor of their origin in distant lands far to the south that demanded a mythic explanation for their journey to the north. This the Hopis supplied in a story, the several versions of which center around two maidens who refuse to marry, despite the entreaties of numerous suitors. Sometimes they are Corn Maidens courted by Cloud Boys: "He went on a cloud. It was a yellow cloud, he was Yellow Cloud Boy." This suitor representing North is followed by Cloud Boys from the other five directions, but in each case their gift bundles are rejected. The identity of the final, successful suitor varies, but sometimes he is "Pavayoykashi, a rain deity in the far south," in which case he is tricked by Coyote.

Coyote determined to win the single maiden away from the rain deity whom she had agreed to marry, "So he traveled south to a country where it was warm and where there are parrots and macaws. He captured one of the macaws, returned and at once proceeded to the house of the maiden saying: 'I have brought something pretty for you.'" Having won her attention with the gift of a beautiful bird, Coyote furthers his plan by stealing the clothing of the rain god, which is also beautiful, resembling that of the Flute players and certain kachinas. Coyote carries with him a bow, and arrows in a lion-skin quiver, and in this guise he tricks the maid into marriage.

The god then tracks Coyote and locates his former prospective bride before returning in anger to his home, far to the south, but before long he comes back north again. "Pavayoykashi bided his time and one time brought a strong wind, some very heavy rain and thunder clouds, in which he was hidden, to the village. He took revenge on his enemy, the Coyote, by striking him dead with a ray of lightning."[14] The maiden then continued her life of "lewedness," which is a theme in all of these myths.

Another version makes the maidens twin daughters of a Walpi, First Mesa, chief, although the tale is told on Second Mesa, where there is a clan lineage called *kyash,* indicating the birds. These maidens also refuse ordinary bundles as marriage gifts. "We should like a parakeet. That is what we want. It is only this bird which we like. Perhaps someone will get it for us and bring it to us. Him we will marry." One of the suitors is the well-known outcast, Poker Boy, who represents the helpful qualities of his grandmother, Spider Woman, and he makes an attempt to satisfy the maidens' desire.

This youth is called Kotsho'ilapdio, meaning fire poker, explaining why he is always dirty and torn. But fire is also a relative of the Sun, and therefore this youth has power. In an attempt to locate the parakeets he calls on the aid of his grandmother. Spider Woman tells him that many have tried to get the birds but have failed, because they are in the east where the sun rises. Because the youth insists on trying, she instructs him to get up early in the morning to run until he comes with offerings to his uncle who lives beyond Rainbow Springs. "He started, going south to Rainbow spring, where his uncle lived." The uncle, not unexpectedly, turns out to be Rainbow, who accepts the offerings and promises his aid.

> *"I suppose you will get it [the parakeet]," the uncle said, "for you are going to your father, and he has a great many of them." "Who is my father?" asked Poker Boy. "Do you see that sun? That is your father. He is a rich man. He has a great many horses, everything of every sort, parrots and all kinds of birds."*

The uncle then gives him a simulacrum of a rainbow, which is cast with lightning speed across the sky in a big arc toward the east. Over this Poker Boy travels to the home of the sun, "far to the southeast." The "southeast" combines the daily journey of the Sun with his seasonal journey south.

"The Sun," it seems, "behaved like a man, after dark he went to lie down." Poker Boy has given everyone there offerings of prayer-sticks and is given a choice of birds that lived in the Sun's house, from which he took two female and one male parakeet. This version of the myth then takes a side trail to include Coyote as an unsuccessful suitor. He has seen the birds that Poker Boy is bringing back from the Sun, so he tries to create a parakeet by dressing up a rooster with painted yucca fibers. But this ruse does not fool the girls for long, and soon the successful youth presents his real offering. Incidentally, this bird has a yellow and green tail and is a "pretty little parakeet," so it is certainly not a macaw to the narrator, whatever it may have been in ancient versions of the story.

The girls

> *came down and saw the birds sitting there, nodding and turning their heads. Both ran to catch a bird, saying: "This is my bird! This is my bird!" Each grasped a bird and folded her arms about it. Poker Boy was between them, a girl on either side of him. . . . All stroked the parakeets from head to tail. "That is the kind we want," they said.*

Poker Boy's success fades rapidly, for although he was a good hunter he was considered poor and ashen by the other villagers. So these evil people suggested, "Let someone take Poker Boy's wives from him." First his younger wife and then both of them took to playing with other village boys, and soon the parakeets were not feeling well.

> *After a while her husband saw the man who was taking his wife and found out who he was. This was why the parakeet did not feel well. . . . The parakeet knew the man who came in at night and said to him: "Our mother has another man now. That is why we do not feel well. . . . Tomorrow morning, we will go away from here; we will go back home."*
>
> *Next day, the parakeet pulled out some of its feathers and gave them to Poker Boy, saying, "We are now going back home; keep these feathers and use them in any dance that you have."*

Poker Boy then sat on a roof, looking at his Sun Father.

> *Everyone was watching him. The parakeets were very restless; they could not sit still. All of them were flying about. This is something they are not wont to do. Everyone was asking: "What is the matter with those birds?" Just as the sun came up they flew away, rising straight up into the air. All of the people went after them but they were not able to take either one of them. "Now both birds have gone to the east, that is why they are no longer in my house,"* says Poker Boy.[15]

This story is subtitled "Why there are no parakeets in the Hopi country," but its import is much broader than that bit of naturalistic information. Although it is told like a folktale (the poor boy is really of high status; he succeeds where other suitors have failed), it is also a major myth with many ties to ceremonies. The shift is apparent in the conclusion that makes the heroines faithless wives, as they must be, because at base such myths tell of Sun Youth's courtship gift of parakeets, or other members of the parrot family, to the corn Maidens. Because of their seasonal nature, the Corn Maidens are fickle creatures who return to the Sun's land in the south, just as summer itself does. One will remember that, before the birds departed, they left some of their feathers with Poker Boy to be used as their representatives in the dances to symbolize the Sun and his fertilizing influence. Therefore, we should take note of specific dancers who wear such emblems and the ways in which certain ceremonies fit aspects of the myth.

According to Fewkes the First Mesa Winter Solstice ceremony has as its main feature,

> *a prayer to Muyinwu, the germ[ination] god, and in one of the kivas certain clans from the south dramatize the advent of the Sun god in the form of a bird. The public advent of this Sun or Sky god takes place on the following morning, when the bird personation is replaced by a masked man, called Ahulani. This Sun god is also called Soyal kachina. . . . He is accompanied by two maids, called Soyal manas, wearing masks resembling those of Anya katchina manas, who distribute seed corn to the women of the pueblo.[16]*

Parrot is joined with Eagle to represent the Sky. Fewkes has a description of the Kerwan kachina, which is only another name for Ahulani, in which we find that the top of his head is adorned with two eagle tail feathers and a cluster of parrot feathers, while at Oraibi one of the Soyal Manas, or Sun Maidens, is impersonated by a member of the Parrot *(Karro)* clan, along with two members of the Bear clan—because Parrot clansmen are said to have arrived at Hopi on the head of a bear.[17]

The Hopi Horned Water Serpent ceremony takes place in February–March with a performance that can be divided into acts. In the first of these, effigies of the snakes protruding from screens appear, and a miniature cornfield is constructed in which sprouted corn grains are set on clay pedestals. The second act is a public Buffalo dance, in which the Buffalo Maids have sun-shields on their backs and a crown of parrot feathers with eagle down in their hair. For a third act, Spider Woman distributes seeds of corn and other crops to the spectators, while a fourth act introduces two masked girls, the Anya kachinas, who grind corn on mealing stones, then dance carrying corn ears. There are two kinds of Anya kachinas, one called Tasaf Anya, of which the male dancer wears variegated parrot feathers on his head, which has a curved beak like a bird.[18]

A number of other kachinas, some of whom we will meet, wear parrot feathers, but those just given were selected to illustrate the close link between the Sun, parrots, and the Corn Maidens. Although these connections do not illustrate the myth, which will come later, they do show how often similiar sets of ideas come together in the ceremonies. In order to supply the dancers with macaw/parrot feathers for these and other ceremonies, it was necessary to find a continuous supply, hopefully related to those the mythical parakeet plucked and presented to Poker Boy.

In order to obtain these feathers a well-developed trade to the south was maintained to supplement those from captive, caged birds. Perhaps the most remarkable instance of keeping these caged birds in numbers was discovered during the excavation of Pueblo Bonito, in a Chaco Canyon site attributed to the middle of the twelfth century. Certainly a more inhospitable habitat for macaws would be hard to imagine. Pepper excavated room 38, whose unequal dimensions were about 12 by 30 feet, to find it filled with ceremonial objects. Then, when working carefully on the floor, a mass of bird droppings was found, which proved to be 10 inches thick across one end of the room; and partly embedded in these ancient droppings were the skeletons of twelve macaws, which Hargrave has determined to be Scarlet Macaws.

While excavating beneath the same floor two more skeletons were found, which had been carefully buried before the collapse and destruction of the aviary where the living birds were kept. Pepper assumes that this was a ceremonial room, or one in which ceremonial objects were stored, and that it pertained to a Macaw clan.[19] Other rooms in the same pueblo also yielded their share of macaw bones. In a later excavation Judd found eight articulated skeletons of the Scarlet Macaw, as well as loose macaw bones. Four of these birds were found in room 249, which was constructed as a special cage for the live macaws, with a vent shaft to let in the little light and air that they got, a lack that led to deformed breast bones on the birds. These had apparently been kept on a roost or shelf where they were fed piñon nuts, squash seeds, and roasted corn.[20]

Nor are these Chaco examples of prehistoric "parrot" raising isolated. At Wupatki, in the San Francisco Mountains region of Arizona, four Thick-billed Parrots, including a complete skeleton which may have had a ceremonial burial or may have been a favorite pet, as well as individual bones of Scarlet Macaws were found, dating from the period prior to 1250. In the same general area bones of four Scarlet Macaws were found at Winona ruin.[21] The trade by which these birds were obtained was very ancient, beginning in Basket Maker time or earlier, by routes that were well known. According to Judd, "we may assume that Mexican buyers of Pueblo turquoise and buffalo hides introduced parrot and macaw feathers as a medium of exchange somewhere around the middle of the eleventh century. To this dead plumage live birds were soon added."[22] Hargrave was able to demonstrate that all but four of the macaw remains found in these ruins belonged to birds below breeding age, indicating that none was raised above the border and that the macaws had to be replenished by trade. Nor did the macaws live long in northern captivity; only one specimen was of venerable age.

In the sixteenth century Cabeza de Vaca told of having seen many turquoises in the villages of the Rio Sonora that had been obtained in exchange for the skins and feathers of parrots that the Opatas used for barter. It has also been claimed that macaws and parrots were bred in captivity at Casas Grandes, in Chihuahua, Mexico, but this aviary may have served only as a way station for live birds from the far south.[23] Parsons indicates that trade and travel between the Zuñi and the Pima-Papago had existed for centuries, which is of interest, because the Pimas were known to have kept or raised macaws.[24] The Hopis also traded with the Sobaipuris until a fight, sometime before 1716, ended those exchanges. The interruption was probably not of long duration; Beaglehole points out a number of references to late eighteenth-century sources, which show that Hopi loom products were found among the Gila River and Lower Colorado River peoples, indicating that there was probably a reverse trade in shells and parrot feathers from Mexico and the Gulf of California.[25] At some point, however, the Apache cut off the pass on the Gila River and brought about the scarcity of macaw/parrot feathers so often mentioned in the nineteenth century.

How the Rio Grande Pueblos got their macaw feathers is less clear—whether by a secondary trade with the Zuñi or directly from Mexico. In any case, Espejo's party found live "parrots" among the Keres in the sixteenth century.[26] Bandelier noted in his journal, for November 26, 1882, that at Cochiti, "it is interesting, how eager they are here for *plumas de guacamayo* [macaw feathers]. They insist . . . *que hacen mucha falta aqui* [that they are much needed here]."[27] In his commentary on trading, Lange notes that the Cochitis went as far as Sonora to trade for horses, so possibly they brought back feathers as well. By this time macaw feathers were indeed difficult to come by, as we see in a statement by Stevenson on the Sia sacred fetish.

> *The ya'ya are most carefully preserved, not only on account of their sacred value, but also because of their intrinsic worth, as the parrot plumes of which they are partially composed are very costly and difficult to obtain, they being procured from other Indians, who either make the journey into Mexico and trade for these plumes with Indians of that country, or the Indians on the border secure them and bring them for traffic among their more northern brothers.[28]*

Such trips to the southland in search of macaw feathers are raised to a mythical level in a story told in the Tewa pueblo of San Juan, slightly to the north of Keres country. The story is entitled, "The Faithless Wife," but we should be prepared for such infidelity even before learning that the wife's name is White Corn Girl. The husband is Olivella Flower Boy, who is Summer chief of the village. (Tewa villages are ruled alternately by Winter and Summer chiefs.) The Summer chief announces to his people that a dance will be held, and they reply: "That is a good dance you have in mind. We shall have lots of fruit, lots of corn, lots of everything we have planted. We need parrot downy feather [*tanyi po,* parrot hair] and parrot tail feathers [*tanyi w'ae*] and we have none." The Summer chief replies that he will go to the south where it is warm and the parrots live to get these feathers. Meanwhile they are to bring the feathers of local summer birds to make offerings for the Oxuwah of the directions. Oxuwah may be either clouds or kachinas.

Olivella Flower went to the west first, to Tsikomo. (Those who like to search out the realistic basis of mythical places can find the mountain by traveling up Santa Barbara Canyon on the Santa Clara Reservation, where this peak can be seen on the north side.) There he is told that his wife has failed him, but he replies, "Even if my wife has failed me, I have to do what I said I would do," so he travels on to a great river. There a water snake gives him the same message. The mythical place where summer reigns all the year around is called *w'aiyege* in Tewa, and because of his wife's failure, the chief took ten years for the journey. But with the help of "our Mother," that is, the Corn Mother, he succeeded.

When he came to the mythical place, "It looked very green." It was like a mesa, but it was way down—perhaps under a pool of water—rather than up in the air, and an otter came to him from the chief of that country, offering to take him down to the house of Parrot chief.

> *He was carrying pollen and he gave it to Parrot chief. Parrot chief said, "Olivella Flower, Summer chief of Tekeowinge, having it in mind you came here. You came this long way because your wife failed you. You have had a hard time, yet you have come. In two days you will be back in your house, because Blue Oxuwah, Yellow Oxuwah, Red Oxuwah, White Oxuwah, Speckled Oxuwah, Dark Oxuwah will help you. Your father is seated asking our Mother to help you. You are to take back what you need." Then the parrots came in, and very prettily they spread their tails. "Take out what feathers you like," said Parrot chief.[29]*

In this particular story the infidelity of the wife is made a literal matter, perhaps by joining it with another tale, so she is driven out to become the mother of Utes, whom the Tewas say allow a woman to have two husbands. At base though, it is the same myth as the one that we have heard from the Hopis: Summer chief's father is the Sun; his mother the Corn goddess. He is able to return in rapid fashion, because he is brought back in the embrace of the Cloud spirits of the six directions, bringing both macaw feathers and rain for the summer's crops.

Parrots are rather curiously associated with salt and salt-gathering expeditions, but there are reasons of both associative logic and practicality which explain this connection. The common places that Indians used for gathering salt in quantity were dead lakes or lagoons—notably the saline marshes east of the Manzano Mountains and the Zuñi Salt Lake that lay far to the south of that pueblo. When these enclosed bodies of water receded, in the drying heat of the summer's sun, they left deposits of nearly pure salt encrusted on their margins and on rocks in the water. One can thus say that salt is a gift from the Sun Father as well as of Salt Woman. On the more mundane side Parsons assumed that because of the great importance of Pima-Papago salt gathering, the Acoma and Hopi traders may have introduced the parrot-salt association at the same time that they acquired the parrot feathers from these people.[30]

Even if this particular borrowing of the connection proved to be false, the parrot–salt alliance would be reinforced by the fact that the Zuñi Salt Lake, to which several Pueblo groups went for their salt, was itself a long journey to the south and hence toward the exotic homeland of the parrots. The salt was found in and extracted from a body of water, and beyond that it is obvious that salt attracts moisture, a quality that explains why the salt journey was, for the Hopis at least, a pilgrimage for rain. Because salt is a product of sun and water, salt is also a mediating term between the two, much as is the rainbow, which is linked with the multihued parrots.

In illustration of these associations we find that at Acoma, where only four clans have important ceremonial functions, the Parrot clan is in charge of the salt pilgrimage. They were joined in this undertaking by a clan of the same name from Laguna, making it a combined venture. The relationship goes back to the time of the Keresan migrations when Salt Woman, a lesser deity said to be a grandmother of the War Twins, is herself wandering with the people. When they reach White House, an important reference point in Keresan tradition, they enter various homes but are not fed by the residents, until they come to the house of the Parrot people.

When Salt Woman is offered food in a house of the Parrot people, she places her hands in the vessel of cooking deer meat, stirring it. "Then the one who was the mother spoke thus, 'Oh my, very sweet is this soup.'"[31] To punish those other people who had been unhospitable, the Twins hurl throwing-sticks at their children, causing them to become chattering Scrub Jays. Salt Woman and the War Twins then go on to Laguna and lastly to Zuñi, picking up members of the Parrot clans for the expedition to the salt lake, which is to be the future home of both the goddess and the War Twins.

> Then here below reached the lake Ma'seewi and his brother
> Uyu'yewi. Then thus spoke Uyu'yewi, "Go ahead, Grandmother,"
> thus he said. Then Salt-Woman shook the lake four times and then
> entirely salt became there around the edge. Thus long ago Salt-
> Woman Tsit'icots'a sat down there.

The Parrot clan today is considered to be the owner of salt, and their permission is necessary when a party wishes to go on a salt-gathering expedition. The bird is also a tutelary spirit of this group: "The parrot clan elder prays to the parrot and kopishtaya."[32]

Because macaws and parrots and their feathers were known to have come from the far south, in Mexico, this point of origin may have influenced their extensive use in fiestas and saint's day dances to which the Pueblos invite their Spanish-speaking neighbors. Although these dances are in a way secular and display a number of borrowings from Mexican-Indian dances, they contain basic Pueblo elements beneath the foreign overlay. Bandelier described such a dance in December of 1885, calling it a *baile de la cabellera,* in which six matalotes and six malinches danced from each kiva. This Cochiti dance was a modified version of a Scalp dance, but the male participants were those who had killed beasts of prey, not enemies.

Malinches are female dancers in a literal sense—not males dressed as females—who usually wear tableta headdresses and in general resemble their Mexican counterparts. In this particular dance the women wore a tuft of parrot feathers in place of the tabletas. Lummis likewise described a feast day dance at Cochiti in which women wore tufts of parrot feathers in place of tabletas. In the native Buffalo dance the malinches again wear fanlike tufts of eagle and parrot tail feathers, "the bases of which are obscured by a cluster of smaller parrot feathers."[33]

The Hopi Buffalo Maid wears a crown of parrot feathers in addition to the sun-shield on her back. In all of these cases the parrot feathers seem to replace a tableta headdress. The latter consists of a board cut out to resemble a cloud terrace, and painted "all-colors—like a rainbow," so there is little doubt concerning why the two can be equated or substituted, or that both stand for the Rainbow.

At saint's day dances the Keres also carry a long pole that is manipulated by the lead dancer in each kiva group. It would seem to be an unusual type of fetish used to join the various elements that are to be brought into harmony by the dance. At Santa Ana this pole is called a *Kastotsho'ma,* and there it is brought out only on Saint Anne's Day. On the upper part of the pole is an egg-shaped swelling that is filled with seeds and is surmounted by a cluster of brilliant parrot tail feathers.[34]

The poles used at Santo Domingo in recent times are somewhat modified, but not in essentials. The pole of the Turquoise kiva is perhaps twelve feet long, crowned with tail feathers. These are probably not from real macaws but seem to be white feathers that have been dyed orangish red, while around the base are Steller Jay feathers. The egg-shaped seed container is painted turquoise, with two black bands, but the collars of eagle down that separate this protuberance from the tail feathers above and the remainder of the pole below are now made of an ersatz material that has been dyed cerise. Below this is a cluster of thirty primary or tail feathers from smaller birds, tied in a bundle at the end of a cord. Most of these birds belong to those treated later in the chapter on birds of summer, although a few iridescent magpie feathers were also there.

The pole itself is wrapped in skin and tied with a thong, and eagle tail feathers are hung at intervals. Also tied to the pole is a cloth panel, perhaps eight feet long and a foot and a half wide, at the bottom of which there is a decorative border, and above that a design of multicolored cloud symbols. The pole of the alternate kiva, the Squash or Pumpkin, has an orange ruff in place of the eagle down; beneath it are several tiny ears of corn, taking the place of the mixed feather bundle, while the design on its cloth panel is a full-sized corn plant. These poles are carried into the plaza in an upright manner, but waved in a near horizontal position.

Because similar poles are used by the Tewas, the Jemez, and the Hopis, it is safe to assume that they had a significance prior to the coming of the Spaniards. Something more of their meaning can be seen in the Acoma pole carried in the Fiesta of San Estevan. There it is called *paiyatyamo,* or "sun youth." Those who dance with it are dressed just like the pole and "at the top of the pole is a bunch of colored parrot feathers like the headdress of the men dancers."[35] The Keres have a demigod of the Sun Father who is also called Paiyatemu; this divinity is closely connected with music, flowers, and butterflies—those bright-colored fragments of summer—which brings us to the Hopi Butterfly Maids.

At Hopi, where butterflies are the "pets" of the germination god, Muyingwu, the Butterfly dance has secular overtones like the Rio Grande tableta dances, which may provide the pattern for the Hopi dance, possibly introduced by the Tewas who fled the Rio Grande in 1696. The Butterfly Maids, variously called Buli, Poli, or Polik Mana, wear an elaborate wooden tableta painted red, green, yellow, and black. On it may be painted the emblem of the Sun and the Sun's flowers, or sometimes corn plants. The top has a cloud terrace form, though the feathers are turkey rather than parrot. The procession is led by a standard-bearer carrying a long pole. At the top of the pole is a gourd painted black, "with red-stained horsehair and parrot and other feathers attached."[36] The cloth panel is painted with a Hopi girl, because only maids past puberty are supposed to take part in the dance. The girl dancers reveal to the spectators the names of their young men, and their male partners are supposed to furnish their entire costumes. Although the dance has no secret rites, in recent times at least, it celebrates the fertilizing powers of nubile girls, as one of the songs clearly indicates:

Come here, Thunder, and look!
Come here, Cold, and see it rain!
Thunder strikes and makes it hot.
All seeds grow when it is hot.
Corn in blossom,
Beans in bloom
Your face on gardens looks.
Watermelon plant, muskmelon plant,
Your face on gardens looks. [37]

There was probably once a male fertility element as well. On the extreme point of First Mesa was a Butterfly shrine mound in which were kept, in Stephen's day, the relics of a "phallic, wizard" society that was already obsolete at the time. Among these relics were lightning-sticks, plant symbols, and two bird effigies. [38] Although it is not possible to determine the kind of birds involved, one resembles a painted wooden macaw effigy found in a Puebloan cache of Gobernador provenience. [39] It may also be noted that the Hopi Butterfly dance is in the hands of the Mustard clan—that plant has bright yellow flowers associated with the Sun.

Though there are secular overtones in all of the dances discussed here, there is also a basic pattern that emerges in different ways but which can be seen clearly if the elements of the pole are listed together. This fertility complex is centered on the pole itself, which may be regarded as a fetish with the gourd of seeds representing its contents; above this the parrot feathers represent the rainbow, and at times the red horsehair or red wool represent the sun's rays that shine through the cloud terraces to make the colors of the rainbow exemplified by the parrot feathers. Sometimes the pole itself is a male fertility spirit, son of the Sun. Butterflies are the pets of both the Sun and the demigod. On the banners are more clouds, or the central corn plant, or the women whose faces look toward the growing fields, as does the Sun's face. As we will again see later, the role of the parrot, or the rainbow, is to tie these elements together and to promote the processes that take place when all are combined.

One other element should not go unnoticed here, even though it is to one side of the central motif. In addition to promoting the fertility of crops, which may be thought of as a cultural aspect, there is also a natural one: the correspondence between the sun and uncultivated flowers. Butterflies are perforce as closely associated with flowers as flowers are with the sun. On the rainbow-like tabletas the Sun face is sometimes shown shining on his flowers. At Zuñi the common sunflower *(Helianthus annuus)* suggests both the sun and the sun's year and has been selected from among a myriad of other sunflowers for special use. This "sunflower is symbolized by a cluster of yellow feathers supposed to be from the parrot, but more frequently from other birds and dyed in imitation of parrot feathers."[40]

Each impersonator of the Rain priests wears the symbol of this sunflower attached to his forelock. As desired by the Council of the Gods, certain Zuñi men gather the rays of these flowers and present them to selected women who grind the rays to a powder, "after the Sun Father has gone to his house and the winds have ceased to move." The ritual use of this sun-symbolizing powder made from the yellow ray-flowers is not stated, but in the hands of the Rain priests it must be directed toward the conjunction of those processes that bring about a return of the Corn Maidens.

The Hopis have two Flower kachinas, each of whom wears a cluster of parrot feathers on top of the mask, which in each instance unites the same concepts found on the poles. Mashanta has a green, cylindrical case-mask with a band about it of all colors, designs to indicate "heat flowing," and a design called "his cloud." On the top there are, in addition to the parrot feathers, small octagonal discs which are flower effigies. On the rear of the mask is a mutlicolored Sun face with a border of red rays.

The second Flower kachina, Tsitoto, is a veritable rainbow, with a mask that is "half ovoid, with semicircular alternating parallel bands of red, yellow, green, and black on each side."[41] A cluster of parrot feathers is attached to the back of this mask, as befits both flowers and fecundity.

Flowers are the natural product of the sun in summer, while the corresponding cultural product is the ear of corn. Behind the ear of corn stands the Corn Mother of the Keres, who is their most important deity. This goddess is represented by the *iarriko,* or corn-ear fetish. The Zuñis likewise have their *mi'li,* or corn fetish; though it too is a corn mother, it has not developed into a personification. Both of these fetishes importantly involve parrot plumes and an extension of parrot symbolism into the realm of curing.

Each Keresan society member owns one of these fetishes, which he places in front of the altar each time that he is to take part in a particular rite. When this rite is held by a medicine society, the fetish, or "supreme idol," as it has been called, has curative value. This is vouched for by a Cochiti myth that explains the origin of the fetish. The myth tells that an epidemic had come upon the people while their mother, the Corn goddess, was still living with them.

> *[She] had reflected upon the means of remedying the ills of her sons. She had planned an* iareko. *She wound thongs of deer hide about an ear of corn and placed at its top feathers of a turkey which at her orders had shaken out its feathers for her. But finding that her work was not perfect, she had called Spider, saying to him, "I have wished to make for my people something endowed with the same power as myself, and to give it to them. I know that you are thoughtful. How does my work seem to you?" Spider said, "It is good, but put at the top some parrot feathers, and at the neck some eagle-down, and all will be well."*[42]

Because none of the parrot connections that we have met so far suggest curative powers, the question arises as to why its feathers were necessary to make this fetish perfect. The answer would seem to be that the parrot ties many hues together, all colors, all directions. We have already seen that with its rainbow aspect it tied the elements of sun, clouds, and rain together, linking them with the many-colored seeds of corn that are contained in the gourd on the pole. The Pueblos have contrived to differentiate not only corn but also bean seeds by colors that are related to the directions. The directions are, of course, also multicolored, one color standing for each point. By bringing all these colors and their powers together, the cosmic influences are joined to shine directly on the village and its fields, in the Middle Place. The parrots aptly stand for this assemblage of colors and thus for the binding of forces together.

These feelings can be followed through devious lines of thinking. A Zuñi explained to Stevenson his thoughts as he tied macaw and parrot feathers to the *mi'li* fetish that he was constructing: "One of the macaw plumes was now attached to the ear by binding to it the end of a slender stick to which the plume was attached. . . . A similar plume was bound at the opposite side . . . a third was placed between the two and a fourth opposite the third, thus symbolizing the four quarters."[43] The yellow of the North, blue green of the West, and red of the South are represented, but white for the East is not specified.

At Hopi the parrot is said to be the bird of the South in the Soyal or Sun ceremony and in the Powamu or Bean ceremony; in the Niman or Farewell Kachina ceremony the parakeet or macaw is said to represent the South. The Tewas have a choice of either the macaw or the Red-tailed Hawk, either of which may stand for the red South. The Keres arrangement is less certain, because the Sia claim the Cardinal for that direction. However, on the map of the Santa Ana cosmos there is a place in the "middle-south," or Gowawaima, which is not the same as the South corner. Concerning this extra South there is a Shiwana or rain-maker song, sung in the neighboring pueblo of Santo Domingo.

> *The parrot is sitting in the tree at Gowawaima. He spreads out his tail and makes clouds that come out and cover him. Today it is going to rain from the north, west, south, and east. The plants sprout with two and four shoots, and grow and ripen quickly.*[44]

In this song the discrepancies seem to be effectively reconciled with the parrot in one South, which is the land of summer. But the clouds that he calls to the Middle come together from all the directions. According to Cushing the Zuñis also contrived to organize a rational symbolism in which the parrot figuratively ties things together, but some qualifications will have to be made concerning his version. He mentions a "mytho-sociologic" organization of the Zuñi tribe, which he held to be the key to their sociology as well as to their conceptions of space and the universe. This system is based on an arrangement of clans, in which the Parrot-Macaw clan plays a central role. But one must keep in mind that the bird itself, as distinct from the clan, represents the South at Zuñi.

Cushing found that the nineteen clans were grouped in directional clusters. To take a selection, the Crane belonged to the North from whence that bird comes. The Bear and Grey Coyote clans were attached to the West, because bears are either black like night or grizzled like the dusk, at which time coyotes lurk. With the South are the Badger, Corn, and Tobacco clans—the first because badgers are often seen digging on the sunny or southern sides of hills in winter, while corn and tobacco are useful plants associated with a summer that comes from the south.

Finally, Cushing has a single most important clan, the Pichikwe, which he translates as Parrot-Macaw, whose people belong to the Middle and sum up all other directions. "The Macaw is characterized as 'midmost,' or of the middle, and also as the all-containing or mother clan of the entire tribe, for in it the seed of the priesthood of the houses is supposed to be preserved."[45]

Some reservations can be made about Cushing's schemata, though it fits very well with the ideas behind the sun-pole and other fetishes and may be another version of the same complex of symbols. First of all the clan name is mistranslated; Pichikwe is properly Dogwood, but this does not alter his picture much for reasons that we shall see. Second, the Dogwood is the largest clan at Zuñi; it is important in the priesthoods and ceremonies, but it is by no means all controlling. On the first point, the Zuñi clans are usually grouped together into phratries, such as Badger-Corn-Tobacco, but the Dogwood clan is so large that rather than being linked to others it is itself separated into divisions. These divisions are the Dogwood proper, the Parrot-Macaw, and the Raven-Crow-Kachina. However, when asked to which division they belong, most Zuñi, according to Kroeber, simplify the matter by saying *"Mullakwe,"* meaning Parrot-Macaw, so Cushing was not far wrong.[46]

On the other hand, it would seem to be the Dogwood clan as a whole, or at least the combination of Parrot and Raven-Kachina people, who represent the Middle, because it takes both of these groups—which are associated at Hopi as well—to round out the system. Here the Raven-Kachina people are the keepers of the myth-dramas that are thought to be represented in the kachina dances. An elaborate myth explains how these two divisions came to be related, but as it is fully developed in the chapter on ravens we will give it only brief notice here.

The Zuñi people were given a choice—and those of Acoma tell a similar story—between a blue egg and a white one, being told at the same time that one of these would produce a beautiful bird for whose followers there would be, "everlastingly manifest summer, and without toil . . . fields full fertile of food shall flourish there."[47]

With such a bright paradise in mind many people naturally chose the pretty blue egg but got for their choice the crow who mocks men and eats his crops. Those who had chosen the white egg became "macaws and were wafted by him with a toss of his wand to the far southward summerland." Cushing also uses the myth as a basis for dividing the Zuñi into Winter people and Summer people; but while such a moiety system fits the Rio Grande Pueblos, it is doubtful at Zuñi. Even for the Keres the parrot takes no part in the Battle of the Seasons; the crow fights on both sides.

At Hopi the Parrot people more clearly tie things together, for there they are in control of the Singers society, the myth keepers, and it is surely by myths that a culture is bound together. At their tribal initiation, each male Hopi must join one of four societies, which includes the Tao or Singers whose cult spirit is Talautumsi, or Dawn Woman, the mother of all crops. There is thus a dual meaning in the Singers; they know the songs that were sung and the myths that were told at the time of the emergence from the Underworld, and they are the owners of all crops. It is a phallic society that carries in its rites representations of the generative organs of humans.[48]

The Parrot clan controls the Singers society at Oraibi and Mishongnovi, while related clans have charge in other villages. It will be noted that the fertility element is only the reverse of that elaborated in the pole representing Sun Youth, where the Butterfly Maids were the human counterparts of the phallic spirit. With the Singers the divine fertility spirit is Dawn Woman, goddess of child-birth and crops. That the Parrot clan should have a role in both cases is natural—for one thing, the Parrot clan is the symbolic mother of all Hopi clans, illustrating that parrots also tie things together in a genealogical sequence.

One of the myths of the Parrot clan explains their control over fertility. This clan began its migrations in the tropical lands to the south where an old man and an old woman, fearful that their clan would die out, wandered into the jungle in search of a power that would make them fertile. There they met a beautiful woman, doubtless Dawn Woman, who had heard their supplications and led them to a nest. "'Kneel down and put your right hand on these eggs,' she told the woman first and then the man. 'Pray now for the blessing you want.'" Soon the old couple felt the stirrings of life within the eggs.

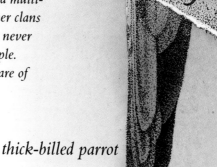

"Good!" said the beautiful woman. "Now you may take your hands off the eggs, knowing that they are parrot eggs and that you are now Kyashwungwa, Parrot Clan people. You will be fruitful and multi-ply, you will have the power of fertility. In time to come other clans and people will ask you for the power of increase. You must never deny them this power, for you are Yumuteaota, Mother People. Remember me and what I say, for I am the one who takes care of all bird people."[49]

thick-billed parrot

MACAWS, PARROTS, AND PARAKEETS

With this mandate it is natural that the Parrot clan tends to control Hopi women's ceremonies, the Lakon at Oraibi, and the Marau at Mishongnovi on Second Mesa. There is no published version of the Lakon at Oraibi, but a Second Mesa account makes clear its purport, though it is there said to be in the hands of the Butterfly-Badger phratry.[50] Only one man is involved, and he carries a fertility stick with ears of corn on the bottom, and with lightning running up the stick to the top which is a cloud. In addition to the chorus of women, four Lakon maidens take part. Their dress is particular and includes a headdress symbolic of a cloud made up of eagle feathers and feathers from a tropical bird, which doubtless means macaws or parrots. Their faces are colored like the sun by moistening yellow powder made from ground yellow petals of sunflowers. Each maid carries four ears of corn that are selected to represent the colors of the four directions, and each maiden—Corn Maiden—stands in the position of one of the four directions. In the center is a cloud design called a "water sifter." Then the yellow maid of the North throws her ears of corn, one by one, into this ring. The other maidens follow suit in the order of a ceremonial circuit: North, West, South, and East.

The male fertility deity, Muyingwu, plays an important part in both the Lakon and the Marau rites. The second rite belongs to the Parrot clan at Mishongnovi, but at Oraibi to the Sand clan, because the latter group are said to be the keepers of the soil. Where the emphasis of the first ceremony was on the fertility of crops, the Marau celebrates the reproductive qualities of women, and the emergence of mankind from the Underworld is enacted. The four central maidens in this ceremony wear a headdress made of red horsehair and parrot and eagle feathers, and they wear anklets of bright embroidery to represent the sunlight. At the conclusion of the rituals the maidens throw bits of dough to the spectators, which they hope will be seized by the men of their choice, after which there is a general tossing out of gifts of food by older women.

However the use of parrot symbolism varies, its meaning seems to follow a definite pattern. On the altars of the Hopi Flute ceremony are carved wooden images of four birds connected with the sun and the seasons; among these is a parrot about twelve inches long, while another is the Yellow-headed Blackbird, or Sun Maid. It will be remembered that the Sun Youth of the Keresan pole was a notable flute player, and at Zuñi as well he is a god of music and butterflies. The Sun who shines above these ceremonies is sometimes said to have been "made" by the birds and animals. After darkness "out came the foxskin for daylight, next came the parrot tail, making it yellow."[51] Thus we see the connection of the parrots with Dawn Woman, who precedes the Sun.

Early in this chapter we spoke of the Ahulani kachina. Another kachina, Ahul, may be a counterpart but certainly represents the Hopi Sun. Of his origin it is said that "Ahul came up at kishyu'ba at the house of Parrot family of the Kachina clan."[52] Although Ahul represents the Sun, his role is to call the Cloud chiefs of the directions. In the Powamu ceremony the chief of that group both calls up and represents Muyingwu, who comes from the Below or Nadir and is thus the counterpart of the Sun at the Zenith or Above. Muyingwu is also called Germinator and is lord of the crops in the Underworld.

The Sun in the Above calls up, with the help of Germinator Below, the seeds that are planted by the Hopis. The parrot family again has a place in tying these two directions together, which is illustrated in Stephen's comments on the general symbolism expressed on kachina masks. The eyes of any kachina, he notes, represent seeds, while the eyebrows above them are clouds. Then, turning to a specific kachina, he continues that two eagle feathers are black, for the Above and storm clouds, while parakeet feathers represent "all colors" for the Below.[53] The "all colors" represent the Below here, because in the Underworld the multicolored seeds of corn and beans are planted before summer. In the opposite season things turn over, and what is Below will become the Above, carrying its color symbols with it.

Although parrots are closely associated with the Sun, it is notable that in most rites where these birds have a place, Germinator also has a part to play, not only for the fertility of seeds but for humans as well. Human fertility is, of course, on the female side with mother, mother of corn, mother of crops, mother of clans, and eventually Dawn Woman. On the male side there is another set: Germinator, Sun Youth, the pole that is a fetish, and the phallic priests. The parrots join these ideas together through their relationship with the Sun, becoming the media through which the Sun's fertility is brought down to an earthly level.

But it will be remembered that the parakeets flew upward again to their rightful place near the Sun where they perhaps still live, in the House of Dawn Woman. Next we will meet a bird that represents the Sky, flying just below the Sun.

3 BIRDS OF THE SKY
eagles, ospreys, and large hawks

To separate the theme of the Sun and Sky is difficult, but even though the two often join or cross flights, they are not the same concept. The seasons also belong to both, because the sun marks their coming and going, and the clouds in the sky hold the rain and snow, which also indicate seasonal turnings. Eagles are of the sky, and, because they can easily spiral upwards until lost to human eyesight, they are said to go through a hole in the Above, possibly to the home of the Sun. The Sun also vanishes from the sky, only to return again.

From the sky, eagles survey everything on the four-directional surface of the earth, so they represent the fifth direction—the Zenith. As Beast god of the Above, Eagle has power equal to other directional gods: Lion in the North, Bear in the West, a diversity of animals in the South, and Wolf in the East. The eagle is the only bird in this select company of divinities. Sometimes these deities are set off against the Underworld serpent or burrowing predators who represent the sixth direction—the Nadir or Below.

As a god, Eagle is often equated with more abstract deities, such as Knife Wing or Flint Bird. These gods are represented in drawings and on altars as a combined bird and manlike being. They dominate the sky and are doubtless distant kin to the thunderbirds of other American Indian groups. As birds, eagles gather together a long series of meanings, beginning with the sun, the seasons, clouds, rain and snow, and lightning with its attendant fertility-bringing aspects. That series ends with mature corn plants and then turns to the curative value of corn.

Curing combines with the exorcism of evil. The Beast gods have power for both curing and war. As the dead become clouds, they relate to the sky theme and to the kachinas, who represent both clouds and the dead. Those who are earthbound use the feathers of eagles to send their arrows on flights through the air, so through their primary wing feathers, eagles are tied to hunting and second-arily to game dances.

The plural term "eagles" implies that several kinds of birds are joined in a single concept. For the Pueblos, as for ourselves, the Golden Eagle and the Bald Eagle are the great ones, but there are others. The Red-tailed Hawk, called "Red Eagle" by the Hopis, is often included in this high company. Mearns, with bird in hand, found that nineteenth-century Hopis identified the Common Black Hawk as a "Black Eagle." The latter is a stream-frequenting bird that seldom travels as far north as Hopi or Zuñi.

The name Black Eagle is often used but probably refers to immature eagles of both species, which appear black. Only in its second year does some white appear on the Bald Eagle. At Zuñi the Eagle clan has two divisions: Black Eagle and White Eagle. The latter obviously refers to the Bald Eagle, while the former may combine both juvenile eagles and the hawk.

Another great bird, the osprey, is referred to by both the Keres and the Hopis as Water Eagle, which is an apt name for this aquatic raptor. And even in our classification the osprey is close to the eagle. It is more skillful at diving and catching fish than the Bald Eagle, which often steals its catch. Both have a snowy head, but the osprey has a black mask and a white breast and in general a lesser size.

Despite the inclusion of ospreys and a large Buteo Hawk or two, the Pueblos are thinking principally of the two great eagles. The wingspread of the Golden Eagle may be seven feet or more, reaching across a body and tail of thirty to forty inches. Its beak is as long as the head. The Golden Eagle flies beyond the range of human sight to disappear, as myths tell it, through a hole in the stone vault of the sky. Golden refers only to the feathers on the nape of its neck, and these can be seen to glisten as the bird soars upwards toward the sun. Elsewhere it is a dark bird.

Golden Eagles have a circumpolar range. In the Eastern Hemisphere they range from the farthest north through Tibet and down to North Africa. On our side of the globe they are found from Alaska to Mexico; in the Southwest most are residents rather than travelers. Here they live by hunting jackrabbits, ground squirrels, and formerly prairie dogs. Their nests are in potholes built on inaccessible cliffs or sometimes in the tops of large yellow pine or even cottonwood trees.

The Bald Eagle is even larger than the Golden, but its flight is never as graceful nor as high. Its heavy wingbeats may appear labored, but it can in fact outfly the fastest duck. Because the Bald Eagle is a water-loving bird, it has special appeal to the Pueblos. This eagle eats fish by preference and does not scorn those washed up dead. It also feeds on waterfowl but seldom takes them on the wing, preferring to round up the weak or injured, or those wounded by hunters. In the Southwest its diet is supplemented by the ever-plentiful rabbits.

There have been many critical comments about the fact that the Bald Eagle was chosen as the symbol of the United States, because, though he looks fine, he is a carrion eater, something of a coward, and robs weaker birds such as ospreys of their catches. There is some truth in the criticism, but there is one definitely American thing about this eagle—its range is confined to Alaska, Canada, and the contiguous United States, with only a slight extension into Mexico.

The unjust charge of cowardice derives from the fact that it will not defend its nest as vigorously as the Golden Eagle. The Pueblo Indians of Taos have a different view of the Bald Eagle's courage, having a special name for the "White-headed Eagle," because it "is an angry bird and brave." The people of Taos have apparently watched its successful attacks on animals such as coyotes and foxes and thus give it a place as a hunter.

According to one Taos story, Coyote was admiring the clothing of Bald Eagles—their buckskin leggings and other nice garments made from the skins of wild animals. "He was thinking to himself how he could get that clothing and the mountain lion quiver and bow and arrows." This pair of White-headed Eagles offered to exchange some of their fine clothes with Coyote, if he would bring them something equally rare, such as a blue fox pelt. Coyote is not really brave but by a ruse got the pelt and then decided to attack the eagles.

> Then he pulled his bow. "This is the way I am going to shoot," he said to himself. So they came flying. They flew around and around high up. And he was carrying on a sham battle, running and yelping, war whooping, pulling his bow. "This is the way I am going to do." Pretty soon one of them flew swiftly to where he was—ss—s! He dodged and jumped and gave a war whoop. Then he shot the eagle. Then his feathers, the soft white one, just spread out, but he flew swiftly up again.

On the next swoop the eagles used arrows on foolish Coyote. "He did not feel the arrow the eagle shot into him (they were very little, fine arrows in their bodies)." The idea that eagles fight and hunt with bow and arrows relates to the fact that eagle feathers are the best for fletching arrows. Other weapons such as the curved throwing-stick relate to the falcons. Coyote was shot many times by these White-headed Eagles, then knocked down and stripped of his clothing.

> "Grandfather Coyote is not strong enough to fight us. . . . He made a mistake when he challenged us to a fight. He did not know we were the strongest of animals against any enemies we might meet." They flew up to their home at Rocky Mountain Point, and Coyote remained cast away in the plain, and the White-headed Eagles remained at their home forever. The eagles are the worst enemies the animals have.[1]

Hunting is merely a subtheme with the Bald Eagle, because it is plain that the Golden Eagle, which can take the young of mountain sheep and antelopes, is a superior hunter. The symbols that give the first eagle a higher place are indicated in such names as Cloud Eagle and Snow Eagle. Among the Tewas of the Rio Grande he is called Chieftain Bird. The pure white head and white tail, as well as its water-loving habits, are valid symbols in an arid region.

Along the Rio Grande one would expect this preference, because Bald Eagles breed in southern Colorado and follow the river through New Mexico. The Zuñis, however, shared the same preference, even though they were far from that river. In the last century the Zuñi preference for white-eagle feathers led to a special process during plucking. A gourd of kaolin was brought in and rubbed on the feathers to make them white.

Next, the bird underwent a rite in which a youth of the house takes

[an] ear of white corn, and biting off several grains takes a mouthful of the kaolin mixture. The man at the head of the eagle holds its mouth open while the other, standing with his head some distance above the eagle's, ejects the mixture of kaolin and chewed corn into the eagle's mouth; then, throwing the remainder from his mouth over the eagle, he rubs that which remains in the bowl over every spot where the white fluffy plumes should grow, as corn comes up, and the kaolin that the plumes may be white.[2]

At present, according to Zuñi ornithologist Ladd, the feathers of both species of eagles are of equal ritual importance and value, but the white, black-tipped tail feathers of the Bald Eagle are more coveted and are saved for use on masks.[3] Because the preference is always for white feathers, one can imagine the surprise when the juvenal feathers of Golden Eagles, which are white based on the primaries and even more so on the tail, grow back as dark feathers. That must have influenced the kaolin and white-corn rite at Zuñi.

The best way to assure a supply of white feathers was to keep Bald Eagles in rooftop cages. Henshaw visited Zuñi in 1872 and mentions this species, but none of the Golden:

Among the Zuñi Indians, these birds are highly prized for their feathers, with which they deck themselves at their sacred feasts and dances. At Zuñi, I saw perhaps a dozen kept in wicker inclosures. They presented a lamentable appearance, as their feathers had been plucked out to serve as ornaments. The quills and tail-feathers are especially valued.[4]

A similar observation had been made in 1851 when Woodhouse passed through Zuñi with the Sitgreaves expedition. Where they got the young is something of a puzzle, because Bald Eagles seldom breed in New Mexico. Probably the Zuñis collected a few young from nests in the White Mountain and Mogollon Rim region of Arizona, where they frequent the small lakes and streams and breed in moderate numbers.

The Hopis live in a part of northern Arizona where the Bald Eagle is very rare, but the Golden Eagle is a sparse resident scattered through all the mountainous areas; in breeding season it also nests in the desert of the Little Colorado.[5] The Golden species is taken from the nest and raised by the Hopis, but they, too, think in terms of the white-cloud symbol. In the Lakon ceremony the women have their bodies and limbs painted and wear a white manta over their shoulders.

"On each shoulder is a plume of eagle tail feathers [which are] white. The women represent clouds and these feathers are the white cloud wings bearing up the black rain clouds."[6] The juvenile Golden Eagles have tail feathers that are white in the basal half and black at the tips, thus giving the white-cloud/black-cloud effect. Adult birds, of course, lack this feature, so there is a tendency to pluck the birds as soon as the first plumage has hardened. But the Pueblos keep caged birds alive as long as there is any hope of extracting more feathers. And every kind of feather from the eagles has found some role in ritual and ceremony. The Hopis distinguish by name: tail feathers, downy eagle feathers, wing coverts, primary wing feathers, undertail and thigh feathers, and "side of bird under wing."[7] Hence they have a pterylography to go with their ornithology.

In Hopi-Navajo country eagles were never abundant, and both groups had ceremonial uses for the bird's feathers. So the shortage of these made it necessary to supplement the supply with related feathers from various Buteos, or Broad-tailed Hawks. Notably these were from the Red-tailed Hawk, which appears in tales as Red Eagle.[8] Talayesva recounts an eagle hunt and sacrifice from the period of his youth, but because no eagles were found at the time, his bird was a hawk.

His father took him out one spring on a hunt that began by placing an offering in the Third Mesa Eagle burial plot. His father found the young hawk, and, because they were in Bear clan eagle-hunting territory, they had to take the young bird to the sister of the Bear clan's chief. She already had five eagles and three hawks tethered to her roof, so she was willing to part with this one—after the proper rites. First she washed its head in white-clay suds, just like a newborn babe, and then gave it to the young man.

This bird was then given the name Female Bear, because all eagles and hawks are thought of as mothers. Then:

> My uncles and fathers told me that the eagles and hawks are spirit people who live in a special home in the sky. Sometimes in the winter and spring these sky people are said to come to Oraibi as kachinas, with heads like eagles, and to dance in the plaza. . . . I was told that at the right time of year the Eagle Chief above sent his people down through a special hole in the sky to build their nests, lay their eggs, and hatch their young among the cliffs of the mountains and high mesas.

The young boy also knew that at the end of the Niman dance, when the quills of the bird would be hardened, and at the time the kachinas were also sent home, captive eagles and hawks would be "sent home" to carry offerings and prayers to the cloud people for rain. For this offering miniature kachina "dolls" and bows and arrows were made for the bird.

> The next morning I climbed upon the housetop with my father and held the cotton leash while he threw a blanket over the hawk. Then he placed his thumb upon her windpipe and pressed hard. It seemed to

take a long time for the hawk to "go home." When she became very still, we plucked her feathers and sorted them. We stripped off the skin and tied our prayer feathers to the wings and feet and around the bird's neck, so that she would forgive us and be ready to return and hatch young hawks the next year. Then we took her out toward the place where we caught her, to the hawk and Eagle cemetery of the Bear clan.

These feelings expressed in recollection are those of a youth who had cared for his captive eagle or hawk for months, and perhaps they explain the many myths and tales in which the young eagle tender returns with his friend to its home in the sky. This boy and his father completed their duties by digging a hole about two feet deep. Their bird was placed on the bottom and his father uttered a prayer. "Now we let you go free. Return to your people, for they are expecting you. Take these prayer feathers with our messages to the Six-Point-Cloud-People, and tell them to send us rain."[9]

Sacrifice is always cruel, but unlike wanton killing it does have meaning and limits. For one thing, this is the only case where birds or animals are directly sacrificed to the spirits, although many birds are taken for their feathers, which will be used in offerings. Eagles were kept tethered or caged on rooftops until quite recently. Federal law now prohibits the taking of eagles, but the Hopis, as of 1975, have special permission.

To put the matter in some perspective it may be said that the number of captive eagles was never great. Stephen reported that in 1893 that there were two captive eagles on First Mesa.[10] Thirty-five is the highest number ever recorded from Old Oraibi. Against this we may set the numbers killed by Anglos. The stockmen of Texas until recently banded together in eagle-killing organizations. In the fall the Golden Eagles tend to drift from Arizona and New Mexico into trans-Pecos Texas. The Big Bend Eagle Club alone made the following number of eagle kills from airplanes: 1941, 657; 1942, 667; 1943, 1,008; 1944, 800; 1945, 867; 1946, 819.

In short, nearly 5,000 eagles were killed by this one group in that short time.[11] Nor did the practice stop immediately. In 1971 a pilot was paid $25 a head to shoot eagles from the air on a single Wyoming ranch. His take amounted to 570 eagles for which he was paid $8,425. The point to be made is that all of the Pueblos together would not have the same impact on the eagle population as a single white hunter who runs them down with an airplane.

In that kind of slaughter there is neither meaning nor much skill. To take a young eagle from its nest in the face of attack from the adults or to grasp an adult eagle by hand and subdue it is something quite different. This act takes both skill and courage, which was, of course, one reason why it had meaning. Another mitigating fact is that because of the difficulty involved in taking eagles, not every village would have them at any one time. In 1881 Bourke listed those he saw: "Eagles are still raised in cages in Picuris, San Ildefonso, Santa Clara, Zuñi, Acoma, and the villages of the Moquis [Hopis] farther west. . . ."[12]

Eagles were either taken from the nest, just before they were ready to fly, or the adults were captured from pit traps of several kinds. These pits were the favored method of the Pecos and Jemez Eagle Catchers society, which specialized in capturing the birds and providing feathers for ceremonies. The Cochitis also used pits, and eagle trapping is there referred to as "this very dangerous business."

Father Dumarest describes the pits as dug in a swale or valley, where the ground would be soft. There are plants around the hole to conceal it. "At the bottom of the pit is a bowl filled with water which serves as a mirror to reflect the eagle. Fastened in the plants is a rabbit to attract the eagle. As soon as the eagle alights, the *chaiani*

red-tailed hawk

can catch him, for the eagle is unwilling to abandon his prey."[13] That is, once the eagle has sunk its talons into the rabbit, it will fight rather than flee.

Ornithologist Jensen gathered other details on these pits as used by the Rio Grande Pueblos. The hole is dug about three feet square and five to six feet deep, always near a tree. After the eagle catcher enters the pit, branches and turf are placed over the top, leaving only one small opening through which he can reach out with his hands. A live eagle is tied nearby as a decoy, while a dead rabbit is placed on top of the pit for bait.

If a soaring eagle spies the tame eagle, it alights in the tree, and after examining the surroundings for some time, it darts for the rabbit. This is the concealed man's opportunity. He reaches out and catches the eagle by the legs and pulls it down into the hole, which is too narrow for the eagle to fight in.[14]

In former times the Hopis had a more elaborate method, consisting of permanent stone structures about four feet high. These "eagle houses" were erected on the tops of certain buttes where eagles were often present. A post was firmly embedded nearby and a rabbit attached to it with a two-foot rope. When one of the great birds had sunk his talons into the rabbit, the hunter rushed out and grappled with it. While in the hut he sang magical songs to attract the eagles.[15]

Hopi eagle hunting, or taking them from nests, is so thoroughly institutionalized that the land extending from the mesas for fifty or sixty miles is divided into eagle allotments belonging to the different clans. The title to particular areas is established in migration legends that tell how a clan came into possession of certain buttes. As we saw earlier, any hawks or eagles taken on another clan's territory have to be presented first to its chief, who has a right to keep them.

There is both a practical and a spiritual reason for this clan ownership. When a nest is located, the finder must wait some time—until the young are nearly ready to fly—and before that time others may also find the nest. More importantly, there is a spiritual link between bird and clan. "Since the birds come from clan owned buttes, they are considered to be children of the clan."[16] As fellow clan members they tighten the bond between living members and the Six-Point Cloud People to whom they are sent home.

Among the eastern Pueblos a similar tie is formed by treating eagle victims like slain enemy warriors who are adopted by the tribe. At Jemez they washed the heads of captured eagles just like enemy scalps, and at Cochiti an eagle taker may be initiated into the Scalp-taker society. The transposition of enemy into friend is a common one. The slain human enemy also becomes a rain maker.

On First and Third mesas at Hopi the eagle victim is buried in a special plot, but on Second Mesa there is a division of treatment, as with human bodies. The bird is given a final meal of rabbit flesh so that its soul will have "ample strength to fly back to the buttes after death." Then it is either burned in fissures on the cliff, as are very young babies, or, if an adult bird, the body is taken to the owner's cornfield. It is buried in the corn because, "the eagle is the most important animal friend of the Hopi and the old bird is like a grownup person."[17]

Eagle is a friend because he protects the cornfield in a literal sense by destroying its pests and also by acting as the all-seeing eye that looks down as the Sun does from the sky and takes account of things done on earth. He is thus closely associated with the Sun god and in fact often appears to fly to the Sun's home above the visible sky. So we turn first to the Sun–Eagle concept.

The origin of the eagle, who first looked something like a crow, is accounted for by a journey to the Sun in a tale told by the Picuris to their children. The protagonists are two boys searching for their parents—the boys are analogues of the War Twins, who are sons of the Sun. They are aided by their grandparents, then by woodrats, and next by butterflies who carry them partway into the sky. Then they encounter a bird who says, "If you can paint my feathers, I will take you up to where the Sun lives." So they paint his beak and legs yellow and his tail white with black at the end—a young Golden Eagle.

Then the two boys sit on this eagle's back, close their eyes, and ascend higher and higher until they come to a strange-looking land.

Now, little boys, I have brought you to the Sun's land. Over there where the white house is, your mother is staying. She is now the Sun's wife, and your father's head is at the Morning Star's house. Every morning the Morning Star plays shinny with your father's head.

When challenged to a contest, the boys hit the Star's shinny sticks rather than the "ball," until all are broken.

When his last shinny stick was broken, the Morning Star dropped dead. "We win," said the little boys. "Our father's head we shall take over where the Eagle is waiting for us."[18]

Then, while the Sun is asleep, the boys steal their mother, and the three are taken back to earth by the eagle they have made with paint.

eagles, sun, and seasons

The simple folk tale is only one of many that relate eagles to the home of the Sun in the sky. When the two are joined, a whole series of ideas appear, and of these some are visible ties. Others are constructs of the mind and have to be thought rather than seen. The influence of the Sun god on seasons is perfectly visible to everyone, and if the eagle is a link between earth and sun he will have a related place.

For the Keresan Indians a myth recounts the Battle of the Seasons in which one side is led by Shakak, the spirit of North Mountain and of Winter; he has a counterpart in the South, or land of Summer. These two Shiwanna are personified storm clouds, and the rains of each are needed. The Sun rules both seasons, and the eagles play a part on both sides. The Winter spirit "wore a shirt like icicles and his shoes were like ice. His shirt was very shiny. To the edge were tied turkey feathers, and eagle feathers were tied on."[19]

On the other side four kinds of eagles fought in the van of Summer's forces, though the spirit himself wore parrot feathers in his hair. By translating the native names the four eagles can be identified as Bald Eagle, Osprey, Golden Eagle, and Red-tailed Hawk. Three of these would be seen more often in summer, and when Laguna still had the lake for which it is named the Bald Eagle may also have been a summer visitor there, even though his white head often represents the snows of winter.

In any case the eagles were associated with the clouds under the sun and the rain that these clouds carry. The product of rain is the staple crop, corn, and so we find the eagles helpful in uniting the two. In the Tewa version of the flight of the Corn Maidens—another battle of the seasons—Eagle finds them and brings corn back to the people.

> *Shrivelled Corn old woman went to her house and she got ready for pina [magic]. She got ready her basket of meal and she and Uroto Sendo bathed. At night they made a circle of corn meal; she brought an eagle feather and put it in the middle of the circle, and both fed the corn meal to the eagle feather and prayed. As she prayed the feather began to stand up. They sprinkled water from the medicine bowl. They said to the Eagle, "Now, our Eagle man!" The feather began to turn into a little eagle and the eagle began to shake his wings. They kept feeding the eagle. "Now, our man eagle, we want you to help us. You are the only one who goes everywhere in the world. We are going to ask you to find out where the White Corn Girls are."*[20]

This eagle finds the White Corn Girl in the East, confined in the body of a coyote. By giving medicine water to her through an eagle feather, he restores her to human form. And when she returns, her husband can resume his hunting. Not only the far-seeing ability of Eagle allows him to find the lost Corn Maidens. Eagles also have power as cloud symbols, and these can bring corn up. At Hopi the combination is found on the mask of one kachina. The eyebrows are drawn as cloud terraces, the eyes are seeds, while on top of the mask are "two eagle tail feathers, vertical, and typifying the black of the Above, perhaps specifically . . . the storm cloud deities, cumulonimbus."[21]

Because of these associations with corn it is natural that eagle feathers are the most important of those wrapped around the corn-ear fetish, which represents the Mother goddess. On the Zuñi *mi'li* are three fluffy eagle plumes, "representing the feather adornment on the head of the Corn Mother."[22] At Sia an eagle feather is placed at the top of the *iarriko* or fetish that represents the Mother goddess, Iyatiku. At Santa Ana this fetish is nearly smothered in a mass of short, fluffy eagle plumes.[23] The Hopi fetish, *tiponi*, was to "represent the great chief and through it they would be enabled to gain his ear." The clan chief was to call it *iso*, for it was the mother of the clan. This object was wrapped in corn leaves and buckskin. "At its top was fastened a bunch of eagle and turkey feathers."[24]

eagle and underworld

Because the eagle subsumes many themes, it is inevitable that the progress of his influence would make a complete cycle: from sky to rain to corn and then to the Corn Mother in the Underworld. Below, there are other associations with that dark world, which is the opposite of Eagle's sky home. When the Zuñis were still living in the fourfold Underworld, they learned that the Sun Father was lonely, because no one offered him prayer-sticks as he passed across the sky each day.

Thinking to climb into this daylight world the Zuñis sent scouts to discover the way. "'Come, let us go over there to talk to the eagle priest.' They went. They came to where eagle was staying." The twins tell the bird that, "all the society priests shall go out standing into the daylight of their sun father. You will look for their road."[25] Eagles do not really belong to this dark realm so Eagle, as well as several other birds, fails to find the road. Reed Youth does that.

A more successful part of Eagle's Underworld associations appears when his feathers are used to root a newly built house to the earth. The people of Jemez wanted to erect the pueblo solid as a rock, so they deposited a reddened eagle feather to be the root toward the north to Wawanatutu (whence the first people emerged and whither the dead return).[26] Similar eagle feathers were placed for each of the other directions.

Having roots in the Underworld, eagles are also joined with the dead, a connection that is reinforced by the fact that the dead rise and become Cloud people who drift across the eagle-dominated sky. At Sia the first chief "was buried in the ground in a reclining position. His head was covered with raw cotton, with an eagle plume attached."[27] The raw cotton represents the coming cloud shape of the dead and at the same time Chieftain Bird, Bald Eagle.

At Hopi an eagle road marker is placed to the west of a grave to show the departed his road to Skeleton house.[28] Eagle feathers are also placed over the hearts of the Hopi dead. Sometimes, it seems, the dead may be reborn not as clouds but as young eagles. One Second Mesa Hopi told Beaglehole that the tiny gifts given to eagles acknowledge their status as clan children, "really, as Dead Hopi who have returned to the village disguised as eaglets."[29]

There is yet another connection between the sky and the Underworld. Snakes represent the latter and in nature eagles are their foes. As always, an opposition is a kind of tie. In prayers and myths the Zuñi Bow priests set the Eagle of the Above against the Serpents of the Below. These great birds are always masters of the snakes and what they represent.

> The Moquis [Hopi] believe that snakes have an instinctive dread
> of their powerful and unrelenting foe, the eagle, whose mode of attack
> is to tap the serpent gently with one of his wings, and exasperate
> it into making a spring. When the snake has lunged out with all its
> force and struck nothing but feathers, its strength is gone, and it lies
> uncoiled upon the ground. From this position it cannot recover before
> the king of the air has seized it in his talons, and soared away with it
> to his eyrie upon some distant mountain peak.[30]

Because this is true, the Hopi Snake dancers believe that rattlesnakes can recognize eagle feathers and will try to avoid them. Hence the whip or wand by which the live snakes are controlled, before and during the ceremony, is composed of two short sticks that support eagle feathers. These are used to brush the snakes and so guide them as the handlers and assistants desire. The Snake ceremony is of the earth, but directed toward the sky. At Shongopovi it is in the hands of the Sun clan and the related Sun's Forehead clan, so the Sun prayer-sticks that are offered during the snake dance have eagle breast feathers and yellowbird feathers attached to them. On the same mesa the *tiponi* of the Snake society is very large. "The tiponi is two feet high, wholly of eagle wing feathers with eagle feathers tied to the tips."[31]

eagles and sky

Logic relates the eagle to the subterranean world, but in the natural world, and with stronger logic, he belongs to the sky. On a sand painting made for the Hopi Powamu, or Bean, ceremony, a house is made for the Sun. This consists of four concentric rings painted in the directional colors. In the center of these circling colors is a Sun face.

> *A small quartz crystal, to which an eagle feather . . . is attached is placed in the center of the sun symbol. This is called the heart of the sun. The four white lines with branch-like projections, and the seven red lines emanating from the sun symbol proper, represent eagle feathers and bunches of red horsehair, both of which symbolize the "sun beard" or rays of the sun.*[32]

Eagles live in the sky and may disappear through a hole in the Zenith, the sky being thought of as a great stone vault. We have already heard that at the right time of year the Eagle chief sends his people down through this hole to build their nests. This distant land of the Eagles has more than once been visited by Pueblo youths who were carried there by either friendly or hostile birds. In *Pueblo Gods and Myths,* a Zuñi version is recounted in which a young man falls in love with his captive eagle and rises with her to this high land.[33] The Hopis also describe such a visit, this time by a boy who was preoccupied with eagle hunting and providing food for his many birds.

Because of his utter absorption with the eagles, he failed to do his share of the family's field work. Because of that his angry sisters beat his eagles and then locked them up. Upon being rescued by the youth these birds told the boy to dress for a long journey.

So the young man painted his legs yellow, with sikahpiki, tied some bells or rattles round his legs, and some eagle's feathers in his hair, put on a kilt, sash, and belt, and decorated his body in different colors. Over his cheeks and nose he made a black line. He placed a number of strands of beads around his neck and ear pendants around his ears.

One of the Eagles said, "I am going to carry you on my back." So he mounted the Eagle, holding himself with both hands to the wings of the Eagle, and [with] the other Eagle taking the lead, they began to ascend.

The three circled first above the village, then proceeded to fly south to his family's field so that his relatives could see the singing youth leave.

The Eagles kept flying higher and higher to their home. Arriving at an opening away up in the sky, they passed through into the world where the Eagles dwell, and from whence they come down in response to the prayers of the Hopi and hatch their young for the Hopi here in this world.

Unlike the Zuñi myth, these eagles abandon the youth on a cliff almost immediately, in retaliation for his sisters' unjust treatment of them. The narrative thus becomes a story of his escape back into this world, in which he has the aid, first of all, of a wren—his own name indicates bluebird wing feathers—and like a Laguna counterpart he is a teacher of bird-hunting methods. The little wren contrives a ladder of her own feathers, plucked out one by one, down which the youth climbs from the high cliff on which he has been left stranded.

On this secondary plain in Eagle-land he comes upon Spider Woman, whom he is able to serve by successful hunting—perhaps his game is the Horned Lark that inhabits similar terrain on earth—for he is less an ordinary youth than a hunt spirit. Each day he makes his journey outward from the Spider's nest as a kind of kick-stick race with himself. Novice hunters in tales are always warned not to go in some particular direction. Here it is the West, where an ogre lives. This figure is partly a keeper of game, but he is also a corpse demon. And when the youth kicks his ball of pitch and hair into the ogre's kiva, he is forced into a gambling contest, which he inevitably loses.

The youth offers his kick ball in payment, because it is his only possession. "'I do not want that,' Hasohkata said, 'but you may lie down outside at the entrance of my kiva and it will not be so cold then,' for it had by this time become fall and the weather was getting cold." The youth was not left in freedom, however, but bound hand and foot and left to suffer in the cold. Spider Woman, who takes care of the foolish, fortunately found the young hunter, covered him with two turkey feathers for a mantle, and then planned to free him.

"So she went out and called out to her people, saying: 'All assemble here, but do not tarry, be quick about it.' Those who responded at once were specially animals of prey, such as the bear, wildcat, panther, mole [gopher], etc." She tells these beasts that they are to go and take her grandchild from Hasohkata, by defeating him at gambling. For the purpose Gopher proved most helpful, because the contest was a kind of cup game in which Spider Woman placed four cups, mouths downward, under one of which she concealed a ball. Gopher was able to move this marker about, so the prey animals easily won the contest, as they did the next, which was a contest of pulling up brush, where the same beast again helped them by gnawing off the roots.

"They returned to the kiva, untied the young man and all again entered the kiva of Hasohkata." After they had taken the things that he had stolen from previous victims, he asks to be left alone.

To this they did not agree. "We are going to kill you," they said. So the Bear grabbed him, tore open his breast, and tore out the heart of Hasohkata, which he took with him. The Wolves, Coyotes, Wildcats, etc., hereupon fell on the corpse, tearing it to pieces and devoured it.

The narrator interjects at this point that their behavior here is the same as these animals display today, which justifies the killing of predatory animals.

There still remained the problem of returning to earth.

So the next day they went to the opening through which the Eagles had brought the young man. They looked down and could see nothing. Everything looked as if we are now looking upward. So Spider Woman placed around the opening sticks and brush of all kinds just the same as around a spider hole. Over this she then spun a great deal of web and before cutting the thread she told the young man to mount her back. Hereupon they began to descend, the thread of spider web unraveling at the opening as they descended farther and farther downward.[34]

eagles and hunting

In that story the descent from the sky is equally mixed with the theme of hunting, particularly bird hunting. The hero of the story is a patron of customs that relate to bird hunting, a lore that he naturally learned in the sky at the home of the Eagles. His rescue by the beasts of prey relates him to the whole circle of hunters, and on earth he spent his time hunting small game to feed his eagles.

Eagles have some virtue as hunters, in the Hopi view, but nothing like the falcon god, Kih'sha, who is the great hunter. Kwa'hu, the eagle, and Kwayo, one of the large hawks, are not very good hunters.[35] They lack the curved wings and the curved throwing stick that is modeled on them. On the naturalistic side the Hopis have observed that eagles and broad-winged hawks cannot swoop under bushes to take their game, but the eagles and other beasts of prey do have the bow and arrow. Arrows are fletched with eagle feathers, and they seem to arrive from the sky.

In only one pueblo has the eagle's hunting prowess been incorporated into the ceremonial pattern. At Acoma the Hunt chief is not a Lion but an Eagle, or Eagle Man.

The game was all gathered and saved for the katsina at the house of Antelope clan. After this had been done, the men who had been taught the hunting songs, made songs of their own, rejoicing over the hunt, and put on a dance in honor of the Eagle Man and proclaimed him leader of the hunt.[36]

Over Eagle Man the goddess Iyatiku placed a man of the Sky clan, who would be the Outside or War chief and at present he has taken over the duties of the lapsed Hunt chief at Acoma.

eagles and curing

In the same pueblo Eagle has a role as one of the gods who cure the sick. Oak Man, according to Acoma myth, was the first Medicine chief, and he was taught to make altars by the Mother goddess. "Iatiku told Oak Man he was to kill an eagle and take the longest feather from each wing, and the down from under the tail, and to tie them on the top of the last two uprights of the altar. He was also to bring the rest of the feathers."[37]

All of the Beast gods have a role in curing, but Eagle has much less importance than Bear, god of the West direction. At Zuñi downy eagle feathers are dyed red and used as the badge of medicine societies. In the prayers of the Medicine cult, eagles are often invoked in phrases like, "with eagle's mist garment,"[38] which parallels the Rain priests' "Eagle's thin cloud wings." When the power of the Beast gods is directly sought for curing, it is the deified eagle, Knife Wing, who is addressed:

And furthermore, yonder above
You who are my father, knife-wing,
You are life-giving society chief.
Bringing your medicine,
You will make your road come hither.[39]

Although Eagle is not mentioned by name in these medicine prayers—other than as a rain bringer—the bird figures prominently in one curing society at Zuñi. It is called the Eagle Down fraternity, or *U'huhukwe,* the first part of the name representing their call; *kwe* means people. The group had four divisions and specialized in pulmonary diseases, although they might be called in for other difficult cases, such as smallpox. The patients are brought into a room where the chief of the society sings and prays to the Beast Gods of the six directions.

The members of the Eagle Down people, with their bodies painted white, then enter the chamber.

> *Suddenly they spring before the altar, and bending their bodies low dip eagle plumes called "eagle hands" into the medicine water and sprinkle the altar, each striking the left plume on the under side of the right one. . . . Dipping their plumes into the medicine bowl, they repeat the sprinkling to the four regions, calling upon the Beast Gods to come. No women dance while the water is being sprinkled, but immediately after the sprinkling three women, dressed in white cotton gowns and red sashes, and holding an eagle wing plume in each hand, take the floor, and thereupon a member of the choir rushes in the wildest manner to the center of the room, dancing with the women for a while, then performing the most curious and weird antics before the altar, while he invokes the Beast Gods.* [40]

It is mandatory that the two dancing doctors never lay down the eagle plumes, so before they draw on the bear legskins, the feathers are placed in the bear paws worn by curers. The dance continues until the first rays of the sun appear, when the men assemble before the altar and pray, while the women go outside and offer their supplications directly to the Sun Father. The Rain priest of the North, who belongs to this society, has under his care the animal fetishes used in the ceremony. These include, in addition to Bear and the other beast gods, a human female figurine about eighteen inches tall and a well-cut stone image of a bison. It would be interesting to know the myths that go with these two images and whether or not she represents Bison Woman. At Cochiti the Buffalo dance, in which the chorus has eagle down daubed in their hair, has curative powers, because the buffalo is "like the bear, only not quite so much."[41] The eagle down in the latter case is for snow, not for curing.

In Acoma, when a boy is to be initiated into a Medicine society, a realistic painting of a bear clutching eagle plumes is drawn on the wall, along with a large painting of a formalized but realistic enough eagle; the doctors of this pueblo also mimic the bird. After the head man has anointed the curers with an eagle plume dipped into his medicine bowl,

> *The two doctors who have been sprinkled begin to gesticulate and grunt "Ah Ah." Then they come out in front. They hop about in front of the altar "squatting like an eagle." . . . They dip their eagle plumes in the ashes [which are called bear] and go about the chamber "whipping the disease away."[42]*

At Isleta, when there is any general malady or epidemic, it is treated by the town chief who calls in from all the directions the fetish animals. "Over the bowl of water from the river the chief makes a cross with his eagle-wing feathers, stirring the water. Sounds of bear, mountain lion, coyote, snake, eagle come from the bowl."[43] The chief then takes his whistle and calls in "all the powerful animals," who are not necessarily the directional beasts; even the coyote's cunning is useful.

In this pueblo the power of the eagle in connection with a curing rite may be a most literal thing and there is a taboo on killing eagles. A man had killed a bear, also tabooed, and thought he was dying in consequence. The chief came to the man's house where he had been in seclusion and used two eagle feathers as wands to draw the man up and out; then he went outside. "His chief helper took his place behind the altar. Outside Ka'a called the eagle, whistling like an eagle; and so he got the power of the eagle and flew away."[44]

eagle dances

In these curing ceremonies imitations of eagles and eagle dances have been set within a larger context, but among the Tewas the Eagle dance itself may provide the structure for a curing rite, though the dance can also be held when there are no patients. Formerly the Eagle dance, like that of the Zuñi Eagle Down society, was held in mid-winter, but it is now held sporadically in spring. In the old days the two dancers had to endure a severe retreat with no fire and no food, except one ear of corn for each of the four days of fasting. The dance itself was of the formal type, and any actual curing was done on the third night by the chief of the Eagle people who brushed the sick with eagle feathers.[45]

Besides curing, Eagle dances may also be held as part of a Game dance series, where they are only vaguely connected with the promotion of game. These dances are more of a harvest home dance, and at Acoma the Eagle dance is a purely secular affair held at Christmas time. Yet a third reason may be behind an Eagle dance—the promotion of a supply of eagle feathers, so necessary to ceremonial life.

At Cochiti the three-year Game dance cycle begins with an Eagle dance performed by the Turquoise kiva people. Two dancers perform with as many girls, chosen on the basis of ability, because the representation of eagles in dance steps is very difficult. The purpose of each dancer is to imitate the flight of the birds as carefully as possible, and, if he is skillful, the steps may indicate soaring, hovering, swooping, and the like.

Roediger summarizes the Eagle costume as it appears in the Rio Grande pueblos.

> The gleaming brown-black of the upper body is interrupted by a vest shaped patch of bright yellow on the chest. This is outlined with eagle down. The lower arm, legs, and bare feet are as yellow as the legs and talons of an eagle, and the face is yellow with a brilliant patch across the chin. The smart, soft, buckskin kilt, the color of cream, displays through the center an undulating snake design, and at the bottom of the kilt are strips of blue, yellow, and black, while the tinklers, made of tin and forming the fringe, click together throughout the dance. . . .
> A sweeping, fan-shaped tail of eagle feathers is attached at the back, and perfectly fashioned wings of long eagle feathers, bound to a strip of heavy buckskin, cover the arms and shoulders from finger tip

to finger tip. The hair hangs loose, and the head is covered with white down or raw cotton, forming a deep, snug cap, to which a long, yellow beak is fastened so that it protrudes just above the wearer's nose.[46]

The Hopi Eagle dancer is a formalized kachina, Kwa'hu, who has even more carefully contrived wings of eagle feathers. In the old days the helmet mask was adorned with a realistic eagle head mounted on top. There was an inverted "V" over his mouth, which is the symbol for all birds of prey, whether eagles or hawks, and he wore a green tablet on his back. More recently the eagle head has been abandoned and sometimes replaced by parakeet plumes, while a yellow beak takes the place of the older mouth.[47]

The Eagle dance as a separate performance has arrived at Zuñi only in recent times, but its introduction was prepared by an extensive use of eagle feathers. All kachinas there have always worn downy breast feathers from eagles, a usage that is explained in a myth telling of a boy, son of the Kachina chief, who when lost was rescued and returned by the father of Eagles. This rather delicate youth became lost in the mountains and was flown back to a spring near the town. There the Eagle plucked out six of his tail feathers, some downy feathers from under his wings, and some "spoon feathers" from his shoulders. These he presented to the boy with instructions to hand them on to his father, the Kachina chief. In accepting these the chief prayed:

> *Father of eagles, give me long life and your strong heart. You travel so far and fly so high that your breath is clear and strong. Make my heart clean like yours. I breathe from your feathers, so make me strong like you. . . . Our fathers, the kachinas, will wear these feathers because the eagle is strong and wise and kind. He travels far in all directions and so he will surely bring us the rains. The eagle feathers must always come first.*[48]

The eagle's high flight contributes to curing ceremonies as well as to rain bringing, because "He never goes where there is dirt and sickness."

The story behind the introduction of the Hilili-Eagle dance into Zuñi is an excellent illustration of an often unknown process in which a number of elements are slowly gathered to form a new ceremony. Because this has happened only recently, the dance has not been integrated into any of the Zuñi fraternities, although it may be called for by the heads of several. The Kachina chief takes charge of presenting it, though the dance is still half-secular.

The original Hilili dance was introduced from Acoma-Laguna around 1892, where it was said to have been a Scalp-taker dance. At the time that it was introduced it may or may not have involved carrying a live snake—not a rattler—but by the turn of the century a multicolored stuffed snake was mounted on the right side of the mask of the dance director, who was the only one to wear this ornament. Early, and perhaps from the time of its introduction, the masked dancers displayed birdlike movements and gestures, perching and waving their winged arms.

The Hilili dance is so called from the cry of these masked dancers and it is said that formerly they cried "ululu." Perhaps this is a reflection or recollection of the cry of the Eagle Down fraternity dancer who definitely represented an eagle and cried "Uh . . . hu."[49] However these associations came together, in about 1910 two Eagle kachinas were introduced from Hopi to become the stars of this dance. Rather oddly, all of the Hopis claim that the Hilili kachinas were introduced into their villages from Zuñi, so perhaps both groups adopted them from the Keres in recent times. A myth grew up almost immediately to account for parts of this new Zuñi dance, which indicates that myths can have a secular origin and only acquire religious meaning with later developments. These will be the fixing of a date on the calendar, a process that is already taking place, and the ultimate inclusion of the dance under a specific society. According to the new myth the Zuñis were at first frightened of the live snakes used by the dancers, but a visiting Hopi supplied a rationale for abating this fear.

Now, my fathers, I thought you people had things for the snakes. We have all worked on our feathers, all who belong to societies. We have made feathers for the snake and planted them in the winter time. I do not know why you are afraid of the snakes, they are bringing with them an eagle dance so that the people have many eagles. There are no eagles here. You have good places for the eagles to build their nests, but you have no one to dance for the eagles. These people will bring the eagles. They [the snakes] are good climbers. They can climb the high mountains, and so they can get the eagles.[50]

This myth justified the rite and in turn provided a concluding episode in which the two Eagle dancers climb up the cliffs of Corn Mountain and there pray for an abundance of feathers for Zuñi use. Myths are also tales, so this one closes with a natural point.

So that is why there are always eagle nests on Corn Mountain and all the people from different villages come here to Itiwana to get eagle feathers. The Hopis brought their eagle dance here and since then we have had many eagles. But the Hopis have given away their dance and so they now have bad luck with eagles in their own country.[51]

eagles and war

The recently peaceful history of the Pueblos has tended to obscure a relationship between the Sun, the Eagles, and the War gods.[52] A segment of the eagle's story could be included in the chapter on birds of war, but only a little of the bird's symbolism tends in this direction, as a part of the interlacing of themes. Other birds are specialized for war. As symbols, Sun and Eagle often stand for one another, and sun-shields, for example, will have rays made of eagle tail feathers. Sometimes these represent a weather rite. Of the sun-shields Voth says, "in the great Flute ceremony every flute player wears such a symbol. . . . He also wears on the head a ring of corn-husks, into which are thrust eagle breath feathers."[53]

The Flute ceremony is held on alternate years with the Snake ceremony, and the latter adds war to weather ritual. In most Hopi ceremonies small eagle feathers are worn in scalp locks, while in a war rite connected with the Soyal or Sun ceremony, the priest waves six old eagle feathers.[54] At Zuñi the "great feather," which is the badge of a War or Bow priest, is made of eagle wing and downy feathers. It was worn on the war path as well as in ceremonies.

"The way it is worn is prognostic. If the tips point backward the kachina comes peaceably, but if the tips point forward his intentions are hostile, for this is the way warriors wear the feather on the warpath."[55] At Taos eagle feathers are placed in the mountains for Red Bear, the War spirit.[56] At Cochiti there was once an office of War priest, and its holder was superior to the War captains. On initiation his face was painted red and, "white paint is brushed over the front part of his hair and eagle down placed on top of it. They give him a bow, arrow, and quiver filled with arrows. A tomahawk is placed in his right hand."[57]

At Jemez the War captains represent the War Twins, while the War priest represents the Sun and stands highest in rank of all the pueblo officers. All Jemez men must belong to either the Eagle or the Arrow societies, which were formerly organized, along with the Scalp-takers, as a standing body of warriors who were trained in fighting techniques and enduring pain. The two societies were joined by the important fact of fletching arrows with eagle feathers.[58]

The Zuñis combine the war and rain aspects of the Sun–eagle concept. The Sun Father is above all and his sons, the War Twins, are represented by the two chiefs of the Bow priests. The more important elder of the pair is appointed to office by the Rain priest of the North. He is turn prays to the Sun Father to send rain. Often the eagle-shaped god, Knife Wing, appears as an intermediary, because his weapons are flint knives and lightning arrows. He taught the use of his flint knives for scalping, which is both for war and fertility— scalps bring rain. Lightning may also strike for either war or fertility.

At Hopi the Eagle, who represents the Above, is one of the pets of the War Twins.[59] The Hopis practiced scalping in only a limited form—only one or two scalps were taken from the bravest in any engagement. These were brought back and thrown into fissures on the mesas with prayers for rain. During the Wuwuchim ceremony these scalps were fed wafer bread, again with prayers for rain. The Sun and Eagle clans had a special duty on Second Mesa. Each war party had a singer from one of these clans, who accompanied them and sang songs before and during the battle. When correctly sung, their magic would lead to a first kill by the Hopis, and that was a sign that they would also win the engagement.[60]

The eagle does not always represent the Zenith as a directional bird, because there is more than one set. In Table 2 it was seen that the Hepatic Tanager or the Yellow-headed Blackbird often stand there, but as a War god it is the eagle. In a Zuñi account of the origin of the War Twins and the Bow priesthood is this prayer:

Come forth, ye War-men of the Knife,
Carve plume-wands of death and the spaces,
Bring out the great drum of the regions!
. . .
Come forth, master priest of the high [Zenith]
Thou first in the kin of the Eagle,
Lay before us the streaked stone of lightning!
Come forth, master-priest of below [Nadir]
Thou first kin of the Serpent.[61]

knife wing

One god of the sky has been soaring behind the actual bird. Knife Wing, or Achiyalatopa in Zuñi, is one of the spirits based on the eagle. He is related to the Eagle monsters of the Keres and the Hopis and distantly to the "Thunderbirds" of other Indian groups. Knife Wing is the patron of societies at Zuñi and in prayers is addressed along with the other Beast gods. As illustrated on altars this god is pictured wearing a terraced cloud cap and with arms or wings that hang with eagle feathers, lightning lines, or flint knives.[62]

These flints, which may be either knives or arrow points, are thought to represent lightning. Because it is possible to strike sparks from flint, it must contain a bit of lightning; and where the great flashes strike the ground, one is able to pick up the flint arrowheads that have been shot down from the sky. Knife Wing's weapons are a great stone knife, lightning arrows, and a bow made from the rainbow. He was first of all a War god, but the connection between lightning and rain is evident.

A myth explaining the origin of the Zuñi Scalp ceremony tells of a slain Navajo woman who refused to remain dead. She pursued her killer to the shrine of the Beast Gods where Bear, Lion, White Bear, and Knife Wing offer their stone knives to the hounded killer. "Then Achiyalatopa said, 'Here is my knife, with this you will take off her scalp.'"[63] She is then laid to rest.

The equating of scalps with rain has been noted, but it is most vivid in: "our fathers the Beast Bow priests, with their claws, tear from the enemy his water-filled covering."[64] Knife Wing as the ruler of lightning thus has a dual role—on the enemy side as a rain maker and with the Zuñi as a war power. Deceased members of the Bow priesthood become lightning makers, or Ku'pishtaya, "mighty warriors who control the lightning arrows," thus joining both concepts.[65]

monster eagles

Kwatoko is a monster eagle in Hopi myths. Stephen describes and illustrates a petroglyph of this spirit, which had been pecked on a block of detached sandstone. Beside Kwatoko are marks to indicate the number of victims counted by some Hopi scalp-taker.[66] In myths this malevolent spirit is slain by the War Twins. He had a heart of stone, but his only weapons were beak and claws.[67] The name derives from words meaning "eagle-sky-high," and there is no suggestion of flint knives or arrowheads; that was left to another monster, Cha'veyo, who wore a string of arrowheads across his heart.

"Kwa'toko was a great eagle, as high as a man and the spread of his wings was as wide as a large house. He swooped down and carried off men, women and children . . . ," and in his story the War Twins are the lightning wielders. "The Twins bestrode their mantles and gathered up their lightning and threw it at Kwa'toko and killed him, and the lightning darted from their hands to the object aimed at and returned again to their hands." The wife of this monster eagle returns in a gentle rain over the mountains that had been their home, after she too had been killed by the War Twins' lightning.

flint wing

Flint Wing is Keresan counterpart of the Zuñi Sky god, though his resemblance to an eagle is never mentioned. At Sia they say,

> *The lightning people shoot their arrows to make it rain harder, the smaller flashes coming from the bows of the children. The thunder people have human forms, with wings of knives, and by flapping these wings they make a great noise, thus frightening the cloud and lightning people into working harder.*[68]

Here the lightning makers are a collectivity of spirits, much like the deceased Bow priests of Zuñi.

In the origin myth from Acoma, the War Twins undertook a search for a lost altar and in the process angered the gods of the four directions by ransacking their houses. When the Twins found these spirits asleep, they began to plunder their weapons. "Shakak on the north side had there the staff with which he makes snow. This they stole. On the west Morityema had the staff with which he made lightning and the balls with which thunder is made." They stole these and also the frost staff of the East ruler. In retaliation these spirits sent a large cloud that emptied in a cloudburst and a hail of flints, driving people to a mountain where a huge water snake arose from the water. But when the War Twins killed the monster the waters receded.[69]

Flint Wing, or Flint Bird, is definitely a monster eagle, and he abducts women. His appearance must be much like that of the Zuñi god, but he is not prayed to despite his connections with sky and weather; he seems more like the Hopi monsters. Flint Wing's story is tied up with that of his opponent, the hunter Kasewat, in myths which have been given various interpretations. Lucien Sebag has given a lengthy and detailed analysis of the stories from a French Structuralist and Marxist point of view, which makes much of oppositions: sky versus earth, hunting versus agriculture, husband versus wife, summer versus winter, cooked food versus raw food, and so on in rigid style.[70] Flint Wing in this view becomes a mediator, even between man and animals, because his shape combines both forms. The points made are instructive but too structured—the

Pueblos tend to have cycles rather than insisting on absolute opposites. The various roles of the eagle seem to illustrate a cycling and an ambivalence of attitudes toward the great bird, rather than a set of contradictions that must be solved like a puzzle.

In the tale of Kasewat, Flint Bird abducts the wife of this hunter. As in the Hopi story he is a teacher of birdhunting methods. He instructs Spider Woman, an Earth goddess, in the art of snaring snowbirds (Horned Larks), and in return she helps him to regain his wife. The wife is Yellow Corn Girl, and Flint Bird is a combined seasonal and weather spirit. "Back of Flint Bird's house there was a spring and a pond into which four streams flowed. They were of four colors [the directions], red, white, yellow, and blue, and when properly treated would produce hail, rain, snow, and wind respectively."[71]

The normal ceremonial circuit is reversed here, because it begins in the Red South rather than the Yellow North. The weather types are literal rather than conceptual. Flint Bird dropped ice into the red stream, and it began to hail on Kasewat with great violence. These are weather contests; in another version the god and Kasewat match skills by throwing clubs at stone balls in the East. In other words, they produced lightning and presumably rain.[72]

Kasewat is a rabbit hunter who also hunts birds; the Eagle is also primarily a rabbit hunter who may take birds. Flint Bird is a deified eagle who abducts a wife. The wife can be either Yellow Corn Girl or Yellow Woman, who stands for the Moon in these stories. Like eagles, the Moon lives in the sky but is abducted every month, during which time the hunter gets no game. Thus we see not an elaborate set of oppositions but rather a group of themes that can be shuffled like a deck of cards. Their individual values are always the same, but they can be joined in different combinations, without losing individual identities.

Although snakes are in opposition to eagles, they may also take their bird form. In another Acoma myth Water Snake entices Yellow Corn Girl away. He takes the form of an eagle to carry her to his home (which is Wenimatse, where the spirits and the dead abide), a land of eternal summer. The War Twins eventually rescue her and the three other Corn Girls held captive: Spider Woman takes the first of them to Hopi, the second to Zuñi, the third to Laguna, and Yellow Corn Girl to Acoma.[73]

These Eagle Sky gods relate not only to the Sun and the Moon but also to the other figures in the sky. In a Zuñi story a wife was abducted by Knife Wing, when he persuaded her to climb on his back. In flight he told her "to look down and see if she could see anything. The girl looked down and saw nothing but dark blue. She couldn't see anything at all. Then the girl became frightened and knew she was in another world."

The husband undergoes contests with the god in the sky and slays him. He cut off his head with a knife and threw it into the East, where it became Morning Star, patron of hunters. He cut out his heart and threw it into the West, where it became Evening Star.[74] In other stories the parts of Knife Wing's body become the Pleiades, Orion's belt, and the other stars that guide hunters and warriors.

As a god, Eagle integrates various aspects of man's luck as it falls from the sky. As a Beast god he oversees both war and the generous arts of healing. He may be a gentle cloud spirit bringing rain or a fierce warrior who rules the weather with hail, whirlwinds, and flood. He controls the luck of a hunter, both by his weather and his seasons. He is often killed, and then we see the fragmented parts of his body rising in the sky at night. Through the Pleiades or the Morning Star, he still rules some human affairs, though shorn for the time of his brilliant lightning arrows.

As a bird, an eagle soars freely above the highest mountains of the four directions in upward-spiraling gyres to survey the affairs of the animals, birds, and men on earth. All of the displays in the sky are meant for the earth.

4 BIRDS OF THE EARTH AND THE DEAD
mountain turkeys and others

Several kinds of fowl suggest by their habits and flight that they are bound to the earth. In the Southwest these are grouse, quail, and turkeys. The Pueblos had names for the first two, the most beautiful of which is "sagebrush softness," a literal translation of the Tewa word for Scaled Quail. Neither grouse nor quail receives more than brief mentions in tales. At Zuñi quail are one of only two birds that are taboo; their feathers are used neither in prayer offering nor in ceremonies.[1] The secretiveness of Scaled Quail is involved, and that is said to make them improper message bearers. The same idea may mean that their feathers were used by the Bow priests only—hence the taboo.

The turkey is the gallinaceous bird that represents the Earth as fittingly as the eagle stands for the Sky, and its importance in ceremony and myth is equal. Turkeys are very easy to domesticate, so whole flocks may be maintained for the use of their feathers. That sets them apart from the macaws or the eagles, which could be kept only in small numbers. Being of and on the earth, they also became man's companions, both in life and in death.

Mountain Turkeys are a subspecies of the Wild Turkey, the race *merriami,* which is confined to the Southwest. These birds are not the same as our domestic turkeys, though they are wild relatives which look much like the bronze variety. A domestic gobbler has an overhung breast, thicker legs, and exaggerated wattles and dewlap; it is inclined to be overweight and sluggish. The Mountain, or Merriam's Turkey, is trim and muscular, allowing it to travel with great speed and even to soar or plane a bit—abilities consistent with its chosen habitat, which is the yellow pine belt of 6,000 to 10,000 feet in elevation.

There it feeds on mast—pine nuts and acorns—and on insects that can be scratched from the forest floor. Formerly these turkeys, which are gregarious for most of the year, traveled in flocks of as many as a thousand birds. When the snow covered the higher mountains, they migrated to winter ranges, where snow did not cover their food. To make these journeys they needed leadership, so the older gobblers directed them to both food and the water that they need in abundance.

Their original range was from southern Colorado through suitable mountain ranges in New Mexico to near the Mexican border, then through the southern mountains of Arizona, the White Mountains and San Francisco Peaks. The Mountain Turkeys faced hazards, predators, and weather but were able to maintain themselves in vast flocks until the middle of the last century. While the birds are very wary during the day, they are noisy at roosting time, and it was simple for market hunters to locate the flock and kill them in masses to sell the meat in mines and towns.

When their wise old leaders are killed, a turkey flock is in perilous condition and does not recoup its numbers. Inclement weather may also kill them in great numbers. If the birds are plump, they can roost out a three-day snowstorm, provided that food is available when they come to the ground. The various pressures combined until in 1925 there was fear for the continued existence of Mountain Turkeys. Protection by law failed to make the flocks restock as had been hoped, so in 1940 steps such as supplemental feeding and transplanting of small groups was begun. In 1942 their numbers were 21,000 in New Mexico and 25,000 in Arizona, the latter scattered from the White Mountains to the San Francisco Peaks.[2] By 1964 the New Mexican population had grown to only 25,000 or 30,000 birds.[3] That is a far cry from the formerly vast flocks.

Indian hunting pressure has never been a negative factor, because the Pueblos are at most only casual hunters of game birds. The feathers were and are the desirable part of this bird, and several students have argued that the Pueblos never ate turkeys, keeping them only for their ceremonial values. Some have even suggested that there is a taboo against their use for food. At the present time Ladd says of Zuñi,

> *There is some folk history relating to pre-historic hunting, but no details are available. Domestic turkeys are kept and wild turkeys are taken by shooting. . . . It probably was eaten during prehistoric times. At present, several families keep domestic, black and white turkeys both as a source of feathers and food.*[4]

Those who hold for the food taboo are notable scholars, so the matter is worth a review. In addition it throws light on the place of this bird in the Indian mind. Parsons was definitely under the impression that the turkey was not eaten except at Taos.[5] That may be true only because in modern times they have become too scarce in many areas to be hunted as game. Lange reports that at Cochiti they are eaten but are killed only as chance game by deer hunters.[6]

Eric Reed reviewed much of the evidence and decided that they were not eaten.

> *Nevertheless, there are abundant scattered turkey bones in Anasazi refuse accumulations in the San Juan area, just as there are "food bones" from various mammals. Charred turkey bones have been found in the upper Rio Grande area. . . . Very possibly the Anasazi who occupied the San Juan region until about 1300 A.D. did eat turkeys; but evidently other prehistoric Southwestern Indians (other Pueblo groups and the Hohokam) and the modern Pueblo Indians of the historic period did not.*[7]

The conclusion is odd even on the evidence in the article, which mentions that one extinct Pueblo group of the lower Rio Grande, the Piros, did eat turkeys. He has also mentioned that in ruins along the upper Gila, south of Zuñi, turkey bones were found in fair numbers to "a surprisingly large amount." Because these ruins were near very good turkey country, one is surprised only if committed to the theory that they were not used as food but only for their feathers.

Gifts of turkeys to the Spaniards also tend to indicate a practical use for the birds. In 1540 Coronado sent a detachment of soldiers from Zuñi to Acoma, where they were welcomed with gifts of all the good things that the Pueblos had: corn, bread, piñon nuts, tanned deerskins, and turkeys. In 1582, when Espejo entered the Keresan pueblo of Sia, he was likewise given many turkeys. It would seem that a gift of corn and other edibles along with turkeys implies that the Indians expected them to be eaten; the Spaniards would not need feathers.

A letter by Coronado is often used as a basis for the supposed food taboo. Part of it is quoted by Reed, but he must have been using a secondary source, because an important phrase is missing. In Reed's version,

> *We found fowls, but only a few. . . . The Indians tell me that they do not eat them in any of the seven villages, but that they keep them merely for the sake of procuring feathers.*

The full passage is given in Purchas as,

> *Wee found heere Guinie cockes but few. The Indians tell me in all these seven cities that they eate them not, but that they keep them only for their feathers.* I believe them not [emphasis mine] *for they are excellent good, and greater than those of Mexico.*

A reasonable, if unprovable, interpretation of what the Zuñis told Coronado and his men would indicate that they kept "but few" in the villages. These would be domesticated flocks maintained to supply feathers for ceremonial use, and naturally enough these would not be eaten. This view would also explain the statement of Coronado's men that turkeys are "kept" more for their feathers than for eating, which does not preclude the taking of wild turkeys as game.[8]

BIRDS OF THE EARTH AND THE DEAD

Reed quotes a later source, which seems to indicate that the small domestic flocks and the wild birds were used differently.

> *In 1626, Fray Geronimo de Zarate-Salmeron speaks of "feather cloaks," for which they raise many turkeys, and describes the placing of turkey feathers in anthills along the way as offerings when traveling, but also speaks of the meat of* wild *[emphasis his] turkeys ("gallinas monteses") along with other game—deer, rabbits, bear, partridges, and quail.*[9]

In the nineteenth century Cushing noted the bread shapes devised by the Zuñis were in the form of game. "The bread tied to the bows has usually the forms of deer, antelope, rabbits, turkeys, or other game animals."[10] Parsons states that, "domestic turkey I have seen Taos men eat, much to my surprise, for south of Taos turkey is a ritual bird, kept that its feathers may be used in prayer offerings; and it would not be eaten, people say, even in time of famine."[11] The people south are first the Tewas and then the Keres, and it must be among the former that she heard of the taboo on eating turkey, because it is certainly not true of the Keres. White says of the Keresan village of Santa Ana:

> *Turkey were hunted in the mountains. Bear, mountain lion, wild cat, and eagle were occasionally killed, but not for food, apparently. It is not known why they were killed, but the killing of these creatures is distinguished quite clearly from the killing of game, such as deer and turkey.*[12]

Of the nearby village of Cochiti, Lange mentions that feathers from the few domestic turkeys kept there today are used for dance costumes.

> *Most feathers for such purposes, however, are obtained from wild turkeys, turkey farms, outside friends and similar sources. Turkeys, wild and domesticated, are, and have been for as long as any Cochiti has any knowledge, eaten by both men and women, as well as the children.*[13]

domesticated turkey

At Sia it is said that when a bear is taken with the purpose of feeding its meat to the chief, it will be hunted, "along with deer and turkey, the men singing as they go."[14]

The Hopis were farther from any Mountain Turkey habitat than other Pueblo groups. The nearest area in which they could be hunted was the San Francisco Range and its northward extension, and this is far across the Painted desert from the Hopi villages. Domesticated birds are expensive to keep; they must be fed corn, piñon nuts, or acorns in quantity, and the first two are foods needed for human consumption. Still, they needed the feathers for ceremonialism and kept at least a few in the villages.

When Stephen was living at Hopi in the 1890s his friend Wiki complained that he had not enough turkey feathers to finish off five or six sets of prayer-sticks. So Stephen arranged to get some through the Hopi trader Thomas Keam. But he was puzzled, because there were still a few turkeys in the mesa top village. He asked why they said that they had no turkeys. "Further talk elicits the fact that the turkeys have already been plucked here, plucked bare of all the kinds of feathers appropriate for prayer-stick trimming."[15]

When turkeys are that scarce, the value for feathers, which will grow in again, would far outweigh any food value. Even in the more fortunately located villages such as Laguna, which is near the Mt. Taylor area that was once good turkey country, the feather value was the dominant one. Gunn says, "At Laguna and Acoma were formerly large droves of turkeys; they were herded something after the manner of sheep. They told the Spaniards that turkeys were reared for their feathers."[16]

In prehistoric times there is evidence that feathers were the predominant reason for keeping domesticated flocks in and around the villages. "One reason for the belief that they were not kept to provide food is that they have been found buried with mortuary offerings. Corn was provided for the turkeys and bones for the dogs which were buried. . . ."[17] That kind of offering does not rule out their use as food, however, because it is common to make offerings to dead game such as deer in the expectation that they will be born again. Hence head and antlers were decorated with feathers and placed in shrines.

A third use for turkeys is unrelated to either feathers or food; that was the fabrication of simple tools from their bones. Of the great ruin in Chaco Canyon Judd remarked,

> *Unworked turkey bones are conspicuous in the trash mounds at Pueblo Bonito. We even found fragments of turkey egg shells. With the possible exception of deer bones, turkey bones were most frequently utilized in the manufacture of that indispensable household implement, the awl. Thus the ban against turkey flesh, if recognized in prehistoric time, did not extend to the skeleton.*[18]

Whatever the uses were, domestication of the turkey by the Pueblo Indians is thought to have taken place quite early. Bones alone, of course, prove nothing, but egg shells indicate that they were certainly raised in the villages. That is confirmed by the discovery of pens with turkey droppings still in them. The oldest turkey burial is dated around 600 A.D. and is from the Flagstaff area. Ceremonial burial of an entire bird in a ritual context does not necessarily prove that they were kept in the village, but it does indicate the bird's ceremonial importance.

Domestication of the turkey seems to have begun by around 700 A.D., at about the time when beans were first cultivated, the date based on the absence of turkey bones from earlier sites. Reed believes that feathers were the first impetus for domestication, and that would equate these birds with the macaws and eagles, which were also kept in the villages so that their feathers could be plucked for ritual use and ceremonial decoration. His view is that in Mesa Verde there was a first phase, to 900 A.D., when feathers were the only purpose, but that from 900 to 1300 A.D. the birds were also used as food.[19]

However the food question falls out, there is no doubt that the central value of the turkeys in Pueblo culture is as a source of feathers for prayer-sticks. In other chapters the kinds of bird feathers used for separate meanings and messages to the spirits will have an important place. Turkey feathers are quite different, because in addition to these special messages indicated by specific kinds of birds, almost all prayer-sticks have turkey feathers attached. These are referred to as the "clothes" of the offering.

The indication of the term was once quite literal, because the Pueblos in early times made and wore cloaks of turkey feathers. When Coronado said that they keep these birds more for their feathers he added, "because they make cloaks of them, since they have no cotton."[20] Actually they did have cotton of a native variety, but it was used for ceremonial garments and belts, or for the Cloud masks of the dead, and not for ordinary clothing.

Pueblo cloaks were not made like the feather mantles of Mexico and South America, which overlap the feathers like shingles on a roof. In the Southwest they were constructed of feathered or rabbit-skin ropes. Either bird or rabbit skins could be twisted around a central yucca fiber string in spiral fashion; then these ropes were tied together tightly to form a mantle. In Basket Maker times—pre-700 A.D.—they may have been made entirely of rabbit skins. Then in later ages these were decorated with outer cords made from bird skins.

By Coronado's time these cloaks were made wholly of turkey feathers and were used for warmth, as robes for sleeping, and from early times the dead were wrapped in them for burial. The sequence before that seems to be that the use of rabbit fur blankets dwindled after 700 A.D. and cords made of feathers steadily gained in use.

Some blankets were made partially of fur cord and partially of feather cord. Strips of bird skin were no longer used in the manufacture of the latter type. Small downy feathers were employed, as well as heavier feathers from which the stiffer part of the quill had been removed. Much turkey plumage was utilized, and it is believed by some archaeologists that turkeys were domesticated at this time.[21]

The idea of having "clothes" for prayer-sticks is obviously related to the cloaks that were made for human use and the need of feathers, for both influenced the domestication of the turkey. In the Pueblo view this took place so long ago and is so central that the question to be settled in myths is one of accounting for the existence of wild turkeys. A myth set in Acoma-Laguna illustrates this reverse order. A full-time turkey herder, a married woman, leaves her village to draw water from a spring. On returning she finds her husband and sister together and responds in a most un-Pueblo way by planning suicide. To a mortal woman that would be unthinkable, but she is basically a Mother of Game goddess. These, like Salt Old Woman on another level, are "givers of themselves" deities.

> *Then she stopped crying and spoke. Southward into the open she went and picked up corn. . . . There below the turkeys came together. She gave to eat to her turkeys. Then Yellow-Woman said, "Take this, my children, eat. This I will tell you. In four days I shall go to the lake to Laguna. If any of you will go with me I shall go," she said. "There is the drowning-place west below Laguna."*

The woman then went northward with her turkeys, the gobbler finally carrying the sorrowing wife on his back. When they arrived at the east end of a lake, now no longer there, the birds and their tender had a final meal together.

> *"Now children, once more let us eat." After she had taken out again the corn she shelled it for her children, the turkeys. "When you have eaten then you will climb from here and when the people increase your clothing will be needed, and also from here on your food will be piñon nuts and juniper berries and acorns on the mountain side."*

The turkeys were too distraught to eat the corn, so after she had her portion this Mother of Game opened all of her remaining provisions. These turned into gnats and mosquitoes. Then she rolled a ball of pollen out onto the lake. There it fell into an opening, because the drowning place is an entrance into the spirit world below the lake. "She went to the middle in the east. The turkeys just flew there down to the east. On the edges of all their wings and tails foam came to be." The buffy-white tail coverts are a distinguishing characteristic of the Mountain Turkey, and escape from a flood or foaming water is often given as an explanation.

The woman's husband came to the lake and found her dress on the shore. He threw this dress into the air, whereupon it was immediately transformed into butterflies. The turkeys, after refusing to eat for the ceremonial period of four days said, "Now once more let us eat the corn that our mother gave us. Presently from here northward let us climb up on Mount Taylor."[22] So it is explained why Mountain Turkeys became wild and why they had different-colored tail markings from other kinds.

At the other end of the bird is a head that is both bald and red; that, too, calls for some explanation, because most birds as well as Indian people have their heads covered. The explanation for this is an account of the first raising of the sun. In the naturalistic sense turkeys are "dawn-busters"; the whole roosting flock will set up a clamor just before the sun rises. Like the sun, buffalo came to the Hopis from beyond the eastern horizon, and so in the Buffalo dance each girl who performs wears on her back a sun-shield made from turkey tail feathers set in a radiating pattern.

In Hopi mythology Coyote was first called upon to raise the Sun into the sky. He pointed out that the Sun only moved when someone died. Two children were sacrified, and it did rise a bit.

But the sun was not high enough in the sky, it was too hot. They first told the wild turkey to try to raise the sun. The turkey made the attempt. His head was burned, and all his feathers came off. That is why the wild turkey's head is red and without feathers. He became tired, his head was too hot, his feathers were gone and he stopped trying.[23]

The buzzard tried next and got the Sun further; he is a powerful medicine man. Then the Golden Eagle did well and was only a little scorched on his neck. The hawks joined, and all the great birds together combined to get the Sun up into the sky. It is easy enough to see why the earthbound turkey was able to get the Sun only a short way into the sky.

Other tales explain the turkey's habitat and habits. At the far end of Hopi's Black Mesa there is high country of the yellow pine zone, which should be perfect turkey range. Apparently its isolation

mountain turkey

from the Chuska Mountains to the east and the San Francisco Peaks to the west prevented these ground birds from occupying this suitable area. The Hopis attribute this absence to a quarrel between Turkey and Coyote. The canine is jealous of the pretty markings on the children of the bird, while his own offspring are most plain.

Turkey suggests to Coyote, the trickster, who is also the tricked, that these marks came from baking in a fire—presumably like the designs on pottery. After this advice, an exodus from Black Mesa is obviously necessary. "'We had better flee away from here on account of your uncle, the Coyote, because he will be very angry and will certainly devour us.' Hereupon she sent her children away to the San Francisco Mountains."[24] The turkey children were exhausted by the time they reached the Little Colorado River, but the hen fled ahead and sent gobblers back to rescue them from Coyote, who is still their greatest enemy even today, in a naturalistic sense.

The Taos Indians have pleasant tales telling about the turkey's crop—"you know they have in front a little bag of their own"—and of their great need for water.

A turkey family lived on a wooded hill. They had fun in the evening in making a bonfire and in playing hiding hoop. They would run around about the hills across the ridges. They would run down to the river bottom for water for their jar made of pine bark or a piñon shell. They would run back up in a squad, pushing and pulling, so as to spill their water and run down again to fill their jar, then up hill again.

At last, late in the evening, they got on top of their hll home, tired out. In the evening the Turkey boys would bother the females in nuisance funny acts to keep them awake. The next day the boys persuaded the females to go pick piñon nuts, across the river on the hillside called Bow Mountain. They went singing.

byu byu tan tan.

They reached the place and filled their bags and started back home. When they got home, they gave their people a little here and a little there. They said, "We are the Turkey people living on Wooded Hillside and we remain there to live for ever. We are turkeys."[25]

Although this children's tale merely accounts for the place where Mountain Turkeys live and some of their antics, the feathers of this bird may be used to convey messages of more serious import. They may be thrown loosely into lakes and rivers or fixed to prayer-sticks, including some of great size.

When the pueblo of San Felipe is to hold a masked dance, the participants must have collars made from sprigs of fresh spruce. Three boys are sent to the mountains, carrying with them some turkey feathers wrapped in a corn husk.

> *They hunt through the hills until they find a suitable tree, which the feather bearer approaches. After praying, he climbs as high as he can and ties one of the feathers to the highest point: "that brings out the rain and the Shiwannas from the mountains."*[26]

On their return journey they leave an occasional turkey feather along the trail leading toward the village, to direct the rain.

Turkeys are of the mountains, as is the spruce. The mountains are also the home of clouds and the Cloud spirits called Shiwanna. These bring the rains to the village to make crops grow, so decorating the tree with turkey feathers makes it into a giant prayer-stick conveying this desire. As we have heard in the Taos tale, turkeys spend their time running uphill and downhill, conveying water. So they are intermediaries between rivers or springs and the rain clouds on the mountains.

A second message is involved in the feather offering; it is also to appease the tree for the damage done when its limbs were stripped, just as feathers are tied on a string between the horns of slain game. These offerings are an apology to the spirits for a disturbance in the natural order of the cosmos. Whatever the message, the bird's feathers carry it. At Zuñi turkeys are called *wotsanna*, little servant, because they perform this necessary communication with the spirits.

One may wish for game, for example. Eagle feathers are perhaps more important here, because they are above the mountains. But Turkey is on the ground below, and his feathers will serve too.

A Tewa tale with the pueblo of Pojoaque as a setting tells of the original Hunt chief. He is the offspring of those earthly spirits, Yellow Corn Girl and Olivella Flower. As dress he wears deerskins trimmed with badger fur, over which is thrown a buffalo robe, because in former times there was a small-sized race of buffalo in this area, which inhabited the Sangre de Cristo Mountains rather than the open plains to the east.

This Hunt spirit is taken to the home of the rulers of game who are in charge of their own kind: Wildcat Man, Wolf Man, Mountain Lion Man, and Yellow Bear Man. These spirits are in turn ruled by Lightning. The Hunt Youth provides all of this group with game for food, but Yellow Bear is angry because he is given nothing but venison.

> So the boy went home to the house of Wildcat Man, and stayed there. Then Awl said to the boy, "Tomorrow you must get up early and bathe and go turkey hunting. We must work and bring all the feathers to Wildcat Man, and he will hold them in his hands and the feathers will talk." Wildcat Man took the feathers into his hands, and talked over the feathers to Lightning Man and from a distance Lightning Man answered, "What do you want with me? This Yellow Bear Man is not doing right, to send away this boy."[27]

The more important feathers that the youth takes to Lightning are from the eagle. We have already seen the connections between eagles and arrow shafts and flint arrowheads with lightning, but hunting is after all done on the earth, particularly in the mountains. So turkey feathers are also a necessary offering. Bear is punished by Lightning's bolt, the youth returns home to become Summer chief—the one who rules the village for one half of the year under the moiety system of the Tewas. He marries the daughter of Wildcat Man, the original of Hunt chiefs.

Turkey serves as at least a messenger in hunt symbolism, but that is the least of his roles. Basically the turkey feather serves as the clothes of prayer offerings. Two erect turkey tail feathers are affixed to each prayer-stick, or when these are offered in pairs a single turkey feather is placed and tied between the two, "to keep them warm." Priests probably once wore feathered mantles on ceremonial occasions, and a priest is much like the feathered prayer-stick in that he, too, is a messenger and intermediary between men and gods.

Turkey feathers are given as offerings to the dead who return to the earth, at least for a time, before rising again as clouds. The turkey relates again here as "clothes," as well as in being earthbound and water directed. Pueblo Indians are buried in blankets, and in former times these were often the mantles made of turkey feathers. Whole turkeys were sometimes put into the earth alongside the human dead. Articulated bones were found alongside a human burial in the cliff dwellings of Segi Canyon.[28] If these were wild turkeys, they were again "of the mountains" and related to the Cloud spirits, which the dead become after an earthy interval.

Several Pueblo groups still use turkey feathers as mortuary offerings. In the Hopi Women's ceremony, the Marau, turkey feather prayer-sticks are made for all of the participants' deceased relatives. "These offerings are carried out later in the day and the Hopi believe that the dead tie them to a string around their heads so that they hang down before their faces."[29] These offerings are not tied to a stick in the usual manner, but are fixed to balls of cornmeal dough or tied to strings and offered to the dead in that manner.

For this offering four women take trays of the cornmeal balls, and the turkey feathers and go to the four directions, beginning with the North, of course. They then perform something like a relay race, each woman making a quarter circuit on the run, "throwing away the balls of food and the nakwakwosis as offerings to the dead and stopping at the place the next woman had started." Corn springs up from the earth, while turkeys are of the earth; together they represent the dead.

At Taos the same feathers are offered without sticks.

> For the dead, turkey feathers are put out, on the north and northeast edge of town, under a stone with a little cornmeal, that is, first the cornmeal is put on the ground, then the feathers, then the stone. Turkey feathers are also offered at the sacred lake, thrown into the water to float away, or left on the bank.[30]

The people of Taos and Jemez present loose feathers to the dead on All Souls' Day at twilight or during the night.

The Keres likewise associate turkey feathers with the dead. A preparation for burial at Santa Ana is described in these terms: "The medicine-man spreads a blanket, usually one that is old and well worn, on the floor and has the body laid on it. Then he puts a bunch of turkey feathers in each hand of the deceased and a bunch underneath his head."[31] At Cochiti on All Souls' Day, "Bundles of turkey feathers are also buried on this day in different places in the pueblo that the pueblo may come under the protection of *uretsete*."[32]

Uretsete is another name for the Keresan Mother goddess, who is symbolized by the feathered corn-ear fetish. Among her duties are those of providing health and of receiving the dead. Parsons adds a footnote to this passage indicating that at Zuñi no dancer would wear turkey feathers on his head, "because as turkeys are hard to raise, turkey feathers are a token of mortality." She then notes that one kachina dancer wears a crown of turkey feathers. He is Shumaakoli, who represents the dead people. Curiously enough his name seems to come from the Keresan word *shuma,* or dead.

Among the important dead are the enemy; the scalps taken from foes join with the peaceful dead to bring rain. At Zuñi the War chief goes out at dawn to meet the four men who announce the return of a War party. A dialogue takes place in which exploits are recounted. That night the scalp is brought in, and a sand altar is made with offerings to the dead enemy, "so that if any of the corn priest's ladder descending children should by mistake cut off your road, no evil consequences may come to him because of it."

> *And furthermore,*
> *You who are my grandfather,*
> *Male turkey,*
> *Weakening the enemy's hearts,*
> *You will remain here always.*[33]

When this prayer has been uttered, the Scalp chief takes those feathers from the turkey gobbler, which had lain on the meal or sand altar painting, and plants them in a hole along with food offerings. The cycles of the earthbound bird begin again. The earth and its stones, corn and other crops, the thirst for water—all of these are combined now with the idea of power.

At Taos the scalp-taker wears a turkey feather. "The scalp on its pole was brought out from Water kiva by the Telana. Save for breechcloth and moccasins they were naked, painted black all over, hair loose, a turkey feather on the crown of the head."[34] Elsewhere the turkey feather is not worn in warrior rituals, but it may be carried by the initiates.

When a Cochiti youth is initiated into the War society, he is required to go into a deep canyon at midnight.

> *When they arrive there, they must sacrifice cornmeal to the Super-natural Beings. Finally, they arrive at a waterfall. There he must take off his clothing and stand there looking northward. He sacrifices again and prays to the Supernatural Being (Mai'mai) who lives in the canyon. He also sacrifices turkey feathers (yectde). He asks to be made brave and to be able to withstand the Apache and Navaho.*[35]

Above these ties that link turkeys with the dead is the happier series that relates them to the earth, man's small plot in the cosmos. At Hopi, Turkey relates to all of the horizon directions, perhaps as their heart. In the Niman or Farewell to Kachina ceremonies in summer, ten sets of prayer-sticks the length of a forearm are made. These include banded turkey feathers, and the sticks are referred to as "all colors," which is to say all of the directions. They also have

> *the curious addition of two long "hairs" from the tassel of the turkey. The tassel is called* unun'humi, *"heart hair." These ten sets are dis-tributed northwest, southwest, southeast, northeast and at the Niman kachina shrine.*[36]

Among the Keres Turkey does not represent north, but in the myth of the Battle of the Seasons he fights on the side of Winter, which comes from the north. Turkeys also come down from the higher mountains when the snows begin to fall, so they combine a seasonal with a directional reference. At Acoma where their turkey-hunting area was literally to the north, on Mt. Taylor, they make prayer-sticks for North Mountain ruler. These are taken to the north of the village, and when the men return, they are greeted by the Country chief who, "has some turkey feathers tied up . . . with which he prays to the north."[37]

Any cycle relating earth, sun, and seasons will inevitably include rain. Turkey is always tending toward rain but not so specifically as the birds in Chapter 5. His relationship to the dead, who are rain makers, joins with the fact that turkeys must live near springs or running brooks to supply them with water. Like the clouds they run up and down the mountains. At Zuñi the Rain priests have a prayer that begins, "This day, desiring the waters of our fathers." The Mountain Turkey is addressed:

> *We have given our plume wands human form,*
> *With the massed cloud wing*
> *Of the one who is our grandfather,*
> *The male turkey,*
> *With the eagle's thin cloud wings*
> *And the massed cloud tails*
> *Of all the birds of summer.*[38]

Here the gobbler is mentioned first among the rain birds, but in the Medicine cult the same image is turned back toward the dead. The words of their prayer are the same, except that the third line is altered to, "the massed cloud *robes* of our grandfather." The image here faces toward the turkey feather mantle, now worn by the Cloud people who are the dead in the role of rain makers.

In Pueblo artwork the rain bird is a familiar element. But because most of the figures are abstract, one can only say that these birds relate to rain. In at least one instance this bird is a turkey.[39] A very important aspect of turkey behavior is the leadership ability of the older males. They take care of the whole flock and lead them in their wanderings. At Isleta this fact has received special notice. Turkey feathers, called *piendirude,* have ceremonial preeminence.

> *Now the chief stands in the middle of the room and throws pollen toward the east. Prayer feather making follows. The chief bids the Mother to set out the basket, and a man assistant to bring down the box of ritual feathers from where it hangs to a beam. A feather is placed in front of each assistant, there are to be twelve feathers, the turkey feather, "the oldest one," in front of the chief.*[40]

The sun, the sky, and the earth have now been placed together. The next element required is rain, and certain birds are specific symbols for this blessing.

rufous hummingbird

5 RAIN BIRDS

swallows, swifts, hummingbirds, and doves

The most important aspects of the cosmos are the sun, the sky, and then the earth. Birds representing these major points of reference are placed above all others in myths, rituals, and ceremonies. Under the sun, between sky and earth, are clouds, and some of these bring rain. Rain tends toward living things on the earthly plane. It nourishes food crops and flowering kinds, as well as animals and men who depend on plant life. Some birds are specific for the theme of Rain, as opposed to those that represent Water.

These rain birds are still in the sky and do not inhabit the water in a naturalistic sense—they have no special adaptations for living in water. Water is a separate concept, because not all of it falls from the sky. Under the earth are subterranean waters which well up in springs that are parts of underground waterways. Rain is simpler and always visible. It is a kind of communication between sky and earth, so the birds that represent it mediate between the two realms.

Swallows live just above the surfaces of streams and pools, which they barely touch except for food and water. They are birds typical of water courses, however small, and they are most often seen there, working their hardest, just before and after a shower of rain. That is for the very good reason that both these birds and the insects will have to sit out a downpour, and insects as well as swallows fly low just before rain.

Hummingbirds resemble the rainbow, the arch over which showers are brought down to earth. Hummingbirds also suck nectar, the moist element from the flowers of spring and summer. At a glance they are as brilliant as the fields of flowers on which they feed. Then, too, they have both great speed and endurance, which fits them to be messengers to the spirits who send rain.

If the chattering of swallows is a kind of speech that represents raindrops and relates sky to earth, doves have another type of voice that relates them to freshets and pools of water that stand in hollows after a summer rain. A song or a repetitive chant is thought to be more potent than simple speech, which is probably why streams begin to sing after a heavy rain. Doves have a song that is a chant, and it is often thought of as an incantation to bring rain; on the next level it is also an indication of where water may be found so that doves may later lead on from the rain birds to the actual water birds.

swallows and swifts

The swallows, all but one, are named by various Pueblo groups, and the swift is often included with them because of similar shape and habits. Zuñi Rain priests have a belief that certain birds must talk to them, and in turn they ask these birds to sing for rain. "Sing" happens to be in the account in English.[1] "Call" would probably be a better word, because none of the Rain priests' birds are songsters; these will appear later with the seasons. One feather used comes from the Long-tailed Chat, who might be said to sing. The notes are beautiful enough, but together with the swallows they are really a call to attention, which is usually uttered near a stream or from the brush and trees of a small pool, left after a rain that makes the washes run.

Four of the eight bird feathers offered by the Rain priests come from swallows. One myth relates the priests to a species of jimson weed *(Datura meteloides)*. On the worldly side Zuñi doctors used it for anesthetics during operations and as a powdered antiseptic for wounds. But for the Rain priests it was used, minutely, to give them the second sight that its powdered root conferred. So they put touches in their eyes, ears, and mouths. This was necessary because they had to go out in the dark of night to ask birds to sing for rain, and also that the birds would talk to them.

A'neglakya and his sister were spirits who wandered about the world, keenly observing everything. Their power enabled them to give people second sight, to put people to sleep, or to make them see ghosts. The War Twins thought that this was too much to know, so they were banished below the surface of the earth forever; where they went down the plant grew up. In this particular account the Rain priests offer feathers from birds representing the six directions. They deposit the offering separately in small excavations made with an ancient beanplanting stick.

They address the Datura spirit and his sister and place the prayer feathers, saying, "I take your medicine that I may talk to the birds of the six regions, that the rains may come and fructify Earth Mother and make her beautiful." In this account only the Purple Martin, as bird of the Zenith, is a member of the swallow family. From a more recent study by a Zuñi we find that the Violet-green Swallow, the Rough-winged Swallow, and the Cliff Swallow have feathers used by Rain priests. Anyone may handle birds or feathers, but only the Shi'wanni may use them.[2]

The Keres have names for the Violet-green and the Cliff Swallows, and Boas uses a different name for a "mud swallow." Presumably that would be a Barn Swallow, although it would also do for the Cliff Swallow. (The Barn Swallow is named by both the Tewas and Hopis.) Two names probably mean two different birds. The swift, even if not a swallow in our sense, has a name in Hopi, Zuñi, and Keresan. The Bank Swallow is named by the Hopi, so only the Tree Swallow is missing. It flies high and appears only during spring and fall migrations, often in the company of Bank Swallows. Perhaps it was never singled out, or again it may be that anthropologists have never discovered its name and distinctions.

Cliff Swallows are probably the most common ones in the Pueblo area, and they make mud houses that might be called pueblos, because they nest in colonies and build their places together. In most of the area the Violet-green summers in the high mountains, but they dip down in Hopi country. Barn Swallows, with their beautifully forked tails and the friendly habit of building nests in human dwellings, are common all over New Mexico but do not care much for the isolation of the Hopi mesas. The other kinds are less common.

Anywhere that water flows or stands there will be some member of this group dipping and circling to catch the insects that waters provide. Swifts, in our view, are close to hummingbirds, but in appearance and behavior they are like more vigorous swallows. This bird never perches and picks up its drinking water, on the wing, at full speed. A grounded swift is so much of the air that it cannot take off again unless it can climb to some high point to launch itself. Unlike the swallow, it feeds high in the air and is not as closely bound to water courses.

Because swallows come in summer, they might have been added to the summer birds, but they lack the bright colors, particularly the yellows of summer birds. It was noted that at Zuñi only the Rain priests may use swallow feathers. The Shi'wanni are a group of fourteen priests who are responsible for bringing the rains that in summer assure the growth of corn and other crops. This order is led by the Kia'kwemosi, who is the Rain priest for the North. It is said of him that, "His breath must be pure so that this region may always be fruitful and beautiful to look upon."[3]

Under him are Rain priests for the other three horizon directions, while the priest of the Zenith is the *Pekwin,* or deputy, to the Sun Father. The *Pekwin* is a literal sun watcher who establishes the solstices and sets from them the dates for all ceremonies. The priest of the Nadir utters prayers that the earth may be good to walk upon. Besides these priests who represent the directions there is also a group drawn from clans. The two Bow priests, representing the War gods, are related to this group as lightning makers.

Rain priests have the duty of fasting and praying for rain, both winter and summer. During the winter there are short retreats in which yucca suds are whipped up in imitation of clouds. In summer the retreats are longer, and the priests roll thunder stones. Also they are integrated and continuous; the priest of the North begins his retreat on June 26, when the young corn sprouts are up and in need of refreshment. He is followed by the other directional priests until August 5; then the clan Rain priests follow, concluding with several from the Corn clan and ending in mid-September.

A prayer that accompanies these rituals and offerings says in part:

Banked up clouds [cumuli] cover the earth.
All come four times with your showers,
Descend to the base of the ladder and stand still;
Bring your showers and great rains.
All, all come, all ascend, all come in, and sit down . . .
All come out and give us your showers and great rains.

Cover my earth mother four times with many flowers.
Let the heavens be covered with the banked up clouds.
Let the earth be covered with mist; cover the earth with rains.
Great waters, rains, cover the earth. Lightning cover the earth.
Let thunder be heard over the earth, let thunder be heard.
Let thunder be heard over the six regions of the earth.[4]

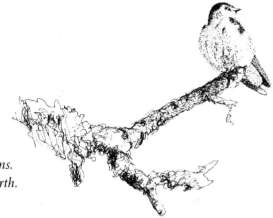

white-throated swift

Swallow feathers are a part of these rain offerings, because as one Zuñi said, "These birds fly around before rain and after. The Rain priests use their feathers. They are hard to get."[5] No matter how hard they were to get, they were necessary, so specially devised snares of horsehair were stretched across a pond and weighted at the ends. In the old days these would have, of course, been made of human hair. When the birds skimmed the ponds for insects, they became entangled and were captured. Mentioned are Violet-green Swallows, Cliff Swallows, Purple Martins, and swifts. Rough-winged Swallows were probably dug from their nests.

In tales the diving-down movement of swallows seems to indicate a bit of mimetic magic in bringing down rain. Long ago all of the birds lived on Corn Mountain, a great mesa behind Zuñi. They held a contest to see who could fly the highest, and it was won by Cliff Swallow, who made a great dive and disappeared into a hole when he came to earth.[6] Because swallows do not really fly high in the sense of an eagle, it would seem that coming down swiftly is the thought.

The Keres Indians make the same rain-bringing symbol of the swallows, above all in myth where the spirit of the South, in the Battle of the Seasons, arrived with a following of swallows. Miochin was his name, and he called together all the birds and animals that live in sunny climes; then, riding on a cloud, this spirit of Summer floated northward to battle. Among the birds of summer, and just behind the first-ranked eagles, were a swallow, a Mud Swallow, and a small swift.[7] The spirit of Summer used lightning as his weapons, and Shakak, spirit of Winter and the North, retreated. A truce was arranged, and the seasons were divided between them.

In another Keresan tale, a secondary point is made. This explains how a spring came to be called Frog's Husband's House. Both the bird and the amphibian are linked to ponds. One day Swallow Man married Frog and was taking her to his house, but he was hindered by the different pace at which the two could travel. Coyote passed by and, hearing of the difficulty, let Frog climb on his back, and they reached the home of Swallow's mother.

> Then the mother of Swallow said, "Have you arrived?" "Yes," said they. "Then climb up," said Swallow's mother to them. Then Frog said, "How shall I climb up? Can I not sit in the spring and my mother-in-law can hand down food to me?"[8]

This was agreed upon, the fancy being that the swallows in their dipping flight over the pool are bringing food to the frogs beneath its waters. Frogs also sing rain songs, so it is fitting that the two should be married.

One scarcely thinks of a song in connection with the swallow family. The gurgling sounds of martins and the twitter of Barn Swallows are pleasant enough, but some of the others are merely chatter. Nonetheless, if one knows the intent of swallows and their interest in flowing waters, as well as standing pools of rain, it is possible to construct from their clipped and muffled notes a song of great beauty. One such song, recorded from Acoma, sets the bird's notes to native words that are so close to the swallow's voice that it can be heard in the imitation.

While this has already been given, it is worth repeating in part.

Beni chi, beni chi, beni nu tsoutr
Soya ta.
Wa wi, wa wi, ha ha, ha ha!

This has been translated as:

Western river, western river, coming from the west,
I sing of you.
Wa wi, wa wi, ha ha, ha ha![9]

The river in this song is the little Rio San Jose, which comes down from the Zuñi Mountains and flows past the farming plots of Acoma. That song is certainly the best that could be said for the voice to any swallow.

The Violet-green Swallow has a shrill note, and the voice of the Bank Swallow is harsh and gritty; the Rough-winged utters an occasional batlike squeak. The Pueblos, like the Greeks, took note of this inability to speak out clearly, so there is a subtheme on speech, but inhibited speech. True speech relates to the mockingbird.

In the Greek story, King Tereus was married to Prokne but fell in love with her sister. He seduced her and then cut out her tongue so that she could not tell. One of these sisters was a swallow and the other a nightingale. When the evil was discovered, he pursued both with an intent of murder, but during the pursuit he was changed into another bird, the hoopoe. That is supposed to explain why the nightingale mourns, and the tongueless swallow only chatters when she tries to recount her wrongs.

Swallows are connected with speechlessness at Isleta. A girl there was born deaf and dumb, which was, of course, a problem to her family; there had to be a reason. ". . . Her grandmother once suggested to her mother that it was because during her pregnancy she had mocked at the little chattering bird called bebatire [dizzy flying] that her child was born dumb."[10] I have not found that name elsewhere, but it is likely one of the swallows, whose speech seems confused or muffled.

Because, as we have seen, some swallows enter either holes in the ground or crevices, there is an inevitable connection that links these rain birds with seeds. The Hopis tell that, when the people emerged from the Underworld, they forgot to bring the seeds up with them. "There was much lamenting, much discussing, until the God of Dew sent the chimney-swallow back to bring the seed of corn and other foods. When the swallow returned, the God of Dew planted in the ground the seed."[11]

The name used by the recorder of that story is wrong, because it applies to a European species, but the sky-rain-earth-seed sequence is a proper one. I presume that the God of dew is Alosaka, a fertility god who combines these things. As for the bird, a Cliff Swallow would be seen disappearing into holes or clefts in cliffs, while the Rough-winged would literally go underground along banks.

Another Hopi story utilizes the habit of some swallows in entering holes. It relates to an earlier phase of the emergence myth, when the entire race was still underground. Those below were looking for an exit onto the sunlit, rain-showered earth. Birds were sent out to find a way and among these was a swallow. "Next time the chimney-swallow, which is very strong and fast, attempted it. As he turned back he felt a current of cool air. He went in the direction whence it came, then thither and yon, but he could not find the entrance."[12] The teller of the myth had certainly stood many times in a narrow side canyon, enjoying the cool draft while Cliff Swallows swooped and turned about him.

hummingbirds

Tireless hummingbirds are the least of birds, but they have a rainbow of iridescent colors and spend their time hovering about the flowers that are a sign of fruitfulness. In particular they like the nectar, the moist element, of the tobacco plant, and this is in the tubular bloom, above the leaves that are used for cloud-inducing smoke. Ritualists blow tobacco leaf smoke to all of the directions in order to induce rain and thus again the sequence of flowers, crops, and food.

At Taos the Broad-tailed Hummingbird is called "flower bird," while the Rufous Hummingbird is named "sun bird."[13] These are the two common species in the Pueblo area. More simply the Taos Indians refer to them as the green one and the red one. The Hopis single out the Rufous as the "Red Hummingbird." At Zuñi there is only one name recorded, and it is placed by Ladd under the Broad-tailed species, which indicates that it is the important one there.

The Broad-tailed Hummingbird is common throughout the mountainous parts of New Mexico; because it breeds in all of the area, it is often seen in summer. Its hood and back are metallic green, while its throat is a bright rose pink. The conspicuous tail is green bordered with dull bronze or black. This species is also found in northern Arizona from April to September. The Rufous Hummingbird is also common, but it does not breed in New Mexico; it occurs during a migration that begins in July and the bird becomes common in August. In Arizona Woodbury notes it as being common in those two important summer months in the Hopi area. The Rufous Hummingbird has a flaming red throat and a reddish-brown hood and back.

At Zuñi the use of hummingbird feathers is limited to the Rain priests. To get these feathers special traps have been devised to catch the hummingbirds. For the purpose several loops of horsehair were tied up and down the bloom of a Rocky Mountain bee plant. These hair loops had slip knots like a lariat, and as the bird traveled up and down the blossom in search of nectar, it might be entangled in one noose and draw it tight when darting away.

At nearby Acoma they tell a story that explains Hummingbird's relationship to rain and at the same time accounts for its brilliant colors. Kaupat'a was a volcano demon (huge lava beds stretch down the east side of the Zuñi Mountains and reach almost to the cornfields of Acomita). That demon played a gambling game with the son of the Sun and lost. The Sun's son blinded the loser, and the blind giant then

> *sang his supernatural song and set fire to pitch from the piñon trees. He stirred the burning pitch and set his house on fire. He stirred it round and round and the lava flowed in both directions to the north and west.*

A number of birds were burned in various parts of their heads or bodies while trying to put out the fire of these molten rocks. All failed, until

> *Hummingbird flew around the great waters to the north, west, south and east, to rouse the tides and put out the fire. He flew through the rainbow and for this reason the hummingbird wears the colors of the rainbow in the feathers around his neck. The clouds came from every direction. The hail fell on the burning lava rock, but could not cool the terrible heat. Rain fell and the lava rock stopped flowing and the fire was put out.*[14]

The rainbow colors, its great strength in flying, and its hovering about flowers—particularly tobacco blossoms—relate Hummingbird to ritual practices. One common method of inducing rain used by Pueblo priests is to blow clouds of tobacco smoke to the directions. The cloudlike form of these puffs is thought to appeal to the real clouds gathering in the sky. Two accounts from Acoma explain the origin of this ritual.

The Keresan Mother goddess, or Corn goddess, hid herself from the people, because they mocked her and because something was lacking from ceremony. In a version of the story based on actual rites, Hummingbird Man learned that something had been missing from ritual practice. The Mother goddess then called the missing part with a name that no one could understand, but Hummingbird Man divines that both the kachina and *kopishtaiya,* or collectivity of spirits, smoke with it, so it is decided that the object must be a pipe.

RAIN BIRDS

"That is it," she said to him.[15]

In the Rain ceremony of the Sia Snake society, feathers of hummingbirds are tied to the offering. Drought is, of course, the opposite of rain, so Hummingbird relates to relief from dry spells. At Cochiti one of these droughts was caused by a failure of belief in the Mother goddess. Only Hummingbird was exempt from the effects, because he had foreknowledge of what to do. "Our Mother had told Hummingbird what to do. 'Child, never tell where I have gone. For four years there will be no rain, not even a cloud. Whenever you are thirsty for honey go to *shipap* and there you shall suck from the flowers.'"[16]

Shipap is the entrance to the Underworld, and by the use of nectar from flowers that grow in that region the bird is always able to remain fat, even when people above are starving. During one drought the Fly as well as Hummingbird were sent as messengers to the Mother. In the Underworld they found that everything was growing beautifully despite the drought above. The Fly kept stopping to eat.

"Then spoke Hummingbird, 'Don't—let us first meet our mother.'" One must observe a ritual fast if a request to spirits is to succeed. These messengers bring pollen, beads, and prayer-sticks to offer to her. "'I suppose you want something?'—'Yes, we want food and your body and storm clouds.'" She tells them first to get Turkey Buzzard to purify the town, the earth, and the thunder clouds.

Smoke is a purifying element as well as a cloud bringer. The smoke from juniper boughs purifies one from contact with the dead, and smoke from hunt fires purifies the heart of a hunter so that he may be in harmony with his game. In this instance the two messengers go to Buzzard's home, where they find that their offerings are incomplete (there is no tobacco), so they return to the Mother and ask where it can be found. "There on a hill, there right in the middle is a doorway. There caterpillar lives. Him you will ask for tobacco."[17]

The Tobacco Caterpillar is a frequenter and guardian of the two species of *Nicotiana,* one of which is day-flowering and one a nocturnal bloomer. Hummingbird as a frequenter of the plant asks

Caterpillar for some of his tobacco. This he takes back to Buzzard, who smokes to the four directions, to his mothers, to the chiefs, and then once more to purify the town. Soon all was well: "Storm clouds, crops and happiness there around were spread."

Another version of the story involves a longer drought and a Gamekeeper spirit called Heluta, who brings in the deer. An earthly counterpart of Heluta also brings in the lines of kachina dancers at Cochiti. Because they and the spirits that they represented are rain bringers, working in harmony is essential. Heluta was challenged to a contest of providing food. The Indians set out abundant corn, but Heluta cannot, by his nature, provide that kind. The people mocked him, and as punishment for this hubris he withdrew himself, bringing drought.

After four years the people were starving, so they first sent a fly to Shipap to find Heluta; he pulled out its tongue so that when it returned, there was only a buzzing sound in place of a message. The people then sent Hummingbird who asks in the name of the villagers that the spirit forgive them. "The children are dying of hunger and thirst. Now they have learned that it is by your power that they live."[18] Heluta takes pity on the populace and asks them to hunt and bring him a deer, a story recounted in *Pueblo Animals and Myths*. Here he plants the dew claws, which bring an increase in the deer, the sort of food he is able to provide. Along with the slain deer offering comes abundant rain to nourish the corn plants.

Hummingbird has the quality of swiftness, as seen in its darting flight, and also of endurance that it exhibits by standing still in the air. Hawks do that when they swoop, but the hummingbird does not drop to the ground; it changes course backward and forward in tireless flight. Racing requires swiftness, and most Pueblo foot races are run to suggest, by mimetic magic, that the clouds come quickly and bring rain. For that reason the race course is often a narrowing spiral that ends in the village itself as the distant circles are brought home.

At Zuñi a kick-stick racer takes it as a good omen if he sees a hummingbird while he runs. Everyone wants to see the human qualities of swiftness and endurance in the children who race forward. At Hopi the father of a young boy makes a special type of prayer-feather offering called a "road marker," a long string to which are tied various feathers. For the boy these are primary wing feathers of *toh'cha,* the hummingbird. His father

> *places the free end of the string of this prayer-feather against the base of the shrine, the feather toward the sunrise, and prays for swiftness and endurance, that his movements may be like those of the hummingbird, as swift and tireless.*[19]

That particular feather offering, called a *nakwa'kwoshi,* is based on a string rather than a stick because such an offering is not as heavy—it is light like a cloud—and swift in its journey across the sky. Messengers must have the quality of swiftness, so, "Hummingbird is Acoma's special messenger."[20] At Zuñi Hummingbird acted as one of the scouts at the time when people emerged from the Underworld. Zuñi priests were seeking a road out to their Sun Father, so Hummingbird was dispatched.

"You shall be the one to look for their road; for that we have summoned you." He has no more success in looking for their road than the Hawks and Eagles. "For the fourth time Hummingbird went close along the edge of the sky. Coming back to the same place, nothing was visible."[21] That mission belonged to burrowing animals and was too much for a small bird and even for the high-soaring ones. Nevertheless, hummingbirds do seek out small openings, such as those of the tube in a tobacco plant; reaching in and bringing forth can be a service.

At Tiwa Isleta prayer-sticks for the stillborn are made during the Winter Solstice ceremony, and several hummingbird feathers are attached to the ends of each stick. The chief then takes them to a sacred place sometime before sunrise and finds a hole into which his assistant casts cornmeal. Next the chief extends the prayer-stick into the hole, waiting for the stillborn to take it from him.[22]

In this rite two ideas converge. Children who die before they are four days old are thought to be born again, so the stillborn will again emerge. At the solstice the Sun is also being drawn out of his

Winter house, to start his journey toward Summer. The hummingbird through its habits and bright feathers serves to represent all of these ideas in combination. The drawing out is done with the bird's long bill, so there is a tall tale, from Oraibi, in which Coyote discovers this bill protruding—"Thanks, I have found a needle. I shall take that home to my mother and she will sew a dress for herself."[23]

On a more serious note the Hopi-Tewas have a story that relates the long bill to curing rites. One kind of illness is caused by foreign objects shot into the body, often by witches. The theurgist who treats the patient removes these by sucking them out of the body. In this story two boys, analogues of the War Twins, set out to find their missing father. Gopher tells them that their father is far away and about to die. When they reach him, the boys gather sunflower stalks and fashion these like the bills of hummingbirds. They then make wings and legs out of the flowers themselves.

Next they make prayer-feather strings, then spread out a buckskin, place a basket on it with the feather strings and the birds that they have constructed. Then, with shaking rattles, the boys begin to sing; after eight songs the hummingbirds come out from under the cover that was placed over the basket. "They began to fly around inside the room. They told the hummingbirds to go and suck out the stick from their father's foot. The hummingbirds began to suck and they could see the stick move. Soon out came the stick." The father was now on the road to recovery, and the boys say to the birds: "You have saved our father. You can go out to live forever among the flowers."[24]

The connection between the sunflowers of summer, the hummingbirds, and this illness has cosmic purport, for the father is the Sun himself, who sickens once a year and must recover his strength through rituals performed by men. The rainbow's colors are created by the sun, and the hummingbird is an intermediary between sun and rain and flowers. As a reward for its aid in rejuvenating a summer sun, Hummingbird is allowed to suck forever the rich nectar provided by blossoms.

In an area where live streams are scarce or nonexistent, doves *doves* are related to rain pools and springs to which they must return at dusk to drink. Their voices may be thought of as both an invocation to this kind of water and an indication to humankind of places where they may slake their thirst. Doves need water, because they live on a diet of seeds that make birds very thirsty at the end of a day spent in gathering. Seeds are the after-products of flowers, and plants need rain to turn out first the bloom and then its seeds. The notes of doves bring these things together and are thought of as rain songs.

Doves are one of the most visible birds in the Pueblo area, particularly along roadsides where a variety of sunflowers and the Rocky Mountain bee plant flourish, even in times of scant rainfall. Several other species of doves in New Mexico and Arizona are found mostly to the south of the Pueblo region, and names for them appear only in Hopi accounts. The Band-tailed Pigeon, on the other hand, is widely scattered in the area. At Zuñi there are two names for dove, and one may refer to the pigeon, a name often used in translating stories.

The Mourning Dove's soft but persistent notes have contributed to its English name; the same thought has occurred to the Pueblos, but it is not the main theme. Equally notable is the rushing noise of a dove's wings in flight, a flight that is surprisingly strong. They may fly at a speed of thirty to forty miles an hour, enabling them to reach distant pools or streams for the water that they must have once a day for digesting the moistureless seeds that they eat. Both their call notes and the habit of searching out springs and pools have attracted Pueblo attention.

Most of the names for dove in Pueblo languages seem to have been derived from the sound of the bird's call: *kaipia'o'one* at Picuris, *ko-oñwi* in Tewa, *ho-o-k'a* of the Keres, *hue-wih* of the Hopis, and possibly the *ginamu* of the Jemez Indians. At Picuris a secular tale recounts the seed-eating habits of doves.

Some of the Picuris youths at the pueblo made their living by going out hunting every day to the mountains, and returned in the evening packing deer. And the two little Doves did nothing but plant every year. They lived, planting corn and beans of various colors in the spring, eating well and not thinking of hunting as the youths of Picuris did. They were seen every day early before sunrise in their fields where their crops were, having their hoes with them, singing.

One year a drought overtook the two Doves, and there was nothing for them to do except sit in the shade, where the youths taunted the birds for their indolence. The Doves appealed for help to the Vulture, but he claimed to like the heat; then they spoke to the seed-eating Crow, who also failed them. The final appeal was to Morning Star, the supernatural patron of hunters. He told the Doves not to be sad, indicating that their mourning notes were caused by drought and were at the same time a plea for rain.

By the time these birds reached home, a few drops of rain were beginning to fall, and the rain produced abundant crops for the Picuris people as well as the doves. It is also a moralistic tale indicating that the Picuris should "not do so much hunting, so that they may learn to work."[25] As a Hunt spirit the Morning Star would have an interest in preserving a balance between time spent hunting and time spent planting and harvesting. He is a protector as well as provider of game. Picuris is a high mountain pueblo with a short growing season; yet even a remote area can be depleted of game if people depend on it entirely.

There is again here the connection between killing a deer and bringing rain—clouds, like deer, retreat to the highest mountain tops. The several Tewa villages that are far below Picuris have the same association of the dove's voice with a rain song. "When a San Ildefonsan was describing the flight noises of the dove and the 'O—'O—'O'—'O of their cry, one of the old Indians broke out into a rain song, which

white-winged dove

led us to suspect that this bird was connected in his mind with rain."[26] From Tewa San Juan comes a snatch of song in which small brown birds, presumably doves, sing while cleaning seeds:

atsiningki apu
kah pu pu pu pu
together it blows
leaf blows blows blows blows.[27]

After the harvest these same notes become a winnowing rather than a rain song, and a dove does have to winnow the seeds that it eats.

The Keresan pueblos of San Felipe and Santa Ana have Dove clans, but clans there have little ceremonial connection, beyond a presumption of mutual help for fellow members. However, the Dove is related to one of the clown societies, as the Sparrow Hawk is to the other. If the Koshare are to be in charge of the saint's day dance, "they tie a piece of corn husk, or one or two tail feathers of the *ho-o-ka* [mourning dove] on the left side of the head of each dancer, who leaves it there for a time and then takes it off and hangs it in his house."[28] This is the "badge" of the Koshare clown group that leads the dance. The Sparrow Hawk feathers are for Queranna clowns.

In a Keresan tale from Laguna the Dove's call appears as an incident during the pursuit of a group of girls, doubtless the Corn Maidens chased by Sun Youth or Paiyatemu.[29] Sun Youth has put a sleep-inducing medicine into the spring where he has led them.

"Wait here a while. Stand here for awhile. Let me look for it here in the north inside. Maybe there is water there. If there is water, then it will sound like a pigeon," said he. "How will it sound?" said the Yellow-Women.
"Thus will call the pigeon,

hu—u ko—wai
hoo oo water, water."[30]

Though this is translated as "pigeon," the native text gives the Mourning Dove's name.

This same song is explained at Santa Ana, where it is said that the call of the Mourning Dove is *"ho-'o G'owai, G'owai!"*—"Water, pool of water!" There is also a woman's corn-grinding song, man singing, which is translated as: "Dove, you liar, you are always telling the Corn Maidens that there is water over here and over there."[31] In these songs the Mourning Dove is indicating the places where water might be found, which it would certainly know, but the bird may also be making a more general supplication for rain as we saw in the beginning.

The Zuñis have a story and a song that illustrate this point. The Shi'wanni, Rain making priests, had failed to bring rain, so Dove decided to try. "He said to the others, 'How are we going to get along? If it does not rain, we shall have no seeds to eat. I am going to try for rain.' They said, 'What are you going to do?'" Then like the Rain priests he made a small pool of water, praying over it and singing:

> *Una a un a taka*
> *una a una u taka*
> *anahona chawito.*

He then took a feather out of each wing, to be used as the priest would have used an eagle feather, dipped them in his pool, and sprinkled to each direction. "As he did this the clouds began to gather." He sang again and repeated his aspersing. "It began to sprinkle."

Unfortunately an old Cooper's Hawk was watching this rite.

> *He said, "There is* nishapako *praying for rain." He kept watching. When it began to sprinkle, he flew over to where* nishapako *was. While he was singing,* anethlau *swooped down on him and ate him up. The clouds all went away again because the one who had prayed was eaten up. Because of the hawk they had no rain. Thus long ago.*[32]

Despite the fact that the Zuñis held this concept of the dove as a rain suppliant, dove feathers were not used on prayer-stick offerings, though they could be used on masks. The proscription on ritual use of these feathers derives from a myth in which the War Twins killed two Navajo girls whose spirits then became doves.[33] In the published versions of this myth, which will be discussed in the chapter on roadrunners, there is no mention of a transformation into bird form, but there is a logical connection. All scalps, including those of Navajo maidens, are potent rain makers, and it is said: "take her scalp with the stone knife, and call the rain."[34] In this particular account the dead maidens apparently spend eternity counting the stars.

The Zuñis do make one ritualistic use of dove feathers, even though prayer-sticks containing them are taboo. They are used on the sacred corn-ear fetish, the *mi'li*. Among the sets of feathers enfolding the fetish in Stevenson's day were "six white o'wa [dove] plumes from the tail of the male bird . . . each one being wrapped on separately."[35] The name *o'wa* is not the common one for doves; it may be a sacred name derived from the bird's notes or from another language, because both Keres and Hopi names have similar phonemes.

At Hopi one of the three women's societies, the La'lakontu, holds a Weather Control ceremony during the month of August, and according to Stephen, "The Lalakon standard consists of the white corn ear, sumac, and dove feathers."[36] The use of these feathers has an etiological tale, but of a negative turn, because it depends on an unsuccessful quest while the Hopi were still in the Underworld. At that time at least two different societies sent out birds to search for the entrance into this world.

> *Before people got the reed [on which they ascended] the Lalakontu sent out the dove [huwi], and it flew around the sky seeking for the* sipapu. *It flew all around the horizon, but could find no opening and came back tired. The people reviled it and called it a fool.*[37]

We have already heard the dove called a liar for announcing falsely the location of a spring where there was none, which must often happen in a dry land. Now it is called a fool for failing to locate the opening into this world. However, the rites of this women's group indicate clearly why the dove appears on the standard announcing the ceremony. The women make meal "roads" to Sun spring, from which maidens bring back netted gourds filled with water. And it is the pool-seeking nature of the dove, and by implication its rain bringing, that joins it to this August ceremony.

A Dove lineage in the Hopi Snake clan keeps the *tiponi* or fetish of the Antelope society, one of the participants in the complex Snake-Antelope ceremony involving rain, seed germination and growth, ripening of corn, and some degree of Sun ritual. Netted gourds of water are also a feature in these rites, but where the Dove stands in so complicated an integration of elements is difficult to say.

The Pueblos are a highly communal people, but they also have room for individual problems, and the Hopis give this same latitude to the dove. In one tale the mourning notes of the bird are attributed to personal difficulties.

> The Shongopovi were living in their village, and south of the village there was a hill called Kwakchome. There was a great deal of this grass called kwakwi *there. A Turtle-dove one time was rubbing out seed from the tassels of this grass, and while doing so cut her hand with the sharp edge of one blade. It bled profusely, and the Turtle-dove was moaning as follows:*
>
> > *Hooho, hoo, hooho, hoo, hooho, hoo,*
> > *Ho-ho-ho*
>
> *While she was moaning a Coyote came along and heard somebody singing, as he believed. So he approached the place. When he arrived he saw the Turtle-dove sitting and leaning forward in great distress. "Are you singing?" he asked the Dove. "Are you thus singing?" "No," she said, "I am not singing; I am crying."* [38]

The plant, *kwakwi,* which figures in this story as food for the dove, is the giant dropseed, a tall grass with a long bloom spike. [39] In olden days it was harvested by Hopi women as a kind of wild grain, mourning dove

and those who hear the story, or who hear doves lament while they are themselves out gathering wild seeds, would sympathize greatly, because both doves and women feel the sharp edges of the grass. Although the significance of a bird may branch out in such a personal direction, the elaboration of a basic theme refers back to the general view—the seed-eating dove calls out above all for water and for rain; rain does not always come, so the bird sorrows.

Songless swallows, on the other hand, bring the rain by their mimetic movements, dipping and circling above the water courses, while the hummingbirds reflect rain through their brilliant colors resembling rainbows, or the rain's product in flowers. All together these kinds might be thought of as a habitat group of rain-making birds.

6 WATER BIRDS

ducks, snipes, killdeer, and sandhill cranes

A number of birds are associated with bodies of water, whether these are pools, marshes, streams, or large rivers. Water is often a product of rain, so some of these birds relate to that theme but never exclusively so. In the bird list there are names for loons, grebes, herons, egrets, bitterns, ibis, and ducks, geese, and swans. Other water birds are the cranes, killdeer, snipes, and their allies, and there are names for these marginal water birds as well.

All of them are naturally adapted to living in or around water, although the ways that they go about this differ greatly. Many of them migrate along the larger water courses, some are entirely water bound—certain ducks even feeding under the water—while others wade in not too deeply or play about on the margins of pools or marshes. There are three prominent subthemes for the group: seed gathering or bringing, guardianship, and a role as messengers. The latter sometimes relates to speech, in the form of myth telling and hearing, or to listening in order to give a warning.

Many ducks feed on the seeds of wild marsh plants, while the Mallard has no aversion to domestic seed grain. Geese enjoy domestic corn seed, and cranes make something of a specialty of it. If this possibility is joined with the migratory habits of the birds, they can be thought of as bringing seeds in their travels from distant points beyond the horizon, from the four directions where the spirits live. These flyways converge on a Pueblo center, and it is thus that ducks become explorers in search of a Middle Place and spiritual home.

They bring with them the seeds that they like, as well as the clouds and rain that also travel with them. Guardianship is a notable quality of any flock of cranes, because one of these birds is always awake and watching. Killdeer are also guards or watchmen at ponds. On approaching any waterhole one will hear a noisy outcry announcing one's presence. In a minor way that habit relates them to War parties that can use such information. A warning is also one kind of speech, but it is not the true nature of speech.

ducks

Swans, geese, and ducks belong together in a single family, as we classify them. They are naturally associated with water, both because of their seasonal travels along waterways and because great resting flocks settle on ponds or marshes. The Canada Goose has a name in all Pueblo languages, while the Hopis named the Trumpeter Swan, which is now extinct in the area, but ducks are the central water birds. Usually the ducks are grouped under a single name in each language, but often additions are linked to the root word for indicating separate kinds. Mearns found names for sixteen different species at Hopi, while Ladd mentions five species as being important at Zuñi.

One is not surprised at the importance of duck feathers in the Rio Grande pueblos, but at first glance Hopi and Zuñi are not placed in what one thinks of as duck country. Actually no village is far from some water course, standing pool or marsh, and the main flyway has a diversion along the border of Arizona and New Mexico. Many ducks rest on the crater lakes in the Flagstaff area and on the ponds that form even in the desert regions.

The Zuñi River flows past the town and more distantly forms a lake where it meets the Little Colorado. This lake and the marshes around it are prominent in mythology. On the other side of the Zuñi Mountains and east of the Continental Divide, the Rio San Jose flows past Laguna, where there was once a real lake, and the farming fields of Acoma, which are distant from the pueblo itself. Although the river is not impressive now, it once served as more of a refuge for water birds. In the 1850s Beadle wrote:

The fertile valley in which McCarty's Ranch is situated . . . gradu-
ally narrows westward, and a gorge not more than two hundred yards
opens into another valley. The last three miles of the former valley
is mostly marsh, and thither the officers from Wingate often go to
hunt ducks.[1]

When the Pueblos hunt ducks, it is not for food but for their
feathers, which rank in importance just behind eagle and turkey
feathers. There is also a belief, at least at Zuñi, that ducks are the
form a spirit takes when traveling home. These spirits are the kachinas who are thought to be present as soon as human dancers who
stand in for them don their masks. When these are removed, the
spirits return to their home, which may be in the cloud quarters or
under the lake waters. At Zuñi the dancers go down to the river to
take off their masks, and the spirits travel to the lake, eighty miles to
the southwest.

Ducks undoubtedly took that route, but the mythological significance is more important. Two spirits play a great role here. Kia'-
kwemosi stands at the head of a lineage of Rain priests of the North;
he had a daughter and a son who were alone and joined in incestu-
ous union, but their offspring were infertile. The brother then decided that he must create a place for different kinds of people.

He descended the mountain and drew his foot through the sands
and created the two rivers [the Zuñi and the Little Colorado] and
a lake, and in the depths of the lake a village. . . . The village is
Ko'thluwala'wa, having the great ceremonial house of the gods
in its center. This house is provided with four windows, through
which those not privileged to enter may view the dance. Only the
deceased member of the ko'tikili *[mythologic fraternity] go within*
the walls.[2]

There are several names for this lake, one translated as Listening Spring, or Whispering Water, the reference being to voices that
may be heard in the depths. Usually it is called Ko'thluwala'wa but in
ceremonies it is called We'nima. The latter is a root word used in

several languages to indicate the home of the dead. Members of the mythologic fraternity go to this underwater village when they die to join the Zuñi spirits there. In a song we find:

> *Our great-grandfather duck came out a short time since*
> *From the old dance village by the mountains.*
> *You have reached the [kiva]; ascend the ladder.*
> *You will enter the [kiva], and here you will sit down.*
> *Hasten and enter; hasten and stand.*
> *Inside you will see your fathers all seated calling for seeds.*[3]

There is no invocation to rain here but an invocation to seeds. Ducks return from the North point, which is ruled by the Rain priest of that direction, bringing seeds, which are emblems of fertility requiring water. Bringing things back and forth from the North and then from the South again relates the duck to mythology and to formal myth-bearers. Kiaklo is the Zuñi spirit who is the Keeper of Myths, and he not only tells stories but is also a great listener. Possibly several ideas are joined here—ducks and geese call out in flight, and they listen attentively while resting on ponds or lakes.

Kiaklo's myth is again centered in the whispering or listening lake.

> *K'yak'lu, the all hearing and wise of speech, all alone had been*
> *journeying afar in the north land of cold and white desolateness.*
> *Lost was he, for all the world he wandered in now was disguised*
> *with snow that lies spread forth there forever.*

This myth was set in the time before the discovery of the center of the world, which is Zuñi. During his troubles and travels he was transformed into a water bird. Because he became all white, one thinks of the Snow Goose or the Whistling Swan, both of which pass through New Mexico with migratory ducks.

> *Yea and his lips became splayed with continual calling, and his voice*
> *grew shrill and dry sounding, like the voices of farflying water-fowl.*

As he cried, wandering all blindly hither and thither, these, water-birds, hearing flocked around him in numbers.

Kiaklo understood their speech, as it was so like his own. "So was she [the duck] of all regions the traveler and searcher, knowing all ways, whether above or below the waters, whether in the north, the west, the south, or the east, and there in was the most knowing of all creatures."

Kiaklo, who is blind, tells the duck of his hopeless search for the Middle Place. Duck tells him that while he knows all, she sees all, and that he should follow her by placing "talking shells" about her neck. "Thy country and the way thither well I know, for I go that way each year leading the wild goose and the crane, who flee thither as winter follows." With the aid of the "rainbow worm," who stretched out across the waters southward, Kiaklo is deposited on a plain near the lake while the duck lit on the listening or whispering waters.

There she swam to and fro, this way and that, up and down, loudly quacking and calling. Lo! the lights of the [kiva] of the Ka'ka [spirits] began to gleam in the waters, and as she gazed she beheld, rising from them, snout foremost, like one of her own kind, the Salamopia of the north, whom the gods of the Ka'ka, the noble surpassing Pautiwa . . . had dispatched to bid the duck dive down and lay before them whatsoever message she might bear.[4]

The spirits who were "like unto herself" are the Salimobia kachinas who are guardians, messengers, and seed bearers from the six directions. Here they arise from the waters of the lake under which the kiva of the gods or kachinas is placed. Their likeness to the duck is symbolized by a full-sized duck bill and head of a duck, with a trail of feathers, that surmounts the helmet mask like a crest. Both Duck and these messengers can fly to the far corners of the world. In ceremonies they act as honor guards in the procession of the gods as they come to Zuñi from the lake.

These spirits ask the Duck to bring Kiaklo to the lake in order that he may learn of the Zuñi past, hear of the future and become the listener and myth bearer. The chief of the council of the gods gives him his instructions. "Then K'yak'lu sat him down and bowed his head, and calling to the Duck, who had guided him, stretched forth his hand and upon it she settled. . . ."[5]

When Kiaklo appears for the tribal initiation, he wears a mask decorated with a frog and tadpoles, a rainbow over the forehead of his mask and three lines beneath his eyes, which symbolize falling rain. "The personator carries a duck skin filled with seed, with a string of shells around the neck, which he uses as a rattle."[6] Shells are of the water, and they do whisper or talk outright when hung in clusters. Two other kachinas who dance at Zuñi wear symbolic ducks on the top of masks; both seem to be borrowed.

The short-haired Chakwena comes from the Keresan pueblo of Laguna and speaks in that language rather than in Zuñi. This personage is a hunt figure described in *Pueblo Animals and Myths.* The mask has for eyes two new moons with the horns turned down, indicating that Mother Moon is pouring out water, and then some yellow on the shoulders for sunshiny days. Also an incomplete rainbow. "The rainbow stops the rain, but they want the rain to go on, so they do not finish the rainbow, but break it with another design."[7]

The Zuñi Hilili kachina appears with the Eagle kachina, which is fitting because both are in the far sky. Hilili wears a duck's head on top of his mask and is said to have come from Hopi, where he is associated with snakes. Snakes, like ducks, are messengers to the gods of all directions and are much of the earth, so there is a joining of sky, earth, and water. Because the particular connections are elaborate, they will be examined in a later book that takes account of snakes and rodents.

The basic message that ducks carry is one of water but joined with earth and sky. Thus they combine with Eagle and Turkey. According to Ladd, the feathers of the Mallard drake are particularly prized for their blue-green color. The blue green of a turquoise is itself a representation of both sky and water, and that is why the color and the stone are so prized. These duck feathers are used for the "blanket" of the individual fetish, called *mi'li,* of the Beast society members. Nearly a century ago Stevenson said that wing feathers were used for the purpose.

These Zuñi accounts state pretty well what ducks stood for—or swam for—but divisions of classification are also of interest. At Hopi, for example, there is a Duck kachina called Pawik. According to Stephen *pa'wikya* means "scoop the water," duck.[8] On Mearns' list of duck names this root is found in the names for Cinnamon Teal, Shoveler, and Gadwall. The first two are still common ducks in Arizona during migration. The Gadwall is now an uncommon summer resident of the crater lakes in the San Francisco Mountain region, but in 1887 Mearns found it common there.

Another root appears in most duck names: *wek-ka.* It is also a part of the names of two herons, two egrets, the White-faced Ibis, and, oddly, two hawks (these are for the Sharp-shinned and as an alternative name for the Cooper's Hawk). Fewkes said that both the Pawik kachina and its name are derived from Zuñi,[9] and an unidentified duck name from Zuñi does end in *ik'ya.* Newman gives *'eya* as the generic Zuñi name for ducks. Unfortunately, linguists have not tackled these problems.

Pawik kachinas are distinguished by juniper seed bandoliers, and they appear on the mesas in late spring and early summer, as do certain kinds of ducks. A Hopi named Masi stated the purpose of these dances in the following words:

> *Duck is the uncle* (ta'), *ancestor of all the kachina and also of the Hopi. He will listen to our song, see our acts, and go direct to Cloud and ask him to send clouds and rain to the Hopi. Our waters are scant now and the sun is very hot.*[10]

The date was June 26, and there were six dancers, the others representing Frog, Swift, Navajo, and Pa-tsro, which Stephen identifies as "quail," but it is the Hopi word for snipe. If the dance was borrowed from Zuñi, quail may be in mind, because they represent dead Navajo, and enemy scalps bring rain.

The appearance of this group as they danced on a June day in 1892 is described by Stephen:

At sunrise this morning all the Duck kachina, donning their full toggery, marched down to the ledge on the east side of the mesa . . . and standing in a line facing the rising sun, sang, Su'nwaia tawalauwa ta'la kui'va [beautiful, singing, light, emerge].[11]

As a group they are referred to as "cloud singers." So the sun and the clouds in the sky join to bring rain and water to sprout the seeds. These are of the juniper, which will thrive in even the driest of years.

Along the Rio Grande the Keres likewise have Duck dances, which are performed by the Wai'yosh, who are also Duck kachinas. At Cochiti the top of the mask is covered with a cloud of white cotton; above each ear are erect eagle tail feathers divided by single parrot feathers. The bill on the mask is a snout that is slightly splayed, while their songs include frequent imitations of the quacking of ducks.[12]

WATER BIRDS

Of the five kachina dance groups at Santa Ana one is called Duck. Some members belong to this group for life, and the Duck kachinas may be called on to dance at any time. That may be during the rain retreats held in June or on King's Day, January 6. In the latter case they dance to honor the incoming officers of the pueblo, which again brings up the idea of guardianship. A song sung at that time begins:

I wonder; I wonder if at Tamaya
The new officers have taken their places.
This is the way I sing: There the rain
Is coming down from the North:
There in the west
The streams are beginning to flow.
Down in front of the rain and the rivers
Lightning strikes the earth,
And from the place
The ianyi comes up
And spreads itself everywhere.[13]

mallard

Ianyi is the blessing and the power of the spirit world. Literally it is the road over which these blessings travel, much as ducks do. In this prayer Lightning has made a road down through the sky and cut a hole in the earth, to complete the roads along which fertility travels. The Santa Ana Duck kachinas are under the supervision of the Eagle society, which is an organization related to the concept of a Sky god for the Zenith—there is a curing deity at the end of each direction.

Between the Rio Grande and Zuñi, the Keres of Acoma inhabit a splendidly isolated mesa, mostly for ceremonies. Their farming villages are along the Rio San Jose and relate to the marshes described earlier. Duck plays an important part in the sequence of their origin myths. In the beginning the Mother goddess Iyatiku gave certain instructions to Oak Man, who was to be the first Medicine chief. Fire was one of the strong things that the goddess gave to the people; fire is a powerful force, and oak is a good wood for it, so a man of the Oak clan was chosen for fire medicine. The Bear and the Eagle were chosen to be his partners, because they represent the curing Beast gods of the Zenith and of the West, and of these, they are most powerful.

"Iatiku then told him to kill a mallard, skin it and take the green feathers from the wings and bring them to the altar."[14] It is not stated what Duck's role is in the curing done by the Fire society, but he is likely a messenger and certainly a teller and a listener in the rites. At Acoma the summer dance for rain, Natyati, takes place in the second week of July, and it includes twenty to thirty Duck kachinas. There is no literal representation of the bird, but they are accompanied by the flute-playing demigod of the Sun, Paiyatemu. Ducks also dance at the summer solstice.[15]

The duck symbolism of the Zuñis, Hopis, and Keres seems to be similar. The Tewas diverge in a way, because the Crane there fills many of the same roles. They do, however, offer loose duck feathers in shrines, one offering consisting of a downy eagle feather, one from the oriole, and two from ducks.[16] The coarsely ground cornmeal offered at these shrines is for the Sun, the Moon, and the Cloud beings, or *oxuw'a*.

WATER BIRDS

The Common Snipe is a wading bird that takes its work *snipes*
seriously. Snipe relates to marshes and pools, where his long,
straight bill is useful for probing the muddy bottoms for food. In
New Mexico and Arizona they are winter migrants. They obviously
belong to water and relate to other water symbols. At Cochiti a
children's tale tells of a game in which Toad and Snipe play hide and
seek. When Snipe hides herself in the river's sand, Toad cannot find
her. Then he ran his stomach against the bird's bill that was sticking
out of the sand.

> *"Hai li li, I've found an awl for my grandfather to fix his shoes
> with." He began to pull. "I am a bird." They laughed and laughed.
> So both found each other and Toad went home to his mother well and
> safe and the bird stayed at the river.*[17]

At Hopi Snipe is one of Cloud's pets and is an important
water symbol. His name, *Patsro,* literally translated, means "water
bird." On the southwest tip of First Mesa, Snipe's image appears in
stone, and there are petroglyphs of two Horned Water Serpents
whose bodies are decorated with snipe footprints.[18] Similarly the
effigies of Horned Water Serpent that are manipulated in ceremonies
have these same snipe tracks, and they are also on the water bowls
that are set out for the ceremony, while the entire bird is pictured on
the curtain behind which the effigy manipulator stands.[19]

The difficulty of interpreting prehistoric drawings is illustrated in the case of these curtains, where the intent is known and
the results can be seen. When the screen was repainted, Stephen
noted that

> *they carefully followed all former outlines, except in the snipe de-
> signs. It was permissible for each one to finish these according to his
> own fancy. The general outline was approximately followed, but if
> one was not assured, he would never guess that all these different
> forms of birds were designed to be the same, the snipe.*[20]

In these bird designs some of the native artists had killdeer on their mind, as shown by the short bills and the collars around the necks of several birds. On this curtain snipes are perched on top of Cloud and Rain symbols. Between the birds are two panels of the one-horned god, Shotoknungwa, who controls lightning. Another grouping has Snipe with Germinator, the two-horned god of fertility. In a kiva mural the one-horned god is holding up an elaborate triple symbol that includes cloud, lightning, and rain. On top of this a snipe is perched, but again the artist has definitely drawn a killdeer.[21]

In sum, Snipe ties together the concepts of the Horned Water Serpent, who controls underground waterways; Germinator, who sends crops up from underground; and the Sky god, who sends down lightning and rain. The Water Serpent dance takes place in winter, and that is the snipe's season in Arizona, so he becomes a water bird of winter. He relates to rain, too, of course, but that concept is tied to summer and the growing season when it is most needed.

killdeer

We have just seen that the killdeer sometimes stands in for snipe as a water bird. Our name drives from its cry, "kill-dee, kill-dee," but the Tewa name is just as representative, *Po-te-yi* sounds right, and the first element means water. The Keres also have names based on the cry: *Shtiwishtiwi* at Sia and *Diwidiwik'a* at San Felipe. These birds will live around any kind of water from mud puddles to lakes. In New Mexico they retreat from the northern part of the state in midwinter but return by March. In the Hopi country of Arizona they are said to be year-round residents anywhere water is found.[22]

The cry is explained in a Tewa story from San Juan, which tells of Coyote stealing fire. When he is about to be caught, he tosses the embers first to an unknown bird and then to Poteyi. "They took the fire. They began to burn their hands and they said, 'r—r rehrö.' Just the same they still say in just the same way, 'r—r rehrö.'"[23] That does not sound as much like the cry as its Tewa name, but one cannot tell how it is sounded in their language.

killdeer

The connection with fire, slight as it may be, takes Killdeer away from water as a theme and approaches the guardian concept, as the tale ends: "And they did not let the fire go out." Two Keresan pueblos have Killdeer kachinas, whose roles seem to be based on a habit of the bird. In nesting season these birds will go into the broken-wing act to lead any intruder away from their nest, which is simply a hollow on the ground. The act is intended for animals who would think the injured bird an easy prey.

At Sia the Killdeer kachina makes the "road" for the dancers, which is to say he leads them in. At San Felipe the Killdeer kachina is a side dancer,[24] though by no means the only one. A side dancer has the role of keeping the main line of dancers in good order, and that includes even keeping bits of costumes in their proper places. Both leading in and attending to order seem to be guardian concepts.

Killdeer, at least at Zuñi, relates to an extension of the guardian theme, which could place him equally with the birds of war, but because scalps and water are often related he has been included in this chapter. At Hopi the name for Killdeer is a compound of "water" and "strong." Strong usually refers to war; we hear of "strong prayer-sticks." At Zuñi killdeer feathers can be used by anyone, but this is not generally done. In former times they were used on war prayer-sticks made by the Bow priests before starting on a raiding party.[25]

There was a very good reason for the association. Any war party was bound to travel from one waterhole to another watering place or stream crossing. Killdeer are perfect sentinels, because no one can approach their water without arousing the shrill cries. If one waits inconspicuously, the birds settle down but will send out their warnings again when someone else approaches. Either way, a war party would want to propitiate the killdeer by offering it prayer feathers.

Cranes are water birds that often eat other water symbols, such as fish or frogs. They also relish seeds, particularly corn, and are also notable guardians by habit. This combination of waters, seeds, and guarding appealed to the Pueblos at every level from children's tales to secret rites. Cranes are high flyers that announce their presence, long before they are seen, by a clarion trumpet call. From the sky and clouds they descend to the water and then to the seeds on the ground.

sandhill cranes

Pueblo observations on cranes begin in the north where they enter the state during southward migrations. There, in the pueblo of Picuris, they tell the following story to children. "Once," it is said, "there lived a flock of Sandhill Cranes up in the clouds in the sky. And they drank the water from the clouds, and also built their nests upon clouds, and lived well."

The leader of this flock urges his followers to go down to earth where the waters contain numerous frogs and fishes. They descend to a spring but soon have eaten all its denizens and drunk up all of its water, so they move to the Taos River and then on to Picuris. But each time they swallow all of the water and the life within it. In actuality the cranes appear anywhere in the state when they first arrive, but after a time the Sandhill Cranes congregate along the Rio Grande.

The story continues:

> *They drank the water of the Rio Grande and ate the fishes, frogs, and other water animals that lived there, and lived well. All the Sandhill Cranes did their very best to drink up the water, but could not finish drinking the water of the Rio Grande, neither could they finish eating up the Rio Grande fishes, frogs, and other water animals that live there. "This river must be very strong, so here we will make our headquarters, here we will build our nests and increase in number."*[26]

The final statement is an error, but that hardly matters in a children's story. Besides, there is a reason for it. Cranes nest either in the northern United States or in Siberia, depending on which race they are—the look-alike Little Brown Crane making the farthest trip. The reason behind this error is that the Great Blue Heron is often identified with cranes by both Indians and non-Indians, so we find Heron-Crane clans and similar links. The heron does nest along the Rio Grande and fish in its waters.

There is a second reason why Sandhill Cranes congregate along the Rio Grande, and a story of more serious purport tells of it. In October these cranes gather in the cornfields of the pueblos along that river to eat leftover waste corn. Bailey quotes one writer of the 1850s as saying: "They appeared from Santa Fe to El Paso and in some places literally covered the cornfields, nor were they disturbed by the gun."[27]

The same must have been true farther north; a Tewa tale from San Juan uses this fact. A young boy was out hunting rabbits when he came to the house of Crane Old Man.

"Good-evening, grandfather," he said. "Yes, get a seat." Little boy was looking round everywhere. He said, "Grandfather, I want to live with you."—"Yes, if you will live with me you will not have a hard time." So that little boy stayed there. It was October and everybody was carrying in his corn. Then Puga old man said, "I am going to San Juan. The people there are getting in their corn, maybe I will get some. All I ask of you is not to go into that room."

The crane, being something of a spirit, knows what the room contains, while the uninitiated boy does not.

In the room that the boy inevitably enters are a number of pottery bowls such as the Indians used for storing their corn, but these contain the spirits that should only appear when invoked in their due season.

He went up to one bowl and uncovered it and up jumped Kossa [members of a clown society], lots of them, and little boy ran after them to catch them and put them back, but he could not catch them. Little boy uncovered another bowl. From it out came Oxuwah. They began to dance. Then it began to rain. Puga old man was caught out in the rain. It wet him and he could not fly.

The *oxuwah* are the Tewa kachinas, and, of course, when they dance it is bound to rain. Rain is a good thing in July and August, but after the corn is ripe and ready for harvest, rain is not good. "Little boy was running after those Kossa, and the Oxuwah were dancing. Puga old man scolded little boy. He caught the Kossa and the Oxuwah and shut them up again."[28] The serious import here is that both clowns and kachina dancers are under the guardianship of cranes as represented by Crane Old Man, who controls their activity.

sandhill crane

A similar idea seems to be a part of kachina ritual at the Tewa pueblo of San Ildefonso, where it is mentioned that during Holy Week a Seeds kachina appears in the Turquoise kiva and scatters seeds from a leather bag. Along with him comes Rain Bird kachina *(kwapiye ohuwah),* who represents a bird that comes only with continuous rain. Parsons adds in a footnote that he represents "a big, drab bird with long legs, possibly the sandhill crane."[29] According to Harrington *Kwa-pije* means "toward rain" and is a "heron-like bird," which could only be the crane. Perhaps the thought here is that the crane who migrates north in spring is in search of rain and that he returns in the fall, bringing seeds.

At Keresan Laguna a story relates cranes to another kind of guardianship. The social organization of cranes has impressed many people. Aristotle noted that they had both leaders in flight and pa-trols on the edge of the flock. When the main body settles down they sleep with their heads under their wings, but the leader keeps his head up and a sharp lookout. Sandhill Cranes have exactly the

DUCKS, SNIPES, KILLDEER, AND SANDHILL CRANES

same ways; the leader tries to find high ground, watches, and trumpets an alarm at any sign of danger.

The Laguna story tells of a monster who kept most of the people locked up—in comparable stories it is usually animals and birds that are locked up and the monster is a Keeper of Game spirit. Here, Fire-Brand Youth is a son of the Sun who is carried by his father to a small band of people still free. After proving his paternity he is sent to challenge the evil spirit.

In order that he might not be surprised by his enemies, Kai-na-ni had set a crane to watch before his door. As Pais-chun-ni-moot approached, the crane was so blinded by the brightness of his appearance, that he was enabled to pass by and enter unannounced into the dwelling.

Migrations of the crane do parallel the journeys of the sun from north to south, which is sometimes used to relate the bird to the solstices. In this tale the point is much simpler. The evil spirit was playing a gambling game but before he contests with Fire-Brand Youth he rebukes the crane. "He went out and spoke to the crane, 'Why did you not warn me?' and struck the crane with a stick so that it stooped. Ever since that day the legs of the crane have been bent."[30]

At Zuñi both the Crane and Bear clans are associated with winter, and in ancient times of Zuñi migrations they were said to have traveled in the North.[31] The origin story of the Crane clan is not very informative. The Divine ones had decided that the Zuñi should be divided into clans. One group, "chose to be the Ko'lok-takwe [Sandhill Crane people], selecting this bird because it happened to be flying by."[32] More importantly, this clan is connected with clowns of the Galaxy society and with them Sandhill Crane plays a signal role.

Soon after the Zuñi had emerged from the Underworld, the gods organized four societies or fraternities (these English names are interchangeable). One of these was the Newekwe or Galaxy fraternity of clowns. The original director of this group chose to be in the

Crane clan, and since that time all galaxy directors have been chosen from this clan. One will recall that in the Tewa story the clowns were guarded by Crane Old Man.

At Zuñi feathers of the Sandhill Crane can be used only by members of the Galaxy society. Their meaning and ritual use is a close secret, so much so that Ladd, himself a Zuñi, did not know or could not tell. There is one public use, on the Galaxy wand called *t'ninne*. That object is a polelike personal fetish carried by each member. It is well wrapped, with a tuft of feathers at one end and two crane feathers attached by strings to the upper part.

During a retreat of the Galaxy society no one else may handle a Sandhill Crane or its feathers; if anyone does so, he is obligated to join the society. At other times a layman who kills one of these birds may bring it or the feathers to any society member.[33] It is interesting that the coot, which also belongs to the same order of birds in our classification, is also restricted to this society. During initiation a stuffed coot symbolizes the stringent taboos that the clowns are under.

The relationship of cranes to the Galaxy society comes somewhat to light in the myths and rites involving the flight of the Corn Maidens. These spirit sisters fled from Zuñi, taking all of the corn in the pueblo with them, either because the people were not performing their religious duties or because the demigod of the Sun, Paiyatemu, attempted to seduce them. Starvation resulted, and various kinds of birds were sent out to find the maidens, but they could not because Duck and his wife had made a nest for hiding them. This was not a real duck but the chief of the gods, Pautiwa, who had assumed a duck form.

Finally Newekwe Youth, who may also be called Bitsitsi when he is the head of the Clown society, or even Paiyatemu if the head clown is thought of in relation to the Sun, is summoned from Ashes Spring, his marshy home. With the aid of his flute he entices the Corn Maidens back to the pueblo where their return is celebrated in the Molowia ceremony held in early winter after harvest. "*Bitsitsi*, the director of the fraternity . . . was prepared for the journey he took to find those refugees, the corn-maidens, by sandhill crane."[34]

The meanings of birds may be expressed either through clans, societies, or a combination of both. The Sia had a Crane clan that became extinct early in recorded history. Both Zuñis and Hopis had Crane clans that lasted into the present century. At Hopi there were once Crane clans on all Mesas, but by 1940 there were only five Crane members left, all in Oraibi. Once they were reported to be numerous.[35] The same applies to these birds in Hopi country, because they are now very rare. But bones were found in the ruin of Awatovi, and one Sammy Day, Jr., told R. Jenks that in September, about 1926, he saw cranes near Chinle. "Seven danced around in a circle on top of a clay hill, one of the birds in the middle."[36]

The Hopi Crane clan was traditionally joined with a phratry, or group of clans, that were in charge of the Wuwuchim initiation ceremony. At the proper age eligible youths must join one of four societies. More of this will appear when we discuss falcons, but the society of interest here is the Agave, because they are guardians in every sense. They patrol the village during important ceremonies and conduct the dead to the nether world. In this repect they relate to the Sandhill Crane. During the initiation ceremony the Agaves erect a standard indicating society participation. It is set up at sunrise on the hatchway of their kiva and consists of, "crane wing feathers and eight strips of corn husks bound on the end of a round stick, forty inches long."[37]

Crane also appears as something of a winter bird in the Powamu ceremony, which is held to exorcise the cold and prognosticate the coming summer crops, sometime in late winter. Another aspect of the ceremony is the initiation of small children into kachina secrets. In addition to those dancers who gently whip the young ones are four dancing monsters. One of these is a giant wingless bird with a two-foot snout who also makes the rounds to frighten children. On his forehead are the tracks of Crane, perhaps indicating that the monsters are also guardians, or simply the bird's relevance to seeds and fertility.

The account so far has introduced birds of the sun, sky, and rain, which combine to bring water and fertility to the earth. On that cosmic stage the seasons turn, and it is the smaller, perching birds whose migrations bring in the seasons.

7 BIRDS OF WINTER AND SUMMER
larks, bluebirds, orioles, and others

The most regular event in the cosmos is the turning of seasons, which provides a great natural clock by which all ceremonial and practical activities are regulated. That passage back and forth from winter to summer is based on the sun's journey. It also relates to the migrations of many songbirds. Most of these arrive in summer, so it is often said that they bring this season, but two kinds have an important reference to winter.

These are the Horned Lark and both species of bluebirds, each of which descends to the lowlands in winter. Other winter birds follow the same pattern, such as the turkey, but its symbolism is much broader. Two kinds of robins are mentioned in the Keresan Battle of the Seasons; the second is perhaps the Rufous-Sided Towhee, but nothing else is heard of them. The traveling birds of summer include a motley array of flycatchers, orioles, tanagers, finches, wood warblers, and vireos. Alongside them is the resident meadowlark.

Horned Larks do not make long migrations, unlike juncos, but in snowy weather they descend in great flocks to lowlands where some of the seeds they use for food are still above the snow. Snow is an important source of winter moisture, and there is also another reason why larks figure prominently in Pueblo myths: They were hunted for food at a time when meat was scarce and other

horned lark

work not pressing. The bird itself is not conspicuous, but this only representative of the European lark family is notable for its song and for certain flight habits.

Like the European Skylark the male Horned Lark is a great singer in flight, particularly during the mating season, when he spirals up the great heights to deliver his abundant melodies. The song begins with a series of repetitious notes accompanied by rapid wing beats, followed by an intermittent song as the lark sails in widening gyres. At the end of this ascent, the bird folds its wings against its body and plummets down to earth. Naturally the Indians noted both the song and the strange flight and included these observations in a number of stories.

The notes are very hard to transcribe with any meaningfulness. The authors of the Arizona bird book give the notes as *chleep* and *chee-lee*, which are in some agreement with the Pueblo names, which probably indicate the Horned Lark's voice. At Hopi it is *Che'roo* or *Chiro*, while the Zuñis call the lark *Tsilo* or *Silo*. The Keres name is *Siya* or *Si'a*, and, curiously, no one has discussed whether or not that could account for the name of Sia pueblo.

At Zuñi there is a little story in which a song is sung by the narrator. "At Kuchima lived the snowbirds [*tsilo*]. The snowbirds were playing. they would fly high into the air and down again. They flew and flew." Coyote is entranced and wants to join them, but the larks use the stock trick, telling him that first he must cut off the head of his grandmother. When he dutifully arrives with the head, the Horned Larks pull out some of their feathers, fastening them to his outstretched front legs.

Their elder sisters said "Let us fly! and as we fly, we must sing."
They sang,—
Tsilo, tsilo maiakwain,
Tsilo, tsilo maiakwain,
Topinte oto, topinte chonchin
Tsi! cho cho cho cho.
Snowbird, snowbird crests
Snowbird, snowbird crests

One bill, one claw.
Tsi! cho cho cho cho.[1]

As a trickster Coyote sets things in motion; in this instance it accounts for the abundance of snowbirds, who said, "'We must not stay here. The coyote might come and harm us.' So they flew away, flying all over the country. That is why there are snowbirds everywhere."[2] The importance of their being everywhere is that they were trapped or snared and formed an important item in Pueblo diets. The Tewas used only two kinds of snares: one for bluebirds and one for larks. Bluebirds are taken

> *by a trap made of stalk of sunflower, horsehair and a bent stick. There*
> *is another kind of trap for snow birds (ko'i), grey birds, with black*
> *striped yellow neck, flocking in winter. These two types are*
> *the only traps in use.*[3]

What these traps may have been like we discover from the Zuñis, who once used two variations of horsehair snares for the taking of larks. In one type a horsehair loop was tied to a rock, which was then buried in the ground with only the loop exposed. A number of these were set close together with seed sprinkled between and around them for bait. The second type of snare was made by burying a willow hoop to which numerous slip loops were tied; the seed was then placed in the middle of this ring. According to Ladd, who describes these snares, this slow method of catching larks has given way to the use of slingshots.

Ladd is also the source of the information that the Horned Lark is the only bird taken by the Zuñis in large numbers, solely for food. The birds are skinned, strung on a long willow rod, and roasted over an open fire. Accordingly, the feathers of this bird are not used by the Zuñis for ritual purposes nor for mask decoration, because "it is a winter bird." The refusal to use for ceremony the feathers of a bird that is eaten may explain the considerable reluctance shown by Pueblos to eating birds—because most feathers are used for ritual purposes, the meat of the birds is unsuitable for food.

The feeling that because the lark is a winter bird he is set apart or in opposition to summer is found among the Keres as well as at Zuñi. In Laguna accounts of the Battle of the Seasons, Winter in the form of the Shiwanna, or storm clouds of the north, fights along with a number of birds in his retinue. His shirt is of icicles, and he is the very picture of the content of winter clouds, whether as snow or ice. What the bird represents is equally clear: "Then there in front parted the birds, Winter's storm-clouds. Also from the South Summer's storm-clouds, the birds, there in front parted."[4]

The Hopis agree in placing the Horned Larks with the winter storm bringers. But because the winter snows are a part of the annual moisture, this is a desirable fact to be induced in rites. In Voth's account of the Oraibi Winter Solstice ceremony there is an illustration of the mask of the *mana,* or female attendant, of the Qoqlo kachina. The top of this mask is covered with red horsehair, which is usually indicative of the rays of the sun and, "to the base are attached bunches of *chiro* [*Otocorys alpestris*] tail feathers, sometimes also those of the *nuwatochi* [unidentified]."[5]

Mearns identifies the latter bird as the junco, the bird that non-Indians most often call "snowbird." Concerning the juncos Stephen makes the following entry in his journal for October 29, 1883. "I saw snowbirds (*nuva'to'cha*) for the first time this year on the mesa top near Tuki'novi. They understand cold and snow. They bring snow." Because both lark and junco feathers appear at the base of this mask, it is apparent that either one of the birds will bring the snows.

It is not possible to tell exactly how many Horned Lark feathers appear on one of these masks, but there must be at least fifty and probably more. The seasonal implication of this kachina *mana* derives from the fact that she accompanies the kachinas, who usher in the winter season of masked dancing. The Qoqlo is the first kachina, on Third Mesa, to appear in groups. His mask has bird tracks painted on it, and on top are feathers from all kinds of birds. The *mana* also appears with the Hemis kachina at the close of the masked dance season, thus marking the limits of the winter half of the year.[6]

While the larks may be seen most abundantly with the coming

of the snows that drive them together in search of remaining seed, they are actually birds that stand heat equally well. During the summer, though, one has not the time for trapping birds, nor is food as scarce then. As a source of food during the worst weather the birds appear in the lore of the Rio Grande pueblos. In a discussion for hunting at Santa Ana, White mentions that, "In myths we frequently find one, or more, grandsons of Spider Grandmother hunting snowbirds for food, but we have never heard of Indians doing this."[7] His difficulty lay in thinking of the snowbird as the ptarmigan, but because it is the Horned Lark, we may be sure that the myths were based on actual practice.

At Acoma they tell the story of Kasewat, a great hunter who was married to a chief's daughter. One day while the whole town was engaged in a rabbit drive Kasewat's wife was stolen by Flint Bird, the eagle-ogre discussed in Chapter 3, and taken to his home in the sky. Our interest here in the story centers on the first part of Kasewat's rescue attempt. He set out on a snowy day and soon found himself far to the south of Acoma, where he came across the house of an old spider who invited him in. "Two or three girl spiders were there. There was a spider boy, too, but he was out hunting snowbirds." By and by the Spider Boy returned with one snowbird that he had killed. After Spider Woman cooked this bird, Kasewat thoughtlessly ate it all, and one of the Spider Girls exclaimed, " 'Oh, he ate it all. He didn't leave any for us.' Kasewat replied, 'Oh, I'll kill you some more birds! Enough to last for some time!' "

He thereupon pulled a few hairs out of his own head and made a snare with which he caught many of the larks to bring home to Spider Woman and her children. "He threw them down on the floor and began to pick and cook them. He showed the spiders how to make a bed with the feathers. He spent the night with them."[8] The purpose of this episode, which seems to be an aside on the main course of the myth, is to indicate that its hero Kasewat is a spirit-patron of hunters who taught them the use of hair snares for catching these birds in quantities and how they are to be cooked in the field.

The followers of Levi-Strauss have other views on this episode, feeling that it indicates Kasewat's inability to accept a specialized role as a hunter, because their analysis sets up an opposition between hunting and cooking. He is in the world of Spider, indicating the Underworld, so things are there in opposition to the normal world of Indian life. As a part of this confusion Kasewat assumes all roles in taking charge of Spider's family.[9] We will examine this interesting analysis elsewhere; here it is only necessary to point out that the situation reflects normal Pueblo arrangements in which the hunters do cook the game, as we have seen when the Zuñis roasted numbers of the birds on spit. They may be prepared differently by women, as we will see.

In a different version of the story, where the analogous hunter is named Shock-of-hair Youth, he traps both bluebirds and larks, which parallels the Tewa practice mentioned earlier. He says, "every day I trap one"; then he enters Spider youth's house, "and below he finished all the nooses." The event refers to a technological advance; he is inventing and constructing some kind of multiple trap—probably like that described from Zuñi—as he continues, "this time my snare will catch by itself snowbirds and bluebirds." With this new device they are most successful in the field: "They piled up the snowbirds and carried them on their backs."[10]

For the following feast the recipe is quite different from the field roasting, in that it consists of putting a snowbird down in a bed of cornmeal. The fact is notable that, in this version of the story of Flint Wing and the kidnapped wife, Spider Woman cooks the dish.

The Tiwas of Isleta also trap bluebirds and larks together. "There is a baited horsehair trap for bluebirds whose feathers are used in prayer-feathers. The snared bird will be plucked and then released. Snowbirds [upoowe] are also snared."[11] One may hope that it was only the tail feathers of the bluebirds that were plucked. Because nothing is said about releasing the larks, they were presumably eaten, or so we must hope. A tail-less lark is a dismal thought.

At Hopi Spider Grandmother herself taught the boys to use the single snare for larks.

His grandmother said to him: "If you had something to do, you would not be thinking evil things." His grandmother pulled out his hair, twisted it around a stick which was about four inches long and tied it to this stick. She showed him how to catch tci'ro. "Go try for some; there are a great many down there by that water." She had two grand- sons, but they never caught anything, but with this snare she was soon provided with an abundance of birds.[12]

It is of interest that certain springs were preempted as bird-snaring areas by the children of specific villages.

Because this account began with the flight song of the Lark, it is fitting that it end there as well. In each of three Hopi tales the plot resembles the Zuñi story in which Coyote wishes to fly like a lark, though it is not the plot that interests the teller but the habits of these birds, and sometimes a chance to sing a little song. In one Second Mesa story it is said that:

Tci'ro had a family of little birds. She took her children to a high point of one of the hills, to give them exercise and make them strong. She had a small basket, and into this she put her little children. They were covered with down. Tci'ro sang to them. She pitched the birds up lightly in the basket as she sang, keeping time, thus, to her song, then pitched them out. They flew away in a circle and returned to her.

The mating antics of Horned Larks are excellently described in another version, where again the male flight is ascribed to the young. "It was a bunch of *tci'ro*. They were flying high up, their mother caught them when they came back, pulled off all their feath- ers, and pitched them up again. When they came back, she gave them back their feathers."[13] The headlong drop of the lark is thus attributed to the removal of flight feathers, which does not really explain the plunge of the bird but accounts well enough for the sudden death of Coyote when the *tci'ro* pull out the feathers that they have given him.

Surely a song belonged in the first version at the point where the narrator says "keeping time, thus," but none is given. Fortunately, however, the story is told by the Hopi-Tewas of First Mesa, and a song is given. This story begins by saying that far away at Grass Hill lived the birds called *koli*, which is the Tewa name for larks and possibly juncos as well. These birds grew *tamu; ta* means grass and *mu* means pod in Tewa.

> *They were happy to have it, so they said to one another, "We better have a dance for it," they said. They sang:*
> isawo isawo
> selomuki selomuki
> selomuki selomuki
> akyamihemi
> umi hemi achc
> *coyote coyote*
> *homesick homesick*
> *homesick homesick*
> *drop down*
> *up down [their call]*
> *Then they all flew up, circling way up in the air. Then they*
> *all sang again*[14]

And so the story goes, repeating the sadly beautiful lark song again and again. That is, after all, the most important thing about a lark, unless one is very hungry.

bluebirds

There are separate names in most Pueblo languages for the Western and the Mountain Bluebird, and at Zuñi the ceremonial usage of the two species seems to be distinct. Both are winter birds because they descend to the lowlands along with the snow and the cold of that season. But they also make their way back toward the mountains in spring with the intent of breeding at higher elevations. In spring they flock together in local migrations and are thus more visible. The passage of large numbers in spring and again in the fall makes them excellent symbols of transitions between the seasons.

The transition from winter to summer, from the barren coldness to summer's heat, suggests another passage. This is the delicate tranformation of a girl from a child into a woman, so at Zuñi and Hopi bluebirds are closely associated with puberty rites. Another kind of transition relates the four seasons to the four horizon directions. These are keyed together by a system of colors, animals, birds, trees, and snakes. Yellow is the color of the North, where any ceremonial circuit always begins its movement counterclockwise: north to west to south to east. Bluebirds often represent the West in this transition of colors and seasons from the yellow of summer to the red of winter; blue stands for the West. Red represents the South, where the Sun spends a winter retreat. The bluebirds can thus represent the transition of the sun and the seasons downward toward winter. Visually, bluebirds with their bright blue on a winter landscape can also represent another turning, as seasons move horizontally, if we watch the sun's point of rising and setting, east and west on the visible horizon.

A second turning represents the Above and Below. It is said by the Hopis that *Sichomo,* or Flower Mound, is in the Underworld, and there all of summer's flowers are blooming in winter. When this world is turned upside down, they bloom on earth, and bluebirds represent this turning, too. In the Hopi Winter Solstice ceremony prayer-sticks are made for the Sun. These consist of bluebird feathers and clusters from the yellow birds that represent summer.

Bluebirds promote the forms of moisture characteristic of winter: "The feather of bluebird is for snow and ice." They are also observed as spring birds. Stephen noted at Walpi, in March of 1892, "two or three flocks of bluebirds fluttering among the grease wood."[15] This flocking together betokens the coming of spring and is objectified in the standard of the Flute ceremony. The standard consists of a short pole painted blue and black, for day and night, and it is topped with skins and hair to represent various phases of the dawn. The pedestal on which the pole stands is a hemisphere representing Flower Mound and inserted in the base are six prayer-sticks with bluebird feathers, "because bluebird is a rain bird, his cry is heard when rain comes."[16] He is obviously thinking of the Western Bluebird, which has a chattering cry. The bird is bringing the summer rainy season.

At Isleta the summer-bringing potential of bluebirds is directly expressed. In that Tiwa pueblo is a society of "summer promoters" called the *Sure*. These use a bluebird feather as a badge of membership. At Hopi the Bluebird clan has certain special functions—its role in war will appear later—but it seems that the clan and the bird are also associated with summer and with wisdom.[17] The wisdom is of a special type and belongs to the clan role, as we will see.

The passage of seasons, or rather the transformation of one into the other, is like the passage from night to day. It also transforms fields from their barren state to fertile status. Women also make this change; a Zuñi ceremony combines all of these ideas in one. Naturally enough, Bluebird, in this case the Mountain Bluebird, symbolizes these changes. "Rabbit skin blanket" is a translation of the ceremony's name, and the connection of this with fertility is given in *Pueblo Animals and Myths*.

The ceremony takes place every four years and is held in August when the corn is about a foot high. The dances that last for several days are supposed to be a reenactment of the first visits of the Corn Maidens to Zuñi. The participants are divided into two groups, one named for the rabbit skin and one for the flute. The latter are related to Paiyatemu, the god of music, flowers, and butterflies—which come from his instrument; he is, above all, a flute player and a seducer of women.

Before the ceremony begins the Rain priests gather at dawn in the house of the priestess of Fecundity. There they prepare special feather offerings made of the tail or primary wing feathers of the Mountain Bluebird. These are joined in pairs at the quill end to form a "V" and are then wrapped with cotton string and attached to a cord with a strand of hair. Each of the many dancers is presented with one of these offerings.

A list of the participants gives a good idea of the intent of the rite; there are four sunrise dancers and a group of female virgins who dance at sunset. Also, a youth and a maid sprinkle the dancers from a water jar. This water has been drawn from a spring high on Corn Mountain, the great mesa behind Zuñi. The two water jars contain reeds to which bluebird feathers have been attached.

Among the important dancers are ten women representing the Corn Maidens and with them a single male dancer—to make the corn ears perfect. That arrangement is the opposite of Game dances in which there will be a line of men representing animals and a single female as Mother of Game. Each dancer here has one of the bluebird feather offerings attached to the left side of her head. The dancing alternates between the two groups, Rabbit Skin and Flute.

One side carries ears of blue corn, while the other holds yellow. These two colors of corn are exchanged at intervals during the dance, indicating the shift from winter to summer. After several days of dancing a finale suggests the night-to-day turning. During an all-night ceremony no one is allowed to fall asleep, and the last group may not leave the plaza until the cloud symbol that they wear above their heads is fully bathed in sunlight. After this elaborate set of dances is done, the bluebird feather offerings are taken to the fields and planted.[18]

The relation of human fertility and bluebirds is overtly expressed in a Hopi rite of passage during the Mamzrau women's ceremony. At that time girl novices are required to undergo a rite ensuring their future fertility. To promote this a ring is made of yucca fibers and called "yucca house." Each girl jumps into this ring and then waits while it is raised to her waist, where it is moved up and down several times and then broken.

Previous to this rite two sets of "maiden prayer-sticks" are made by the girl and tied to the yucca ring. In constructing these she,

> takes a very minute feather from a small bluebird
> wing and with infinite pains splits the small shredded
> long strip of yucca and knots in it the feather. . . .
> In the middle she ties two of these minute blue feath-
> ers with a tiny shred of yucca, a mere thread.[19]

western bluebird

Stephen again mentions the "devilish small threads" and the patience involved. Because larger feathers would have the same symbolic value, we presume that these indicate the exacting nature of duties in approaching womanhood.

At Hopi, bluebirds have associations with war and so could find a place with the more specialized birds of war in Chapter 12. But the relation is bound up with the seasonal theme and with the special duties of the Bluebird clan. Sun, who controls the seasons, is also a patron of warriors. During the Winter Solstice ceremony a warrior prayer-stick is made to which two bluebird wing feathers are attached along with a cluster of pine needles. To this is added a corn husk food packet with a pinch of specular iron.[20]

Pine has cold-bringing powers, and the food packet represents the opposite season, so the implication may be more seasonal than warlike. However, the feathers appear in other warrior bundles, such as those of the snake dancers where they are combined with feathers from turkey and hawk. Importantly they are related to the duties of the Bluebird clan. According to Andrew Hermequaftewa, a contemporary chief of the Bluebird clan on Second Mesa: "I belong to that clan which was appointed to follow all others. We watch for everything. We guard them along the life plan of Masau."[21]

Here we see how wisdom enters the association—the guarding of tribal knowledge and way of life is the issue. But in past times the matter was more literal. Bluebird clansmen brought up the rear in any migration or passage from one settlement to another. By theory these migrations were led by the War Twins, then various clans in ranks. After these had departed,

> the Bluebird clan, or the clan appointed to follow and look after all things that they had with them waited until the next day before they followed them. According to instructions they went into every house to look for the things that might have been left behind, and after gathering up everything—the things that the Hopis should have taken along, they followed them and they kept behind them in this manner from then on.[22]

In these migrations the Bluebird clan came last, because it was a guardian of the ways and in a hasty move things left behind might be sacred objects essential for the proper functioning of the ceremonial calendar and perhaps important household items light enough to carry. Sometimes they would have to be warriors, but probably the passage from place to place, from time to time, from season to season, from night to day, and from childhood to maturity is the Bluebird's basic role.

There is a final symbolic link—that of bluebirds and spiders. At Hopi, Spider Grandmother is the ancient of the Bluebird clan, and she delegates to them her authority. As a goddess she overlooks human affairs of both sexes, whether men's hunting or women's cooking. In the Laguna story of the hunter who snared larks and bluebirds, he brought them to the house of Spider. At Zuñi the connection is most literal: Bluebird feathers are used to cure spider bites. A tent is erected over the victim, and bluebird feathers are burned on hot coals. This smoke is inhaled and the bite treated with a mix of water, coals, and burned feathers.[23]

One very drab bird also belongs with the spring and the transition from winter to summer. In the Hopi Powamu or Bean ceremony, held in late winter, one of the rites is the formation of bean sprouts in a warm kiva—the sprouting is an augury for the summer's crops. The priest who asks for blessings and good crops says that he represents the cowbird, and its feathers are on the prayer-sticks. Voth gives the scientific name for the Brown-headed Cowbird, so he must have observed the bird, although the Hopi name used is a general term for blackbirds.

In northern Arizona they arrive in late April and early May; at this time the anticipation given in the bean-planting rite in winter becomes a reality. When these birds actually appear, the Hopis say: "The *tokotska* has come, it is time to plant."[24] Then the earliest varieties of corn are planted. It is good to know that the cowbird has at least one use, because it is a parasitic bird responsible for the decrease of yellow warblers and vireos in that area.

birds of summer

Birds representing summer are more generalized in terms of species than those representing winter or spring, but they are more specific in associations. The Pueblo summer is controlled by a bright yellow sun, which shines through rain clouds onto an earth covered with a profusion of yellow flowers. The Zenith is often represented by Tawa Mana or Sun Maiden, which can be the Yellow-headed Blackbird. The pollen that fertilizes squash and corn is also yellow, and by chance a considerable number of songbirds who bring the summer are likewise marked with yellow. The feathers of these become offerings to the sun and the warm season.

The birds of summer are most often cheerful singers who bring a note of contentment to a time of hard work for humans. According to Don Talayesva, "My grandfather told me that all the songbirds are the Sun god's pets, put here to keep the people happy while they work." Another Hopi gave the opinion that

the fifth song is a petition for a profusion of sunflowers, and the sounds he produced are to call swarms of birds to come out and sing upon them, because, he says, when sunflowers and songbirds are numerous, there are always copious rains and an abundant harvest.[25]

hooded oriole

At the time of the summer solstice the yellow Sun has reached his northern home, and in the Southwest summer quite literally presents a yellow background. With respect to flowering species, the yellow-blooming kinds equal all others combined. In terms of mass, acres of yellow sunflowers, groundsels, and yellowish rabbit-brush dominate the entire summer landscape. Man, the yellow sun, and the yellow flowers are thus naturally linked to seasonal birds, which sport yellow markings. In a Zuñi myth man and birds are extended kin, in that these birds derive from the flesh of human beings.

In this myth a semidivine youth who is fathered either by Rain or Dew pits himself against a number of monsters. His last opponents are Eagles who have been feeding their young on the flesh of maidens and youths. The hero slays these and brings back from the sky a bundle containing the feathers of young Eagles. On earth his grandmother, who is undoubtedly Spider Woman, gives him an admonition.

> *You have gathered a beautiful store of feathers. Now, be very careful. Those creatures who bore these feathers have gained their lives from the lives of living beings, and therefore their feathers differ from other feathers.*
>
> *Heed what I say, my grandson. When you come to any place where flowers are blooming—where the sunflowers make the field yellow—walk around those flowers, if you want to get home with those feathers.*

For a time the young hero follows her advice and passes around the great plains covered with sunflowers, but after a time he grows impatient with these natural gardens that separate him from his home and despite the warning walks straight ahead.

> *So he took a good hold on them and walked in amongst the flowers. But no sooner had he entered the field than flutter, flutter, flutter, little wings began to fly out from the bundle of feathers, and the bundle began to grow smaller and smaller, until it wholly disappeared. These wings which flew out were the wings of the Sacred Birds of Summerland, made living by the lives that had supported the birds which bore those feathers, and by coming into the environment which they had so loved, the atmosphere which flowers always bring of summer.*[26]

The Hopis have a different account of the origin of birds and of the Sun's control over them. In the times of the very beginning all was then water except for an island in the West where Huruing Wuhti, or Hard Beings Woman, lived. In the east was the Sun—he was her father and she was his mother and they said, "We shall own all things together." To the Sun Hard Beings Woman said, "Now let us create something for you." Then she got out her bundle, just as a priest would when setting up his sacred objects for an altar. In her bundle were all kinds of bird skins and feathers.

So this earth goddess already had all of the component parts of birds, except that they lacked the breath of life. She then rubbed scales from her own cuticle, placing these parts of herself on the feathers and skins. Next she covered them with a bit of native cloth while the Sun kindled a fire at the east side of the pile. "Huruing Wuhti then took hold of two corners of the cloth and began to sing, moving the corners to the time of her singing. The Sun took hold of the other two corners to the time of her singing, but he did not sing."

These two deities swung the corners of the cloth four times, until signs of life stirred within. They

> *began to emit sounds, whistling and chirping the way the different birds do. Hereupon Huruing Wuhti took off the covering saying: "We are done, be it this way." There were all different kinds of birds, those that fly around in the summer when it is warm.*

As she took off the cover, the birds commenced to fly, passed through an opening, and flew into the open air. But all soon returned to gather in front of the two.

> *"You shall own these," Huruing Wuhti said to the Sun. "They are yours." "Thanks," the Sun replied, "that they are mine." Huruing Wuhti then handed to the Sun a large jar made of a light transparent material like quartz crystal. Into this the Sun placed all the birds, closing up the jar.[27]*

When these songbirds are absent from us, the Sun has them locked in a crystal cage elsewhere. In summer they are released again to gladden tillers of the soil and the Earth mother who created them to please the Sun. The Sun owns these birds, but they in turn bring the summer. At Zuñi prayer-sticks include among other feathers, "the path finding tails of the birds who counsel and guide summer."[28]

The Hopis have a word, *sikatsi,* to indicate the yellow of the sun, of flowers, and of birds. When applied to birds it indicates any that have yellow feathers. Stephen translates this word as simply "yellowbird," and under it are included flycathers, wood warblers, and goldfinches. Most of these also have specific names in the Hopi language—used more narrowly *sikatsi* seems to refer to the Empidonax group of flycatchers.

The Yellow Warbler, the Yellow-breasted Chat, and the Yellowthroat are all important to the Pueblos, but there are a number of other warblers marked with bits of yellow, which makes their feathers suitable for prayer offerings. In the Hopi Winter Solstice ceremony *sikatsi* feathers are attached to a standard indicating that the ceremony is in process. Although the ceremony is held in midwinter, it is forward looking toward the summer that will follow. Yellow is the color of the North, and that is also the direction and the color with which every ceremonial circuit begins, as the priest points to the yellow North and then, in counterclockwise movement, to the blue of the West, red of the South, and white of the East.[29]

In the Winter Solstice ceremony on First rather than Third Mesa, Stephen notes that yellowbird feathers are offered at Sun Spring along with underwing feathers from the eagle. Then in the June dances, yellowbird and eagle feathers are offered on a "reed" prayer string, the yellow breast feathers this time being very tiny ones. The yellowbirds have several summerlike associations. For one thing, they scatter pollen.

> *The yellowbird is used because this yellow bird constantly scatters the fructifying pollen, its color shows that, and when there is no rain, there are no yellow birds; when there is plenty of rain, there is plenty of grass seeds and multitudes of yellow birds are seen eating the seeds and scattering the life-giving pollen over the land.*[30]

Among the Pueblos the Northern Oriole (formerly called Bullock's Oriole) is the summer bird par excellence. It is the common

LARKS, BLUEBIRDS, ORIOLES, AND OTHERS

oriole of the Pueblo area, and beyond its beauty this bird has other attractive qualities. It likes the company of man and will catch insects in orchards or pick the worms from corn ears. Each time the oriole appears in ceremonies, it points toward summer. At the end of January the Hopis have a brief ceremony in which a priest brings in a small ball of snow into which he has thrust four oriole feathers. This is done "so that the snow should melt and make the fields wet."[31]

In the Powamu ceremony, which is held a month or so later, there is a most unusual prayer feather offering in which the oriole feathers are blown through a tube. The ceremonialist constructs four black tubes from pieces of reed. An arrow-shaped piece of corn husk is attached to one end. These blowguns are colored by rubbing them with honey, then with corn pollen, and lastly in a skin said to contain buffalo fat (which is closely related to the Sun). In the end of one tube are tiny oriole feathers, while another contains bluebird feathers and specular iron.

At a given moment in the ceremony the priest ascends the ladder part way, so that his head appears above the hatch and blows the yellow feathers and corn pollen from the tube towards the North, after which he blows a few sharp notes from the whistle. Next he returns to the altar, picks up the reed with the blue feathers and repeats the same performance for the West and then the other directions. This is "a prayer for warm weather when the summer birds come."[32]

At Zuñi oriole feathers are particulary prized, but their name is combined with the Western Tanager and the Black-headed Grosbeak, so it is the color that is important. There a cermony is held at the same time of year. It is called after a participating kachina whose name means, "downy feathers hanging." Upik'aiapona is the very incarnation of the welcome season; his mask has a green face to represent the green world of summer, while the mouth is painted all colors to signify the variety of summer's flowers. "He dances for the spring, so that the spring will come quickly with fine days." The date is February 8.

The body of this kachina is painted black but with "yellow

breast and shoulders for the oriole because he comes early in spring. The yellow on the arms is for the yellow flowers and the corn pollen."[33] The yellow also relates to three species of tanagers in which the females are all yellow though the males vary. Male Western Tanagers have black tails and wings set off against a red head and bright yellow body. The Zuñis link it to the oriole, because on prayer-sticks wing or tail feathers are often used and these would be black in either species. If downy breast feathers are used, they would be yellow. The Hopis also link the two birds by using a single name, sometimes with an additional prefix for distinction.

The Western Tanager is a transition-zone bird that passes across the mesas only in migration. It is common along the Rio Grande in the summer, and at Sia it has become the bird of the North, a role played by the oriole at Hopi and recently at Zuñi; in the 1880s the Yellow-breasted Chat filled that place. At Keresan Santo Domingo a song about this bird relates it to the masked dancers. The song tells that these birds lead in the *shiwanna,* which is to say the rain makers of the summer season.[34]

Two other tanagers have females which are yellow, though the males are all red. The Hepatic Tanager male is a rather dull red, so it is probably the female, which under the Hopi name, Asya, stands for the Zenith in both the Winter Solstice and the Powamu ceremonies. Mearns confirmed the name, but often the Tawa Mana or Sun Maid represents that direction, and it is the Yellow-headed Blackbird. The Hepatic Tanager does not appear in northeastern Arizona today, so if its feathers were used, they likely were brought in by trade.

The Summer Tanager belongs to willow-cottonwood habitat and is not found north of Albuquerque. The only pueblo in that area is Isleta, and there we hear of "an all red bird" whose feathers are used on prayer-sticks. It is called *Tushure,* and in the same sentence an all-yellow bird called *Tujumare* is mentioned.[35] Because the two sexes would be seen together, there may be some link. But further inquiry by bird watchers will be needed before drawing any conclusions.

Goldfinches are also seasonal birds that blend in with the yellow of summer, as do a number of warblers. By the concept of turning seasons, it happens that the warblers may stand along with Tawa Mana in representing the Zenith, but in one Oraibi New Year ceremony a warbler represents the Below. While seasons change, there is one unseasonal bird of yellow colors that is resident. The Western Meadowlark is always there, but its songs become more abundant as spring and the mating season approach.

Meadowlarks bring their cheery notes to open grassy flats, where in spring they are numerous enough to fill the air with joy. There is something curative about a warm spring day, particularly in the Southwest, where March is a roaring beast and April brings no daffodils. At Zuñi yellow breast feathers from meadowlarks are limited in use to a curing society, the Shumakoli. By reasonable chance the director of that society is also one of the Rain priests.

Rain and spilling out the water or the song also relate. A story from the Tewa pueblo of San Juan tells of a coyote carrying water in her mouth for the thirsty pup. Meadowlark intervened:

"One day as she went by that bird Oguya said, 'I am going to stay and make her laugh.'" The Meadowlark then sang:

> *poo henge henge*
> *kia oguya tee kewena*
> *tu aaaa*
> *Water, spit it out, spit it out*
> *This is the way tree up*
> *It says.*

Coyote does laugh each time she goes by and so finally has to sew her mouth shut in order to hold the water. When Coyote finally arrives home, she finds her children dead of thirst.[36]

Without song and without water everything would die, but a meadowlark keeps supplying both, as well as flashes of the yellow color that represents the fruitful summer.

From brightness and the birds of summer we turn abruptly to darkness and to those birds that represent the night.

8 BIRDS OF DUSK, NIGHT, AND THE MOON
poorwills, nighthawks, and owls

In the last chapter where the basic contrasts were winter and summer, the similar change from night to day also figured in some myths and rituals. A ceremonial standard consisting of a pole painted half-black for the night, and half-blue for the day was capped by skins representing the white Dawn and others for the yellow Dawn, as well as hairs dyed red to represent the rays of the rising sun. These are, of course, sunrise matters, but the day has another passage, another transformation, this time at dusk, before the day becomes night and the moon takes the sun's place.

The darting flights of nighthawks are most often seen when they are feeding in late afternoon and as twilight falls. They diligently hunt insects then, so they are often linked with hunting, but their ties are more importantly with the moon. On nights of full moons the poorwill calls through the hours of darkness, from whence its older name of "night-jar." In our classification nighthawks and poorwills belong to the same family, and the Zuñis use one name for both, based on the wide mouth which is used to scoop insects from the air.

At Taos Nighthawk is thought of as a hunter, a fact that we also recognize by calling the bird a "hawk" even though it is no relation and stands close to the owls. In a Taos tale Yellow Corn and Blue Corn Women were married to the same bird. The yellow and blue colors could indicate either night and day, or summer and winter.

In the cottonwood tree was living Nighthawk their husband. He was a great hunter. He would go out to hunt early in the morning and late in the evening he would come home with a whole deer which he had tied up by the legs in the bundle.[1]

It makes no difference that the bird hunts only insects; diligence and persistence count.

The story of Nighthawk's cradle is also told at Taos and sounds as though there is some ritual meaning behind it, quite possibly relating to the moon. The daughter of White Corn Old Man and Woman asked her brothers to take care of their sister when she went out to relieve herself at night, but this they failed to do. "There Nighthawk was watching for her. As she came out Nighthawk picked her up and took her to his house on the rocky cliff." When the lazy brother finds this place his kidnapped sister asked, "Why do you come here? Nighthawk is very fierce, he will kill you. You better go back and tell our father and mother they have a grandchild."

The grandparents bring this baby a bow and arrows for his use when grown and a cradle for him. Nighthawk comes home with a big buck on his back and says, "Smell of people!" The wife is able to assure him that the people are her parents.

Nighthawk saw the cradle hanging from the ceiling and there was his boy lying in the cradle his grandfather made. He was not satisfied with that cradle. "That is not what I use. What I use for a cradle is an old, dried up, discarded shield." . . . So he took it down and put up his kind of cradle.[2]

One has to guess that this old shield is part of a rite to make the moon, because a similar hide was used for the purpose in a Hopi tale. "They then selected someone . . . and directed him to stand on the moon symbol. Hereupon the chiefs took the cloth by its corners, swung it back and forth, and then threw it upward."[3] The "cloth" was a painted buffalo hide stretched over a hoop; presumably it went into the sky along with its animating "someone." There are many descriptions of making the sun with a similar sun-shield.

The form of a nighthawk, with its stiff wings, can often be seen swooping across an early rising moon. Perhaps some hunting was done by moonlight, as mentioned in *Pueblo Animals and Myths.* Certainly raids often took place by moonlight, so we find that the Zuñis used the primary flight feathers of nighthawks for "strong" prayer-sticks. These might be used for either hunting or war; in the Scalp ceremony, sticks made for the War gods have erect feathers of the "night-jar."[4]

Scalps are closely related to rain as we will see in detail later. The Common Nighthawk is called "rain flopper" by the Hopi. He arrives there late in the season for a migratory bird and during courtship makes a booming sound at night, which is good mimetic thunder. Nighthawks are drawn to water or damp places much as swallows are, for the simple reason that flying insects are more abundant there. So at Hopi they are listed as Cloud's pets along with Frogs, Fish, Turtles, a Swallow, and Water Eagle.[5] Certainly this bird would fit just as well in the chapter on rain birds. At Zuñi nighthawk feathers are among those offered when a newly made field is consecrated.[6] These are flood water fields made to capture all of the runoff from neighboring hills.

poorwills

Poorwills are birds of the night and would be seen flying only when silhouetted against the moon. For a curious reason poorwills are also associated with sleep. Sleep belongs to the night, but after reading any cycle of ceremonies one marvels at how little sleep the Pueblos got at night. The poorwill utters a call that gives the bird its name in English. Mrs. Bailey describes it as a "moth-like, mottled bird," which sums it up very well, because it flies as silently as an owl. Poorwills nest on the ground, where they are perfectly camouflaged when brooding or sleeping.

Fisher mentions poorwills and nighthawks as he found them in the Hopi area in 1893, and his notes, worth repeating, indicate how an Indian would see the birds.

A fine specimen of poorwill was secured on the evening of July 19 as it was flying over the canyon bottom in front of the house. It would have been impossible to have seen it but for the light color of the ground over which it passed, like a fleeting shadow, in pursuit of insects. The Mokis [Hopis] who saw the specimen were much interested in it and designated it by the name of Ho-witz-ko. Nighthawks were common and were heard booming every evening.[7]

The Hopi name means "the sleeping one," but the birds, unlike people, sleep on the ground during the day. Jaeger, who transcribes the name as *Holchko,* takes the name as further evidence that poorwills hibernate during the winter, a point he has proved for southern Arizona. He found a Navajo who, when asked where the birds stay in winter replied, "Up in the rocks." Then he adds that a pastoral people run across them in this winter dormant period on the ground.[8]

In any case, their closeness to the earth has at times made poorwills directional birds for the Below. At Hopi a skin of the bird is placed about the altar of the Flute ceremony to represent the Nadir. The Keres of the pueblo of Sia have a similar idea. There it is said that the Nadir is represented by *ga wa,* which is "a night bird like the Poor-will, shpiyuka, but larger."[9] The only bird that would fit that description is the whippoorwill, which is found to the south of Pueblo country; but because the cardinal from the Gila River, much to the south, is also a Sia directional bird, it is possible that these Indians did some observing far afield.

owls

Owls are by nature ambiguous creatures—they are of the night but are seen by day. For humans night is a pleasant time of rest and sleep, but it can also be a time of fear when only fires hold back the utter dark. There is something sinister about the voice of an owl, and we find him associated with Skeleton Man, the god of death. But that god is also a fertility spirit, and owl shares this relationship with him. Darkness reminds one of a different and daytime darkness, when storm clouds hover over the mesas and fields.

There is a curious division relating to owls, probably because they are obscure at best. Most of the other birds seem to follow a consistent pattern through the various Pueblo groups and languages, but Owl does not. In the central Rio Grande pueblos this bird is related almost exclusively to witches and witchcraft, an association that may have been reinforced by Spanish neighbors. In the western pueblos of Zuñi and the Hopi villages, owls are more neatly balanced between the evil and the good sides of their nature, with the fertility motif probably uppermost.

Owls tend to be lumped together, but the Pueblos have names for at least seven kinds; of these at least three species are important: the Burrowing Owl, the Screech Owl, and the Great Horned Owl. At Hopi the Long-eared Owl probably has a separate role. Different owls have unlike dispositions, and that, too, allows humans to project their own ambivalences onto these birds. The Great Horned Owl has been described as tigerish, whereas the Screech Owl may be violent, or so gentle that it can be picked up and stroked. The Burrowing Owl is quite different from some of its fellows, being active by day as well as night; this bird is more droll than sinister.

It is readily observable that most birds are diurnal, preferring the sun's light, while most animals are nocturnal. The important exceptions, squirrels among mammals and above all owls among birds, reverse the normal pattern. How this came about may be told in folktales or in important myths such as the Zuñi origin account, where the division took place just one day before the migrating people reached Zuñi. There was a gambling contest to see who would have the day, but part of the issue was prejudged, because the Squirrel played on the side of birds, while Owl joined the beasts.

A literal translation of the Zuñi text reads: "Now, my children, your sun father his daylight you will scramble for. On whichever side the ball is hidden when the sun rises your sun father his daylight you will win." The contest is one based on the gambling game of "hidden ball," in which tallies are kept by a "rat" who holds straws. When one side wins by guessing where the ball is hidden, its rat gets a straw to hold, but in this contest sunrise adds a winner-take-all motif.

And owl has the ball, he dances around. The two Aihayuta [War Twins] gave squirrel their club, near sunrise. "Now, with this club you will hit owl. That's the one who has the ball," said the two Aihayuta. As owl dances, squirrel hits his hand with the club. He drops the ball. Bear gets the ball. Eagle won the game. "These [birds] go around in the daylight. Their feathers are to finish prayer-sticks."

The victory was preordained, because the War Twins who intervene are sons and agents of the Sun Father. Owl is a sort of innocent victim, wandering about in a daze in the daylight. The Twins tell him:

But you, Owl, you have not stayed among the winged creatures. Therefore you have lost your sun father's daylight. You have made a mistake. If by daylight, you go about hunting, the one who has his home above will find you out. He will scrape off the dirt from his earth mother and put it upon you.[10]

Owl, like a kind of awkward, winged Satan, is exiled from the Sun's world to become the creature and symbol of the dark. For this reason, at Zuñi, according to Ladd, no owl feathers are used on prayer-sticks; these are offerings to the Sun, who notes where each is placed while he passes across the earth. The feathers of the Burrowing Owl are not used for any pupose at Zuñi, but the large wing and tail feathers of the Great Horned Owl are used to decorate some of the kachina masks. These feathers are also joined together in the form of a rosette for ceremonial use.

As an exile from the Sun, Owl has acquired a great knowledge of the night and of what transpires when the Sun is gone. Owls are the eyes of the night, and sometimes in tales we find Owl acting as a knowledgeable neutral. In a Picuris story concerning a witch-wife and a convocation of sorcerers, the wizards find that they cannot climb the rainbow, but keep sliding back. Because of this failure they know that some noninitiate is within their ranks.

"Suppose we call the Screech Owl, for he is the only one who can

see, even in the dark," Then they called Screech Owl. "Screech Owl, we have called you because you are the chief of the night, since you are the only one that can see in the dark. You can even see a little ant very far in the dark." . . . "Hu, hu," said the Screech Owl as he flew outside.[11]

The Common Screech Owl of the Southwest is not particular about the elevation it inhabits, as long as there are hollow trees available for daytime security. Both the Picuris and the Hopis have a special name for it. The Flammulated Screech Owl is a little smaller and prefers places where yellow pines mix with oaks. The owl of owls is, of course, the Great Horned Owl, which is a resident bird throughout the Sonoran and transition zones of New Mexico and Arizona. Its body may be up to two feet long, with a wingspread of four feet, and if you add that to a fierce hunting spirit, its nightly presence is demanding, if unseen. In addition to the familiar "hoo, hu-hoo, hoo, ho" of the adults, the young are able to call out a thoroughly spine-tingling scream.

Sometimes true stories are told, which include the owl's voice, and these are but a step away from myths. They tell one at Taos where owl feathers are not put to any use because people fear this purveyor of omens. The voice could represent the Horned Owl, but it would also do for others, depending on how it is uttered. A party of Taos Indians set out on a trading expedition to Indians on the plains, which are not far from that mountain junction.

When they were about half way, when they were camping at night, Owl old man was talking away in his nook, just as if he was telling something. . . . Owl called all night. At daylight they packed their horses and in the afternoon they found the Indians and did their trading. They started back where they lived, and halfway back, the old owl at night began to call out from a tree:
  hum hunhun hum
  chutxiapulu
  ka'wa'ko
  old dirty shirt
  blood deep

Meaning that they were to be in a bloody-shirt fight, that their enemies were coming behind them to fight. "We must look out," they said. So they thought they would take another road to escape. They did not want to fight. So their enemies missed them.[12]

Because Owl makes the day his night, he is not always alert then. At one time he was a guardian of a Tewa Keeper of Game spirit. She was against the people; her role made her withhold what the people most wanted.

Owl (mahu) was taking care of that Mean old woman. If anybody came he would always let her know. The little warriors who wanted to overpower her did not come at night, but crept upon her during the day when her watchman was asleep.[13]

For the same reason, when a Zuñi baby will not sleep during the day, an owl feather is selected from the box of feathers each family keeps and placed alongside the baby.[14]

There are stories to account for the origin of owl's sleepiness, which are not like that in the origin myth. The birds had a contest to see which could fly the highest. Sometimes it is said to be Eagle or again the Cliff Swallow who came down and went into a hole. "They put the owl to wait and see when Kyapchiko came out. Ground Owl got tired and he closed one eye. He got tired in the other eye and he closed both eyes."[15] For this dereliction all of the birds began to hate Owl, which is true of the larger owls but not of this one.

The "ground owl" mentioned is quite distinct in every way from other owls and so has a separate name in most Pueblo languages. It is active in the daytime even though it may look as sleepy as other owls. Burrowing Owls are a scant ten inches long and have nearly bare legs which, coupled with the habit of nodding and bobbing the whole body, combines to produce a priest or a clown—which in Pueblo terms may be the same. It sits on the mounds of prairie dogs or any other burrow and sometimes on a neighboring shrub to watch what goes on. The head of this droll one can pivot in almost a full circle to watch, so it is very knowledgeable.

Among the numerous Owl kachinas the *Shko'o'ko* of Cochiti derives from the Burrowing Owl, even though there is nothing realistic about either mask or dress. One reason that the Pueblos knew so much about this little owl is that when various small animals were dug from their burrows, these owls would be found resting or in spring nesting there.[16] The Indians were also perfectly aware that the relationship of Burrowing Owls and prairie dogs was not one of predator and prey, even if they might eat the young of the dogs at times. Their basic diet is one of insects and mice.

Because of the visible companionship between this owl and the animals, the Zuñis call Burrowing Owl "the priest of the prairie dogs." In a valley to the south of that pueblo, according to one tale, these owls lived on peaceable terms with prairie dogs, rattlesnakes, and horned toads.

> *With the Owls they [the prairie dogs] were especially friendly, looking on them as creatures of great gravity and sanctity. For this reason these prairie dogs and their companions never disturbed the councils or ceremonies of the Burrowing Owls, but treated them most respectfully, keeping at a distance from them when their dances were going on.*

The owls then were a dun black, for we have here a "how it came to be" story. The birds danced then as they do now.

> *Each dancer, young man or maiden, carried upon his or her head a bowl of foam, and though their legs were crooked and their motions disjointed, they danced to the whistling of some and the clapping beaks of others, in perfect unison, and with such dexterity that they never spilled a speck of foam on their sleek mantles of dun-black feathers.*

It may be noted here that the bowls of yucca suds carried in dances are a part of cloud-inducing magic.

The story is not based on ritual, so it turns to a familiar trick played on Coyote. He wishes to join their order, but the Owls insist that he first cut off his grandmother's head and dance with it. When he did, they

laughed until they spilled the foam all down their back and bosoms . . . and ever since then the Burrowing Owls have been speckled with gray and white all over their backs and bosoms, because their ancestors spilled foam over themselves in laughing at the silliness of Coyote.[17]

These lighthearted stories are the mortar that binds together the more serious building blocks that form a structure: they true up the solid adobe. The Zuñis have another humorous story involving the "ground owl" and the darkling beetle, which belongs to the genus *Eleodes.* These beetles are most often seen on cloudy days and because of their black color and slow movements are associated with storm clouds by both the Zuñis and the Hopis.

There was a year during which the prairie dogs were enjoying a particularly bountiful supply of their favorite food, portulaca, because of abundant rains. But then these rains became floods and drowned their food. The prairie dogs consulted the wise and solemn Owl who lived on a hill in their dog village. For a remedy he took a tip beetle and forced him to disgorge his evil smell into a bag. These beetles have a defensive reaction, which consists of standing on their heads and disgorging a fluid that trumpets their inedibility.

The Owl began to whack the bag with a stick. Each time that he hit it the clouds scudded farther off. With a final blow he emptied the bag of its contents, and the sky became perfectly clear. So potent is this odor, "that even the Raingods themselves could not withstand it." Thereupon the prairie dogs trooped out of their holes and in shrill voices praised

their great priest the Grandfather Burrowing Owl. And for that reason prairie dogs and burrowing owls have always been great friends. And the burrowing owls consider no place in the world quite so appropriate for the bringing forth, hatching, and rearing of their children as the hole of the prairie dogs.[18]

During the day many owls look confused and nearly blind, which sets them at cross purposes with ordinary life in the daylight world. Death is another contradiction to life as passed in the light of day. We find that Skeleton Man of the Hopis, who is the god of death and of fertility, has a frightening call that resembles the hoot of an owl at night. He is said to walk about only at night and to be proscribed from the Sun. His light comes not from the Sun but from a fire by which he warms himself and around which certain crops grow in the darkness.

At first thought Burrowing Owl is not the best symbol of darkness, because he also has a daylight side to his nature. But this owl does live underground and thus with the dead. There are other links that bind the two together. Clans are joined together in phratries. One clan is named for the god Masau'u or Skeleton Man and a related one is called Kokop. According to one authority the latter name is an unidentified bird, "which belongs to Masau'u and brings black clouds and rain."[19] The name is now often translated as cedarwood.

burrowing owl

Both are probably correct. The Hopis call the Burrowing Owl Ko'ko, or Ko'koht in the plural. Cedarwood is an important material for building hasty fires—actually it is juniper, which grows in abundance on the Southwest mesas, but that is no great matter. As a deity of the night Masau'u is the patron of all fires, just as Owls are the guardians of darkness. They are joined in part by the voice of the night.

The Hopi Talayesva mentions that these nocturnal notes can bring people up sharply.

> *At one of the dancers a clown imitated the mockingbird. He was clever and made the people laugh. First he mocked all the birds, then talked like a Navaho. . . . Finally he mocked Masau'u, the Fire Spirit who guards the village at night. That call, like the cry of an owl, surprised everybody.*[20]

The god of death is often like a scream in the night, but he is also a god of fertility, which is one of the good things to come from under the ground to a life above ground.

Dark below is related to dark clouds above, so Owls are asked to bring them from the cardinal points; for this purpose discs are cut from gourds. These are painted with the directional colors, and then a hole is cut in the center where the owl prayer feathers are threaded. According to Parsons these discs, which are made for the Niman kachina ceremony at the end of July, are implements of a ritual rainmaking game that is also played at Acoma. These discs, or sometimes balls, are rolled between prayer-sticks that act as goal posts, in order to make thunder and lightning.[21]

The opposition between night and day, plus sleeping, involves the Owl in another fertility rite. Kick-stick races are run to speed the Sun on its journeys and also to hasten Clouds toward the villages. At Zuñi one racer was about to take part in this rite honoring the Sun, but beforehand he went out to Owl Spring where Owl was about to go to sleep for the day. The runner addressed the bird:

> *"They are going to run a stick race with me today and my grand-*

mother told me to come to you to find what to do. I'm bringing this pay to you." And he gave him the prayer meal. "Thank you, I shall be glad to help you," his grandfather said. "Pull a feather from my left wing and carry it when you run. When you carry this close to them in the race my sleeping will overcome them and they will be too tired to race." [22]

So in this roundabout fashion Owl gets to be something of a rain bird.

Success in the race will bring rain, so seeing an owl in this case is a good omen. "Now my boys, listen carefully. If we hear the owl, or hummingbird, or water making a noise in the stream or bank falling in, it will be a good sign for us." [23] Owls also relate to making edible the corn that rain produces. Indian corn stands midway in softness between very hard corn such as "flint" and very tender sweet corn. It is all a matter of how much of the starches are converted into sugar.

During the Zuñi Winter Solstice ceremony two kachinas hoot on the roof of a kiva or ceremonial house and throw down cooked ears of corn to those below. Perhaps this bit of ritual is based on the origin myth, where it is said that

the world was filled with falling snow. Their days were at an end. Their corn matured. When it was mature it was hard. Then the two said, "By whose will will our corn become soft? Well, owl." Thus they said. They summoned owl. Owl came. When he came he pecked at their corn and it became soft. [24]

Owls feed by swallowing their food whole, bones, feathers or fur, and all. After the edible parts are softened and digested, the remains are regurgitated in the form of pellets, which one may presume is the basis for this story. At Hopi the Great Horned Owl is related to fertility through bringing hot weather and a good peach crop. "For hot weather in order to make a good peach harvest, owl and yellow bird feathers are used." In the Winter Solstice rites owl feathers are used to summon the same midsummer heat.

Again it is noted that, "For the peach trees owl feathers are used, as the owl—as also the owl kachina—is said to have special influence over the growth of peaches." Owl feathers are also important for peaches, "because the owl feather is used at Powamu. No pine needles are fastened to the owl prayer-feathers because the pine brings cold."[25] The link between owl and peaches is rather obvious. Hopi peaches are scattered about the mesas, and both the flesh and the pits are much desired by chipmunks and various ground squirrels. Horned Owls in turn like these rodents and make their voices heard on summer evenings.

There are two important Owl kachinas at Hopi, one for Horned Owl, called *Mongwa,* and another for Spruce Owl, or *Salab Mongwa.* There is also a Screech Owl kachina called *Hotsko.* Spruce, which here is Douglas fir, is important in all ceremonies, and the owl that would best fit that is the Long-eared Owl. Its bones were found in a small house ruin in the Wupatki National Monument, so it had early Pueblo connections. Both of these horned owls are important in the Powamu and the Horned Water Serpent ceremonies where figurines of the birds are made.

A simpler ritual occurs when the Horned Owl kachina comes to First Mesa from Second Mesa, bringing five clowns with him. He hoots and pretends to shoot the clowns with a bow and arrows. They in turn capture him and tie him up, until some girl slips past them to free Horned Owl. Once free, he flogs the clowns with a rope that he carries. Because clowns are Fertility spirits, the rite resembles many of those recounted by Frazier.

So far these accounts from the western Pueblos present Owl in a favorable light. But everything about him is as reversible as night and day, and there is another side to the story. The smaller birds hate Owl as a night predator, so it is no uncommon sight to see them mobbing a sleepy owl during the day when it appears to be defenseless, even though it is impervious to threats. Because these little birds are often those who bring the summer, Owl by driving them away may also drive away the summer clouds that bring rain.

Owl is also acquainted with the mysteries of the night through which he can see, so he brings knowledge for good or for evil. At

Zuñi a story relates to War chiefs, but it is also told to children and is illustrated by old pictographs south of the town. The symbols consist of a new Moon in one corner, along with the Evening Star. Across from these in the lower right is a figure of Horned Owl. From the Moon to the bird are a series of zig-zag lines representing its flight.

> The story relates how in ancient times the owl would occasionally come to the war chief and tell him where Navajo hogans were located. The bird would lead the chief to the houses of his enemy. He would then don a headdress of piñion jay and quail feathers, the latter making him invisible, and enter the hogans where the Navajo were sleeping. After he had counted the number of sleeping forms he would return to Zuñi and gather a group of warriors together to capture the Navajo or steal their belongings. The owl did not always favor the Zuñi, however, as sometimes he would fly on ahead and warn the Navajo that their enemies were coming, and when the Zuñi arrived they would find a deserted hogan.[26]

During the Winter Solstice ceremony of the same people, a kachina who represents the chief of the council of gods, Pautiwa, appears carrying an object representing a Navajo scalp, to which a feather from Owl and one from a Crow are attached. The interpretation of this rite is that when there are hostilities, the Navajo pass around at night, like the Owl, and inform the enemies of the Zuñi. Owl at Zuñi is not so neutral as Owl in the story from Taos, even though his hoot works both ways. Nor is he as friendly as at Hopi where Owl Boy is the son of Warrior Woman, a defender of the village for several Pueblo groups.

There are marginal roles for Owl, as in the gambling game of hidden ball. Certain men go out toward the cardinal points to listen for omens. If they hear summer birds, success will come to their side; but if they hear an owl or a coyote, they will lose. How that works, unless they go out in daylight, is a mystery, because there are nights in New Mexico when it seems that coyote pups priested by owls dominate the world, at least between thunder bursts and lightning flashes.

When this gambling game is actually being played, each participant prays silently to himself: "We sing with our hearts, not with our lips." The song is sung to both Owl and Crow; the latter can hide corn in the mountains and find it on need, while Owl can hide the ball in his claws and totter about so that no one knows he has it.[27] A gambling game is balanced if it is honest, so the Owl is a neutral arbiter, but Owls have another role along the Rio Grande.

Going about at night is a hazardous proposition for anyone who does not see in the dark. For one thing there are witches as well as owls outside in the unknown. There seems to be plenty of evidence that witches and their devices existed before the arrival of Spanish settlers in the Southwest, but the two forms probably reinforced each other. Witchcraft as a practice lies outside the framework of legitimate Pueblo religious activity, but because witches exist, religion must take account of them.

Emergence myths always make a note on how witches slipped into our upper world, along with the good people. Because most sickness and misfortune is caused by witches, countermeasures must be taken against them. For this reason curing societies work against the effects of witches. In order to gain power over these enemies some shamans wear dyed owl feathers in their hair.[28] More frequently the witches themselves use owl or crow feathers, or often as not they turn themselves into these birds.

Turning oneself into an owl is only one among many transformations open to witches. They can take the forms of any animal or bird, but usually it will be that of an owl, a crow, or a coyote. At San Felipe there are said to be many, many witches who take bird and animal forms, preferably the shape of an owl. No matter what guise they take, witches wear either owl or red feathers (probably flicker), and so no one there is allowed to pick up these feathers if he finds them.[29] This proscription arises from the fact that they might be used for evil ends.

A story from Cochiti is typical of lore concerning witch transformations. One night a hunter who had no connections with witches found himself in the mountains. Not wanting to risk the trip in the dark, he sat down in the rocky recess of an arroyo.

While there, crows and owls began to alight upon the neighboring trees, and then changed themselves into the forms of men and women. One of them approached the rock, without noticing the hunter, and the rock opened, showing a cave inside. Soon that cave filled with sorcerers and witches which all came in the shape of owls and crows. Among them were the friend of his and finally his own wife.

The hunter returns home and finds the "natural eyes" of his wife. These he soaks in urine so that they will be unusable. Meanwhile the evil group have plotted to kill him the next day by using a witch in the form of a deer, but the plot fails and the hunter eludes death.

He then went home and found his wife sitting in the dark with her face covered. Seizing her by the hair he found that she had the eyes of an owl, not having been able to use her own. He threw her down, and she died.[30]

Witches keep the same dark hours as owls do, so their images are used by people who believe themselves to be witches. In the last century Father Dumarest heard an account from a Cochiti Indian who confessed to having caused a smallpox epidemic, for which he was apparently executed. On the following day the town chief made a search of the man's house and "found in a pot a stone image with owl eyes, feathers of owl and crow, and pieces of cactus."[31] Because the Father buried two of those involved, the story is true in part and indicates that if you thought yourself a witch, the Owl would be a tutelary spirit, and a fetish jar containing an image and feathers would be a part of some nocturnal rites.

At the Tiwa pueblo of Isleta witches travel in the form of lights visible at night; these probably represent detached owl eyes. In a witch-wife story there it is told that as her husband was asleep the wife "dug into a wall niche and took out a pair of owl eyes, took out her own and put in the owl eyes."[32] The Zuñi have rationalized the use of two birds by saying that, "A wizard attached crow and owl plumes to his head that he might have the eyes of the crow to see quickly the approach of man and the eyes of the owl to travel by night."

Sometimes these witches with feathers on them might be observed, which happened when one Zuñi went out to gather wood. He heard a cry that was like an owl, yet had a human resonance in the notes. Looking about, he observed a fellow townsman. "'Aha!' said he, 'Why have you those plumes upon your head? Aha, you are a sorcerer.'"[33] Such things were taken most seriously. One curious case involved a Zuñi War chief who was himself a prosecutor of witches and a dominant personality in high office. While conducting a trial he was suddenly accused of keeping owl feathers inside his own moccasins, which turned out to be a fact, and he was impeached.[34]

At Hopi, witchcraft has not been developed to the same degree as farther east—for one thing, they believe that disease is sent by wild creatures rather than by witches. As we have already seen, owls have much to do with fertility there and probably also with war and hunting, as the story of Owl Boy suggests. There are both Hopi and Hopi-Tewa versions of the myth. In the first an only child was whipped by his mother— which would not happen in real life because of a complex discipline system in which the maternal aunt would have much to say. He was whipped because of his meanness.

One day the mother pushed him out of the house altogether, but Owl then came along and observed his plight.

> *"Oh, my dear, I am sorry your mother whips you and does not like you. I think I shall take you home with me." She walked through the village with him, then spread her wings and flew. Owls have no nest. They go into a big hole under the rocks, and there they live and have their young.*

The last bit of information would seem to indicate that the Great Horned Owl is the kindly bird.

The boy's father is angry but cannot locate his son. Sometime later a man hauling wood heard a song:

Tća'weyuna, Tća'weyuna
Tća'weyu'piiwe . . . .
Annnnaaa.

"The boy was now like an owl. He had short feathers on his arms and over his entire body." The first line of this song refers to the Warrior goddess, Chakwena; the second refers to her milk. Quite evidently the boy is really the son of this figure.

His human parents have a chance to retrieve their lost son, but the mother in Orpheus fashion bungles the attempt. When they come for their son, Owl tells the couple to keep the boy in a dark room for three days so that he will become a Hopi once more. Even the numbers here are out of keeping with the Pueblo system, but in any case the mother peeks in too soon and the boy cries out: " 'Oh, mother, you do not want me to stay here! You have ruined me! I suppose I must go back.' Then he cried, 'hu u' u' hu! u! u! hu! u! u!' He flew against the door two or three times and broke out. She tried to catch him but could not."[35]

In part this is a cautionary tale—mothers should not put boys outside at night, and children have been reminded that if they misbehave, owls may carry them off. At Jemez this is a common threat to children, but the story has other directions as we hear in a Hopi-Tewa version of the same events. The transgression this time is in entering a kiva at night, and that a boy must not do until initiated. A big owl carries this boy to a home on the cliff, where he lives with the little owls.

The boy, however, has difficulty mastering a diet of raw rabbit meat, so with the help of Spider Grandmother, to whom he is led by Chipmunk, he learns the human methods of hunting. One day Owl comes to say that the boy's parents are sad; he is returned, and this time the proscription is the proper four days. His mother breaks it, of course, and there is a midnight noise from the room. In the morning his father went in, "and there in the center of the room was a big owl." The weeping father made five feather strings, such as one would tie between the horns of slain game.

The boy's father tied two feather-strings around each leg and one around his neck. "Now you may go back to your people. You are no longer our son. You are an owl. If an enemy approaches, come and tell the people." He [Owl] shook his head like this [nodding]. "If sickness is coming, you can tell the people."[36]

Some things an owl does know and all owls are hunters, some even warriors, or at least friends of warriors.

At Zuñi a hunter of large game might carry the wing feather from an owl. When game is discovered, the hunter takes this feather into his mouth and expectorates in the direction of his game.[37] The mothlike silence of the owl when it hunts is being invoked here to aid the hunter of game, who must approach it silently. Mrs. Bailey mentions that the Indians of northern New Mexico fletch their arrows with owl feathers, and it is true that except for the twang of the bowstring an arrow makes its course toward the game almost as silently as an owl's flight.

Unfortunately Owl's relation to hunting is all too often related to the lethal end of the shaft and he is a victim; the hunter becomes the hunted. The Hopi tell that Red Eagle, meaning Red-tailed Hawk, was a friend of Owl. But the latter would not go out during the day, so they never hunted together. One day when Eagle found his friend asleep, he scratched Owl a little, but the latter paid no attention. Next Eagle lifted Owl's eyelids a bit and finally pulled his whiskers. The awakened Owl agreed to join in a hunt with his friend.

Eagle swooped down on a rabbit, caught it, and returned to Owl who was again asleep. "Why are you sleeping here again; they will certainly kill you." But the Owl did not hear anything. Two boys out hunting then appeared and Eagle flew up, but Owl was sitting on the rim of the bank sleeping. "One of them put an arrow on his bow, aimed, and shot the Owl through the head, so that the bird tumbled down into the wash."[38] Such is the lot of owls—as signs they are ambiguous, and man's attitude toward them is ambivalent.

9 BIRDS OF BALANCE BETWEEN NATURE AND MAN

crows and ravens

Crows and ravens have roles as ambiguous as the owls and in fact share some characteristics. Witches may take the form of either crows or owls, and both birds have connections with war. Crows and ravens, however, are more closely tied to man. For one thing they share the same daylight hours, and they also share man's food, which may be negative but it is certainly a tie. Because they do join in at harvest time to glean a bit of corn they can also be thought of as birds of agriculture.

There is another way in which these big black birds form a link between nature and man—their coming and going can be related to the presence or absence of flocks of black clouds. Almost synonymous with the rain clouds are the kachinas, who are spirits that also come and go. They represent the dead in a general way, living in the mountains but passing over the villages occasionally to bring rain. The real kachinas are imitated by the masked dancers in ceremonies who, while they wear masks, are the real kachina spirits.

Kachinas thus relate the spirit world to the world of man, and crows or ravens are tied to kachinas in a number of ways. Before considering these it might be well to mention the birds as they appear in the Southwest. For one thing there are two ravens, the White-necked and the Common Raven. The Hopis, say, "two birds, one name," and that is curious, because the White-necked Ravens behave more like crows, in that they congregate in numbers and will move into a harvested field, and the white on their neck is usually not visible unless a wind ruffs their feathers. Formerly their range was much wider in New Mexico.

Common Ravens are much larger than either of the others and are often seen in pairs or singly, flying high and hawklike over the rugged country where they nest. Occasionally ravens concentrate in northern Arizona. The crow of the Pueblo country is the familiar one, but the area is not agricultural over wide expanses. So great flocks of crows are seen only when an isolated crop has been harvested. In New Mexico they are found in the central and northern parts during the summer, often nesting in the cottonwoods along the Rio Grande. In winter crows flock from Albuquerque south and forage from there into western areas, including Zuñi.

The status of the crow in Hopi country is expressed by Woodbury as "uncommon, but sometimes numerous," which is to say that when and where there is food for them, the crows appear. There is quite a bit of interchangeability between crows and ravens in the Pueblo mind concerning ceremonial usage. The Zuñis do not use the feathers on prayer offerings, "because they eat dead things," but the feathers of both birds are used on masks. The most extensive utilization is for the large ruff or collar around the base of many masks; the feathers of fifteen to twenty birds are needed to make one. Either species of bird may be used.

At Zuñi a sacred name, *kokko qu'inna,* applies to both birds.[1] *Kokko* is the name for the kachinas, so that link is basic. As for the birds in their natural contexts, the crow is Q'alashi and the raven K'otolo'a, indicating that the joining of the two birds is not from lack of knowledge. At Hopi a story entitled "How the Crow clan became also the Kachina clan" tells how the kachinas and crows became linked.

The home of the Dark people who originally composed the Crow clan was somewhere at the base of the San Francisco Peaks. Every night they heard someone whom they took to be a spirit coming down from the peaks to visit the village, so they sent a youth up to find out who he was. With the help of Spider Woman the youth overcomes a mountain lion, grizzly bear, and rattlesnakes to arrive at a kiva on top of the peaks. When he asks the identity of the people there, they "answered him and said that they were Kachinas, and being Kachinas they had control of the weather, like the rain and the storms."

This youth is then taught the kachina dances that are to become a central part of the Hopi religion. It is revealed that Germinator, or Muyingwu, is the god who makes his home on the peaks. He teaches the youth to make the masks. The final instructions are that the youth and his relatives will now be Kachina clan.

> *Well, the youth said that they were already the Crow clan, but the head man said that they had a Crow kachina and told the boy to tell his uncle, the Chief, that they must make pahos [prayer feathers] to the Kachinas whenever they held a dance. . . . And so the Crow and Kachina Clans brought these dances to the Hopi.*[2]

Crows appear in dark clouds that are similar to those that gather with their lightning flashes around the San Francisco Peaks in summer. Sometimes these black clouds bring rain to the villages. But the kachinas within the clouds really produce the rain, so crows and kachinas are likely associations. As Germinator pointed out, the Hopis do have an individual Crow kachina whose name is Tumas. Some regard her as the mother of all kachinas, but she is specifically the mother of Tunwap or Whipper kachinas.

A number of sayings illustrate the closeness of crows and kachinas in the Pueblo mind. When those Hopi kachinas who toss gifts to children are about to arrive, "people tell the children that the crow has on a blue moccasin. The children watch the crows as they fly by." The same concept is found at Acoma but not among the eastern Keres. At Acoma when presents are given to a child the parents say:

> *"This has been sent you by the kachina. The crows brought it from Wenimats!" Children seeing crows, look at them to see if they are carrying presents. The "stockings" of the katsina represent crow stockings. Parents point out crows to the children, saying, "See, the katsina are going to come!"*[3]

Connections between crows and specific kachinas at Zuñi originate in a different point of view, given in a myth backing the Zuñi Winter Solstice ceremony. At that time two kachinas appear—the Black god and the White god, or Kwelele and Shitsuka. The White god is a great hunter, while the Black god is a Keeper of Game who impounds all animals behind stone walls on a high mountain.

Shitsuka, the White god, is able to free this game. After the animals fled, on the opening of the corral,

> One of the Kwal'ashai hearing, ran to tell the other, and all left the house to see, and they cried: "Who has let out our game?" Shits'ukia at once spat out the medicine Pau'tiwa had given him over the Kwal'ashi people, and they all turned into ravens and croaking, flew away, to return no more to their homes.[4]

The translator calls them ravens, but the Zuñi name stands for crows.

That myth explains the provision of game, which is a seasonal matter. Winter snows release the animals from the high mountains and send them down. Whiteness undoubtedly relates to the snow, which does the trick for the hunter. Crows also make a seasonal migration out of the mountains and southward. In a version of this story recorded a half century later, the sacred name that combines crows with ravens is used. In it the young man who will free the game makes a pun is using a word which refers to both Kachinas and crows-ravens: "I will make them all black crows tonight, and don't you let them eat any corn." The White god then takes a handful of salt which he puts in the fire, covering it with ashes.

> Soon the salt got very hot and popped. Then the deer started to run out and the mountain lion ran after them. . . . Then all the crows went down to the man's cornfield, and Pautiwa's daughter was busy all night chasing the crows away, running from side to side waving her arms and calling out. After a while the crow flew away and the deer ran all over the country.[5]

The Pueblos do most of their big-game hunting late in the year, at the time harvests are in and after the crows have arrived.

The black and white opposition can be as simple as the weather opposition, for example, at Isleta where the North direction is represented by black and the crow is associated with it. There it is said, "A crow cawing is calling cold weather."[6] More than that is involved, however, as the myths that hold that crows or ravens were once white is worldwide. The Greek god Apollo changed the crow to its present color, and presumably the white/black dichotomy illustrates man's ambivalence toward these birds. At Zuñi the crows formerly had white shoulder bands, but a certain Crow was offered a smoke by two warriors and being a greedy fellow he took such a deep puff that the smoke filled out all of his feathers, staining them black.[7]

At Hopi, "A kachina boy soaked sunflower seeds and made black water which he poured on the crow and made it black, before this all crows were white." At Acoma the reasoning is different and relates to the Volcano demon—"Crow was snow-white. He tried to beat out the fire with his wings and he was changed by the heat till he became black."[8] In the last instance he was trying to help mankind, but that is only half of his role. Crows may drive away the little birds of summer, and that in turn will drive the black clouds away from the cornfields.

Summer suggests one more close association, which is added to the crow-kachina link. In Chapter 1 we spoke of parrots as birds of the Sun, and parrots are also joined to the crows through a myth which was mentioned there. At Zuñi the Dogwood clan has three subdivisions, or perhaps four: Dogwood proper, Macaw, Kachina, and Crow people.[9] The matter has been much confused by the fact the *kokko* can be used for either the spirits or for crows. At Hopi the same connection is made but through linking clans in a phratry.

We have already heard how crows and kachinas joined. The parrot and crow story is simpler and says that during the migrations of the parrot clan this bird was guiding them. When they stopped for the night a fire was built under the tree in which their bird was perched. In the morning it was noticed that the smoke had blackened it so that the parrot looked much like a crow.

Some people said: "It is a crow, and we will take the name Crow for our people and descendants." That is why some people are Parrot clan and some Crow clan, but they are one people for they travelled together and did everything as a group.[10]

A myth from Zuñi and Acoma, briefly mentioned in Chapter 2, explains the crow and parrot or macaw link on the basis of a choice of eggs. It is both a seasonal myth and one that explains the double role of crows. As a matter of fact, the Crow fought on both sides in the Keresan Battle of the Seasons, which is about as ambiguous as possible. The myth of the eggs takes place during the times of migrations when the people were wandering all over the face of the earth.

The nexus of the story is a choice between an egg that is a beautiful turquoise blue, and one that is dun colored like the earth— sometimes there are pairs or more. In the nineteenth-century Zuñi version the myth related directly to the Dogwood clan, who are said to be the first people to offer feathered prayer-sticks. The *Pekwin,* or deputy to the Sun Father, placed the two eggs in a sacred basket of meal. He placed this basket on the floor before the fetishes of the Rain priests and asked everyone to choose one egg or the other.

"All chose the beautiful blue egg; none would have the more homely one. But alas! when the eggs were hatched the raven came from the blue egg and the macaw from the other."[11] The Macaw people were then sent southward into Mexico, the land of summer. In another version the eggs are reasonably paired and one set was to produce not only a beautiful bird, but this bird would be surrounded by a kind of everlasting summertime in which crops would grow without effort.

And from the other twain shall issue beings of evil, uncolored, black, piebald with white; and whither these shall fly and ye follow, shall strive winter with summer . . . and contended for between their offspring and yours shall be the food. . . .

The people naturally select the turquoise eggs, which they put on *common raven*

the warm side of a cliff
to hatch. The pin feathers
of the chicks showed color,
"but when their feathers
appeared they were black
with white bandings; for
ravens were they. And
they flew away mocking
our fathers and croaking
coarse laughs."[12] That teller
was thinking of the White-
necked Raven, but the same
story is told with crows.

The Acoma version is related
to their different migration traditions,
which say that they came from a place
called White House in the North. One
of the War Twins who led them south,
"had two eggs, one a parrot egg, the other a
crow egg. One was blue and the other was white,
but no one knew which was the parrot's egg. They
decided to go to the south, where lay a place

CROWS AND RAVENS

called Ako. They wished to go there and raise parrots." They were to find this new place by a contest of echos—when Masewi called out "A-a-a-ko-o-o-o," that would be the place, if the echo came back "A-ko."

When this spot was located, the people were asked to choose between the eggs.

> *The people divided themselves, some preferring the blue egg, others the white one, but both parties were, of course, trying to select the parrot egg. Most of the people chose the blue egg, so Masewi threw it against the cliff. Swarms of crows flew out.*[13]

In all of the things we have heard about Crow-Raven he has been thoroughly entangled in the affairs of men, and in that realm not everything goes well. Crows may bring dark clouds or they may drive them away. It is much like the Zuñi myth in which these black birds were responsible for withholding the game and for dispersing it to the hunters' benefit. Sometimes crows are not ambiguous—simply bad luck or evil.

At Cochiti they see only the negative side, and the crow as a bird of omen may bring drought. A society in that village is normally the guardian of the rain makers, and in case of a prolonged dry spell the members go into a retreat. Then each day they journey to a spring to bring back jars of water. On returning they tell what portents they have observed along the way. Good signs are rabbit and deer, but to see a crow is bad news.[14]

Presumably this bad luck would mean further drought, but crows are also associated with witchcraft at Cochiti, as we learned in the chapter on owls. At both Laguna and Zuñi crow feathers are also linked with witchcraft, and on Hopi Second Mesa bad people, presumably witches, take the form of crows.

> *You do not believe it because you do not know. But a Hopi merely turns over and becomes a coyote or a crow; if you observe their features carefully, you will be able to see the nose or beak . . . pressing under the skin of the man's forehead when in human shape.*[15]

Among the Hopis Crow sometimes becomes a veritable personification of evil, which is about as far as ambivalence can go in the opposite direction from the kachina association. Crow is spoken of as a spirit who lives on a mesa to the southwest of Old Oraibi. "He would be walking up and down on the edge of the mesa watching the people as they were planting their corn in the valley. 'Thank you,' he would say, 'that you are planting corn for me.'" This crow watched the people carefully, and sometimes he would charm them so that they would sicken or die. "The Crow, or Sickness, would also despoil people in other ways, some into whom he had breathed his bad influence would, for instance, begin to steal." Another spirit, though unseen, influences people for good, but it is noted that "it is not so strong as the crow." [16]

At Zuñi the baneful influence is not tied to wrongdoing or sickness but back to the weather again. As we have seen, the migratory birds of summer bring the rains but crows "drive away other birds and so keep away the rain." [17] That is one possibility, but the Crow-Raven is again joined with the Owls—not only in witchcraft but in making corn edible, as is told in the Zuñi origin myths. The people planted their seeds and waited, watching their priests as heavy rains caressed the earth and matured their corn. But this corn was not palatable; it was bitter.

> Then the two said, "Now by whose will will our corn become fit to eat?" Thus they said. They summoned raven. He came and pecked at their corn, and it became good to eat. "It is fortunate that you have come." [18]

This myth states that those who share man's food have a common bond with him, even if they are in a way enemies. The same concept applies to human enemies as well and thus to war. If a Zuñi has killed a Navajo, he is obliged to house and serve food to that man's descendants any time they appear at Zuñi; accounts show that this was actually done.

War associations follow crows and ravens all around the world, because they eat dead things. At the Zuñi Winter Solstice ceremony when Pautiwa, chief of the gods, enters the pueblo, he brings in his left hand a twig with crow and owl feathers attached. These represent a Navajo scalp, and at intervals he kicks them with his left foot. On a smiliar note two kachinas at Zuñi, one of whose name is an expression of distress, follow the same thought.

> *They wear crow feathers because the crow always comes when everything is quiet and no one is looking for a fight and they bring bad luck. Then the crow comes and flies around the village four times, saying "ka ka" and the people say, "What does it mean?" Then he says, "I came to tell you the Navaho are coming to kill the people."*[19]

With that timely warning the Zuñis won the battle, and ever since, that kachina has had the enemy's blood on his face.

I suspect that the bird in question was a raven rather than a crow, partly because ravens habitually use the two-note call and because they have similar roles elsewhere. At Hopi the raven implied the killing of enemies. Stephen mentions a War dance at Walpi on First Mesa where,

> *Sha'wi . . . carries a long slender pole on the end of which is impaled a raven. This pole, they say, should be a lance; this display was formerly made during war time and implied that the Hopi were roused to anger and that the raven would feed upon the enemies to be slain.*[20]

The Towa Indians of Jemez pueblo, who had more than their fair share of wars because they were caught between the Spanish and various other Indian groups, had a war fetish that consisted of a smoothly ground black stone club. It belonged to the War society whose priest was an actual leader in the field. With it he was said to have knocked off the head of enemies, and to this fetish belonged "several long black feathers, crow or eagle, tied together at the base."[21]

With the crows and ravens we have made the descent from the spirit world of kachinas to the realm of such mundane concerns as bad luck and war. But before speaking further of human activities, something must be said about the nature of speech.

10 BIRDS OF SPEECH

mockingbirds and shrikes

We began this book with birds of the sun and have now descended to the very human realm of a bird who grants the gift of speech. Speaking is the dividing line between man and other members of the animal kingdom. Both birds and animals practice hunting or gathering, and some might be said to make war on one another. These creatures do communicate and certainly retain knowledge, as instanced by the lead turkey gobbler or the guardian crane. But speech is different in that it can be abstracted from any particular speaker and maintain a life on its own. Songs and prayers for example, are in the matrix of human culture and must be relearned with each generation. Mockingbird is a great help in showing how this can be done.

Speech has another kind of independence in that there are many languages. Quite often the words may be used by a person with little or no knowledge of the exact meanings, but he does know that the words have ritual power. The Pueblos often speak of these unknown words in a chant as "ancient." A mockingbird is sometimes thought of in this way as he has learned the figures of other songs without understanding their content.

In a way there is a distant tie between sun and speech—those Sun birds the parrots were known to have the capacity for human speech, though nothing much was made of the point. On the other hand, prayers and songs are often addressed to the Sun, and knowing them is a sign of wisdom and that is why Mockingbird is asked by a Hopi chief to travel with him in search of Tawa, the Sun god.

One account of the bird's gift of languages ends with this Sun-oriented journey.

> *"Well," said the chief, "you are a pretty wise bird. Now you and I will travel the same direction toward the rising sun and the sun may be our god, great and wise. With its light we can see and walk. Wherever this place is where the sun rises, I would like to see who will get there first for there we may learn who is our true god. If not, the sun itself is our god for there must be some spirit, somewhere, that really does look after us. If either you or I should get to the sun first, the great star will appear and many other stars will fall from the heavens, by which those who are still on the journey will know that one of us has reached the journey's end."* [1]

This wise bird who taught the Hopis their ritual songs in the Underworld, and then divided up the languages among different peoples, has a companion. The shrike is more of a messenger than a speaker, but that is a related form of communication. He and Mockingbird were joined together in important events at the emergence. The two do look something alike, and sometimes the shrike is called the "French mockingbird." The shrike has some strident command notes as does the mockingbird. There the resemblance ends, because shrikes lack the ability to imitate other birds. The colors of the two birds are much the same, but Shrike wears a black mask; that becomes an important point in one story.

Mockingbird's learning and teaching of songs and speech can be taken with varying degrees of seriousness. At Taos his wisdom is slight and only associates him with Echo Boy. Near that pueblo a childless husband was gathering wood at the foot of Taos Peak, where every day he heard someone singing. On the fourth day he found a boy, "dressed in white deerskin and nice moccasins with mockingbird feathers in his hair. The man said to him, 'What a pretty boy you are, and you are living in this wood. I will take you to live with us.'"

The adoption proved to be a failure, because the child's only speech was mimicry. "The woman laid down a buffalo hide for him to sleep on. 'Now you go to bed!' The little boy said, 'Now you go to bed!' All night the little boy danced and sang, and they could not sleep." For this the couple put the boy back where they had found him (there have been nights when similar thoughts have occured to all of us). When he was returned to his home, the boy

> told him he was not a little boy, he was kaiuuna [a spirit]. That was why he was dancing and singing. He said to him if he needed clothing to come and ask him and to tell the people to come to Taos Peak foot to ask him for whatever clothing they needed.[2]

It takes a voice or a song to ask the spirits for those things that the people need. Clothing, like speech, is a mark of the human kind. Farther south along the Rio Grande another Mockingbird Youth appears among the Keres, but his meaning has to be a matter of guess. The Santa Ana Indians have a map of the cosmos in which the world is a square with the cardinal directions in the middle of each side. Then, at each corner of the square there are houses for the spirits. Two of these are well known; Spider Grandmother is in the Southwest corner, while Thinking Woman resides in the Northwest. Butterfly occupies the Southeast and guards the village chief, while in the Northeast lies the house of Shpati miti or Mockingbird Youth.[3]

One can only surmise that, because the two goddesses form one side of the world, the two chiefs, the village or "inside" chief and the "outside" chief, form the other side. That would associate Mockingbird with the younger War Twin. His role would be in this case to tell what was going on beyond the confines of the village, and we find Mockingbird in this informative part in a story from one of Laguna's farming villages. There it is said that Fox and Rabbit played a game of tricks, in which Rabbit first makes gloves of pitch so that Fox sticks to a tree. Then in turn Fox entices Rabbit to jump into the lake. But when it seems that he may die, Fox and Chipmunk decide that they had best rescue Rabbit before he drowns.

mockingbird

> *On top of some willows they saw a mockingbird [*spadyi*]. The mockingbird was singing. The chipmunk understood the song. The mockingbird was saying that rabbit was out of the lake, that rabbit was safe.*[4]

Sometimes Mockingbird has the opposite role, which is simply a matter of not telling.

In the tale of White Bison, in which the great beast kidnaps a Zuñi wife, the husband is aided in his search for her by various birds and small animals. In this instance the role of Mockingbird is simply to desist from his common practice of telling everyone all that he knows, indicating that he is usually the interpreter of all that goes on in the animal kingdom. But this secrecy is needed:

> *"Do you see that little white house? There is your wife." When they reached the house, the* katetacha *[magpie] said, "You stay here until I go to Mockingbird [*kaichoo*] and tell him not to tell Bison."*[5]

Then, just to make sure, Poorwill, the sleeping one, spits on the talkative bird and puts him to sleep.

BIRDS OF SPEECH

It is said that at Zuñi a mockingbird's tongue will be cut out and held to a child's lips. The mockingbird is then released. As his tongue supposedly begins to grow back, the child's tongue will also begin to wag. According to Ladd, the child is fed the tongue so that he will have, in time, a knowledge of many languages.[6] Mockingbird's talkativeness and his habits can also suggest arguments or even fighting. When the Zuñis play their gambling game of hidden ball, which may go on for several days, they first look for signs. "If he hears a mockingbird, he knows there will be trouble, perhaps the two sides will have a fight and one will be hit with the ball of the game."[7]

On Hopi Second Mesa the bird's tongue is used to help a child in learning ritual dance songs.

To make a child talk, one should catch the [yaupa] bird, which talks a lot, remove the bird's tongue and feed this to the child. One informant said that this also helped a male child to learn dance songs with ease.[8]

It is to be hoped that the remedy was used only when the child had considerable learning difficulty. At Acoma the same idea has been humanized.

If the child is slow in learning to talk, his parents will put some shelled corn in a mockingbird's nest and leave it there for a few days. Then they take it out, grind it, and put it into the child's mouth, slightly moistened.[9]

The myth bearers at Hopi are the Singers society, and they are closely linked to Mockingbird. All Hopi males must belong to one of four societies around which various gods, myths, and rites are integrated. The first of these is the Tao, or Singers, society, which pays tribute to Talatumsi, Dawn Woman, goddess of growing things, and also to Germinator, the male corn spirit. Next there is the Wuwuchim society, whose name does not translate; their patron is the god Tai'owa, a flute-playing Sun deity who resembles the god Paiyatemu of other Pueblo groups. Third is the Kwan, or Agave, society, in which the Shrike is important, whose patron is Skeleton Man, the death and fertility spirit. Last is the Al or Horn society, whose members pay tribute to Tuwabontumsi, Sand Altar Woman, the wife of Skeleton Man and patroness of all game animals.

The Singers are curators of the emergence myth and its songs, but they also do a great deal of actual chanting during the Initiation ceremony. Stephen describes them in the last century as wearing a white embroidered kilt and mantles with scarlet borders. After singing in the plaza they go down into the kivas, eventually arriving at their own kiva where they pass around the roof, "and then down, maintaining the song until the last disappears."[10]

It was Mockingbird who taught these songs at the time of the emergence from the fourfold Underworld, which makes him a tutelary spirit for the Singers. Fortunately there are several versions of these myths, so we can piece together the roles of Mockingbird and Shrike. In one version it is said that Spider Woman, the Little War Twins, and Mockingbird, who had found the entrance into this world, climbed up the pine tree that grew from Below. "The Mocking-bird sat close by and sang a great many songs, the songs that are still chanted at the Wuwuchim ceremony."[11] All four societies take part in this ceremony, even though it bears the name of only one of them.

To begin with, the people were living, crowded and unhappy, in the Underworld. In order to escape they plant trees and canes that grow into the next level above, on which the Hopis clamber up and then out into our world. They were aided by various insects, animals, and birds, but in most versions it was Shrike who finally found the exit and led the way. It was mentioned earlier that these two birds resemble each other and that a shrike differs by wearing a mask. That relates him to Skeleton Man, who also has a mask.

In a First Mesa version of the story it is simply said that a dove first tried to find the opening but soon tired and that *mochini* found it. On Second Mesa the story is more elaborate, including Eagle, Hawk, and Swallow, who make trips to the top of the tree that is growing into this world, but they, too, tire.

*Toward the last, it was only the shrike that could go up and he made
the trip four times. But the last trip he made he stayed up on the top
limb, and with him on the top limb of the tree went through the opening. Of course, the old shrike felt very safe because he knew that he
could come back down, resting on the limbs of the tree.*[12]

There is a naturalistic reason here in that shrikes like to perch
in treetops, where their keen eyes can spot insects or lizards for
many yards; sometimes they make a ladderlike descent of the tree.
But a more important connection is ceremonial, because the god of
the Agave society wore his mask and was tending his crops alone in
an upper world which was dark, except for the god's ring of fire. It
was Shrike's duty to go out into this dark realm and see if anyone
lived there. He finds Skeleton Man, who was not wearing his mask,
which he could not reach in time to hide himself.

" 'All right; you outwitted me. I cannot put on my mask.' He
soon gave Shrike something to eat. He had watermelon, muskmelon, pumpkin, and squash to eat. He gave Shrike a great many
things to eat. The bird got his fill. Ma'shawa took the pipe and
tobacco from Shrike, smoked it and handed it back." In the subse-
quent conversation between bird and god, it is brought to light that
the Hopis could not have come out, if Shrike had not come upon the
god suddenly.

*You saw my mask; I could not reach it. That is how you outwitted
me. If I had heard you coming I should have put on my mask, and
your people would not be able to get out. But I have failed to have
my mask, and you have won from me.*[13]

At the time of the earthly encounter the Hopi people were
singing in the uppermost underworld, waiting for a message.

*The chief now started to climb up. Shrike, Town chief, War chief, four
of them, began climbing up. Shrike had been going out often to carry
messages. The Mockingbird [ya'ba] sang all night. He sang, sang, sang.
He sang in the Hopi language. He can say anything that a Hopi can say.*

The place of exit was large and square, and the masked god said to Mockingbird,

> *"Remain here. As they come out, you touch each one first, and I shall touch them next." Town chief was in the entrance and Shrike on one side of it. Mockingbird was singing and talking. [Sometimes he speaks Navaho and English as well as Hopi. He sings 'Yes! Yes!'] Down in the earth the people were singing. They began to climb up. . . . Meanwhile Mockingbird was singing and called out: "This is your language. Your tribe is the Hopi." He gave us our language. He placed together all who were of the same language.*[14]

The division of languages is a very difficult thing to account for, because one meets people very much like oneself and yet cannot understand what they say. Part of this is because Mockingbird ran out of songs. In the Underworld everyone spoke one of the four branches of the Pueblo tongue, but as others came out they were given such languages as Apache, Mojave, Navajo, and Mexican.

> *The people kept coming out, and before they were all out the songs of Mocking-bird were exhausted. "Hapi! pai shulahti! Now! [my songs] are gone," and at once the people who were still on the ladders commenced returning to the underworld. . . .*[15]

Because speaking is a prerequisite of teaching, speaker and teacher are often one, and teaching also involves learning. It is said that Mockingbird quit speaking Hopi, and he certainly does not use the language today.

> *After a while he ceased to speak Hopi and began teaching the emerging people American talk, then he ceased speaking that, and in turn taught other emerging peoples the speech they now use, Yota, Payutsi, Yochemu, Navaho. This is why peoples speak different tongues, Mockingbird thus taught them.*[16]

The division of languages is logically joined with the dispersal of peoples, because it is obvious that place and distance have something to do with the variety of speech and also with food and other everyday habits. When the people entered this world they were crowding over one another. "One of the men said that the only thing that he thought was, if they only could speak different languages and learn to eat different kinds of food from one another, they might start away or become parted in many divisions." It was thought that Mockingbird could make this division of languages, so they all started to sing the calling song to bring the bird to them.

The bird said, Yes, it could be done, and asked the chief if he would like to speak another language. He would not. The method used by the bird is not a matter of singing, but another kind of priestly magic.

> *During the night the mockingbird went from camp to camp and at each camp he would take something out of the fireplace and then turn right around and bury something in the fireplace again. He had a sort of buckskin pouch and whatever he took out of the fireplace he put into this pouch and he was holding on tight to this pouch for fear that something would escape out of there.*[17]

It was not long before dawn that the bird finished the task of exchanging languages. He then told the chief to dig a hole and bury in it the pouch that contained the essence of a common speech. The chief was then to build a fire over the spot where it was buried. When the white Dawn, the yellow Dawn, and the red Dawn came, the people arose to find that they had no common understanding. There were now many different languages. Mockingbird can learn or teach different tongues, or he can separate them.

Both Mockingbird and Shrike have minor roles in relation to hunting. Feathers of the first bird are used in the making of prayer-sticks at Zuñi, including the "strong ones," which would indicate that his ability as interpreter among all of the animal kinds gave him the ability to tell what was going on out there. He talks both night and day, so what he learns may be of use in either hunting or war.

Shrike lacks this importance at Zuñi, and his feathers are used only when no others are available. These cannot be used for sticks offered to either Sun or Moon.

One narrator has mentioned that the shrike, "is a very brilliant bird, but an evil one."[18] That probably accounts for the reluctance to use his feathers as offerings. The same view is shared by many non-Indians, who call him the "butcher bird." Shrike is a predator who sometimes impales mice or small birds on thorns or other sharp points, for the simple reason that he is a perching bird and has no talons with which to rip his food.

A hunter he is though, and that makes him a friend of Kisa, the Prairie Falcon. Kisa one day challenged Shrike to a contest to see who could kill the most rabbits. "Shrike is stong but not speedy." So Kisa would dart ahead and kill a rabbit.

> *Soon Hawk had killed ten, and Shrike had not killed any. . . . The next rabbit ran under some brushwood. Shrike knew how to run under brushwood and killed it. So the two birds kept together all the while to see who was the faster. Thus they hunted all day. The rabbits ran, and they went fast. Soon Hawk was tired. Shrike never tires; he is strong and stout.*

Falcon then grants the victory to Shrike—"Shrike is always the better hunter and Hawk cannot beat him"[19]

"Human hunters should be tireless" is the message, and it matters little that a mouse or a little bird, on occasion, is the only game for Shrike, who is a great hunter with the movements described, but usually insects are his prey. The falcons and hawks, to which we turn next are something else again, and their hunting parallels that of man.

II BIRDS OF THE HUNT, OF RACING, AND OF CLOWNS

falcons and lesser hawks

The title of this chapter indicates the diverse roles of these birds, but it also shows how closely each is tied to human activities. Hunting is certainly as old as speech in the affairs of men, and many hawks and falcons are great hunters, at least of small game. There is even a Hawk deity specialized for rabbit hunting. For the most part, however, the great beasts of prey have preempted the field as patrons of hunting. After all, no small hawk is equal to Mountain Lion as a symbol of this power.

Because hawks are in the shadow of greater predators, the lesser ones are equally tied to other concepts. These birds are swift and tireless, and that makes them an example for youths who run races. Races are run more for rain than for sport, so falcons and accipiters could just as well be considered rain birds as hunters. In fact, Sparrow Hawks hunt such small things that they are hardly thought of as hunters at all and relate to novices in Initiation ceremonies or to clowns.

Clowns have the role of scouts on either hunting or war expeditions, but on the civil side they also act as attendants during ceremonial dances. They hover about the lines of dancers, taking care of both order and minor arrangements of costume. Sparrow Hawks, which we now call American Kestrels, are very small falcons that hunt mostly grasshoppers and lizards; in this search they will hover over a field much as a kite does. Bird and clowns are joined on that level.

The Pueblos seem to link the larger falcons with some of the accipiters, particularly the Cooper's Hawk, on the basis of habits. The Broad-winged Hawks, or Buteo Hawks, were joined with eagles and ospreys; that is quite a reasonable division between the two kinds of birds, insofar as their observable behavior goes. Anyone who has seen a Cooper's Hawk hit a pigeon in flight and explode it, or a Prairie Falcon fold its wings and go into a bulletlike dive for some small rodent or perhaps an intruder near its nest, will observe a similarity between these birds.

At Hopi the Prairie Falcon is *Kisa,* or *Kesha.* Cooper's Hawk also goes by a similar name. Kisa is the name of a Hunting Hawk deity of the Hopi, and he is said to be the originator of the curved throwing-stick. This stick is sometimes called a boomerang, but it functions like any thrown stick—a rabbit killer for the skillful. It differs from the straight stick in the possession of certain magical powers. Its special virtue, and that of all sticks made after it, consisted in the fact that when stood up vertically with the grasping hand on the ground and its curve pointed toward the rabbit, the animal was magically drawn toward the stick and was thus easier to kill.[1]

These curved sticks were ornamental as well as magical. In actual rabbit hunting a man would tuck a half dozen straight throwing-sticks in his belt and use these, because they are more easily replaced when lost or broken. Kisa first invented the curved throwing-stick, which resembles a falcon's wing. "He carried it under his wing and hunted rabbits with it. He plucked a feather from each wing and fastened them at the marks towards the point." The "he" here is the hunter rather than the bird.

The throwing-stick is

> *modelled after the wing of Kih'sha, and referred to as his wing* [masha'adta]. *Long ago the Hopi had bow and arrow but no* puchko'hu; *a Hopi youth went to Kih'sha and from him got the first* puchko'hu. *Kih'sha is the great hunter. Eagle [Kwa'hu] and Kwa'yo [unidentified hawk] are not very good hunters. Eagle, Kwa'yo, Lion, Wolf, Bear: all the preying animals have bow and arrow; so also has Kih'sha, but he alone devised the* puchko'hu.[2]

Although Kisa is a name applied to both the Prairie Falcon and the Cooper's Hawk, only the first has the swept-back wings that would fit the concept of a curved throwing-stick; he is also the one who would be hunting rabbits. The other is a bird hawk. The Peregrine Falcon has the Hopi name of Masi Kisa or gray falcon.

There is a story of hunting from Taos in which Spirit Rats gave battle to Hawk Boy and Eagle Boy. The identification of the hawk is uncertain, but it is not the Redtailed. Because the same name appears in connection with racing, where swift flying is the point, it is probably not one of the soaring hawks. These two boys were great hunters of all living animals—big and small, it is said—but we only hear of them setting stone traps for rats; these would be woodrats. They turned these over to their grandmother to eat. "All these dead rats had to be fed with corn meal, but grandmother never did her duty by the dead rats, she never fed them."

The boys follow a trail of blood from their traps to a mountain in which the death house of the rats is lodged. There they overhear these creatures planning to kill them for having failed in their ceremonial duty of making meal offerings to their victims.

Now the dead rats came out of the ground door, prepared with war paint, war clubs, and shields. The two boys were Eagle and Hawk. As the dead rats came from underground they at once began to throw their war clubs at the birds, injuring their feathers to keep them from being able to fly and to make them tire soon.[3]

According to Ladd, the feathers of both the Cooper's and the Sharp-shinned Hawks are used on "strong" prayer-sticks, and these are used by the Beast societies for animals, which is to say they are placed for hunting success, or if set out by the Bow priests, they are a war offering. But it is in another context that falcons and accipiters are most important.

Racing, particularly kick-stick racing, is done by youths who run in concentric circles, usually coming nearer the village with each course. These races may be run for the Sun or to invoke the rain clouds to come nearer the village. Hawks and falcons are certainly swift and so become patrons of the races. In one such race a song is sung four times, and each time different birds of prey are mentioned in the refrain. It begins with "be racing," which is addressed first to a messenger who places distant black balls to mark the rim of the course. Then it is addressed to the races themselves; next the abdomen and back are mentioned, because kicking and running strain both. The song then addresses the birds of prey:

Hohongwika
Kuwakwa lawaiyi
Yahayahatimahai
Nanamuuhunwai ahahaiahahahai

Cooper's Hawk
With joyful words
Be happy
Be racing.

For the second direction Prairie Falcon is invoked, while the third might be Snow Eagle. The final name is derived from rabbit, hence "rabbit hawk," but without further identity.[4]

Two young people, Hawk Youth and Hawk Maid, dance at Hopi. From their names, Kih'sha ti'yo and Kih'sha mana, they evidently relate to the god Kisa, but they relate to the Sun by appearing during the Winter Solstice ceremony, and to the increase of game, for which reason the priest may not hunt rabbits during the ceremonial days. These representatives of Kisa are projecting a future abundance of small game, and a seasonal and weather element is brought in by a vigorous and beautiful kiva dance in which the maid carries a squash-blossom frame. As she dances, the frame is shaken until one by one the blossoms fall to the ground.[5] Thus these dancers race for the Sun, just as racing, which is a part of the ceremony, brings both rain and seasons.

In the chapter on macaws and parrots we learned of a tie between salt and its power to attract water. The Oraibi Sun chief, Talayesva, tells that when he was a young man there had been an extended period of drought and his father sought to break the dry spell by making a long and sacred pilgrimage to the Zuñi Salt Lake. They could have obtained salt with much less trouble from a trader whom they met on the way. But in order to bring rain it was necessary to complete the journey as far as the lake.

At some point, "in the Zuñi forests," his father stopped and made meal cakes to offer to the Hawk deity. Unfortunately their pack burro ate these offerings, so Talayesva had to divide his own with his father. The rite for the spirit consisted of racing to a shrine on a distant mesa, an effort that was difficult for the old man, but the son played tortoise and hare until the two reached the shrine.

> *We raced up a mesa with the dough and placed it with prayer feathers in a small hole for the Hawk deity. As we moved down the southern slope, my father said, "There is a long slab of stone; jump upon it and spring to the opposite side." As we completed the jump he said "Well, we have performed the rites correctly, and our reward will be rain."*[6]

The slab of stone is a larger version of a similar slab or "foot drum," which is found over each kiva's *shipapu*, a small hole that represents the place of emergence from the Underworld. When one stomps on the drum, he is calling thunder.

While the Zuñis were still in the Underworld, they sent out certain birds to scan the then-unknown world above. It was the same mission as that given Shrike at Hopi, but the god whom they were to find was the Sun. "When our fathers, our mother, the society priests, go forth standing into the daylight of their sun father, you will look for their road." The first one to go out was the Eagle, but he was unsuccessful. Next one Hawk and then another were sent out. The English text leaves much to be desired, as it says "Come, let us go and talk to our grandson chicken hawk." Fortunately the native text is included, so one does not have to settle for the meaningless name.

The first to follow the Eagles is *shok'apiso*, the Marsh Hawk, the incessant harrier who is the most common fall and winter hawk in New Mexico. The next one to be sent out was *a'nelaw*, which indicates the Cooper's Hawk.[7] These hawks explored the shores of the encircling ocean in each direction and talked with the Sun Father, but they found no road and reported back that nothing was visible. Although that was no success, it does indicate the searching nature of these two hawks.

sparrow hawks or American kestrels

These little falcons, whose common name has recently been changed, have two roles. They are not great hunters, usually taking grasshoppers, lizards, or mice and only occasionally a bird. They are numerous and so friendly that the Zuñi often keep them as pets. Sparrow Hawks are obviously the little brothers of larger hawks and falcons, and that relates them to novices in the human sense. We have already heard of Hawk Youth and Hawk Maid. Shortly after this pair have retired from their exhausting dance, Kwa'chawkwa, or Hawk Man, appears waving wings and carrying a scapula in one hand. "He waves his wings and clanks [the bones] over the novices."[8] The name of this maskless impersonator means "secondary wing feather of hawk." And when he appears in the Oraibi version of the ceremony there is a touch of realism:

> Suddenly a screeching sound was heard outside as that of a hawk. It was made by Talahoyoma, who was answered by the same sound by Loluomai from the kiva. This sound was produced by a small bone instrument which was entirely concealed in the mouth. . . . Talahoyoma took a mashaata [wing] in each hand, screeched, and then, as the singing and rattling commenced, waved the wings vigorously backward and forward to the time of the singing, often slowly raising them with a quivering movement after a forcible thrust forward, and occasionally ejecting the screeching sound.[9]

Hawk Man is rattling his cluster of scapulae over a group of novices, many of whom are called ke'le, or Sparrow Hawks. Sometimes the diminutive is added and they are ke'lele—little Sparrow Hawks. If they are going to join one of the societies, feathers from the bird are worn in their hair, but if they are not to be society members—which is to say they will become clowns, who live a different life in both this world and the afterworld—no Sparrow Hawk feathers are required. But at Hopi the situation is reversed, and the same bird's feathers are associated with clowns.

At Zuñi the little falcon's feathers are used by the Shi'-wanakwe, which is held to be the most ancient of societies.[10] The newekwe clowns are descended from this group, and they have a progenitor called Bitsitsi, who also makes a scream like a hawk with a concealed whistle. Clowns act as scouts in both hunting and war, but hovering seems to be the important concept. Sparrow Hawk is joined with the Black Eyes of Isleta; with the Queranna, one of the two clown groups of the Keres; and with the Ts'un'tatabosh at the surviving Towa pueblo of Jemez.

The connections are uniform even in different language groups, and each time one batch of clowns is associated with Sparrow Hawk. At the Tiwa pueblo of Isleta divisions of organized groups represent Winter people and Summer people. In summer Shure or Gopher people are in charge. Black Eyes are Winter people and are also a "fun" group of clowns, who talk backward, saying the opposite of what they mean. This group makes use of the feathers of a bird called *tiriure,* a name referring to the quick motions made when the bird is hovering in one place in the air, most likely the Sparrow Hawk.[11]

Among the Keres there are always two clown groups: the Queranna associated with winter and the Koshare with summer. The songs of the Queranna clowns bring the people back from harvest, and in kachina dances they follow at the end of the dancing line, while the other clowns lead. At Cochiti they hold a dance during harvest, because their concern

sparrow hawk

FALCONS AND LESSER HAWKS

is with weather and plant fertility. Their badge of office consists of a tuft of Sparrow Hawk and Blue Jay feathers tied in the hair.[12]

At Sia in the last century the Rain ceremony was given by the Queranna society, and there is an illustration of the altar used. This has two posts on top of which are carved bird effigies, while between the posts is a cord from which bunches of feathers are suspended. These consist of tail feathers from a female Sparrow Hawk and the Long-Crested Jay.[13] In the village of Santa Ana the same clowns wear these feathers; they also adorn the fertility pole that was described in the chapter on macaws.[14]

There is no myth or other information to explain this widespread association, which goes back to ancient times. Sparrow Hawk bones have been found in sites dating to the twelfth century.[15] These diggings indicate a smaller bird with a smaller skull than the present hawk and also that fir trees and lakes once occupied the site where now there are neither. So the bird has changed and the environment has changed as well, but over the centuries ceremonial use of Sparrow Hawk feathers has remained.

Sparrow Hawk is the least of falcons, so it is clear why the bird might be used as a symbol of young initiates, and Eagle has referred to him as "younger brother."[16] The connection of Sparrow Hawks with clowns is less visible, except for the hovering, which is like a dance attendant. One comes last in a file of men either when attending dancers or when in a file of warriors. The use of Sparrow Hawk with jay or war feathers suggests the latter, which will be examined in Chapter 13. On the other hand, with the Queranna clowns at least, the connection is with fertility of fields and with harvests. So we turn next to a bird that stands for the most humane of man's undertakings—the growing of crops and tending of planted fields, which we call the art of horticulture.

12 BIRD OF HORTICULTURE

magpies

The Black-Billed Magpie has no pan-Pueblo theme; only at Taos is he closely related to the Corn Maidens. In part, the limited range of the bird in Pueblo country explains the diversity. At present magpies are not found at Zuñi or Hopi, though an old Indian told Mearns that they were common about the Hopi villages until the 1880s. For both Zuñis and Hopis magpie feathers are important but are imported and related to weather and seasonal matters.

In summer, magpies range as far south as Sante Fe and then in winter travel farther on down the Rio Grande, so the tales of this long-tailed bird travel a similar route. The two most important natural characteristics of magpies are the habits of scavenging for remains of game animals and their equal willingness to settle down and live around human habitations. Also they talk a great deal among themselves and can even be taught a few words of human speech.

All in all, they follow the path that mankind has taken from hunting and gathering to a settled life with planted fields. As for the gathering part, it was well known that the bison who inhabited the plains north and east of Taos always had a flock of magpies following along. The stories relating to the combination come from Zuñi and Acoma, where there were no bison. But we know from Coronado's account that these Indians went out onto the eastern plains to hunt the great beasts.

At both Acoma and Zuñi are stories about a wife who was abducted by Bison Man, details of which are given in *Pueblo Animals and Myths*. In the Zuñi account she is taken up onto a mesa, beyond the reach of her husband. It is Magpie, or *Katetasha,* which might be translated "long-tailed-bird," who takes the husband on her back and in easy stages flies him up the cliff. Magpie then enters the house of Bison, rescues the wife, or wives, and all are brought down again on the bird's back.[1]

The various Keresan towns and villages have central myths that relate Magpie to the East as a directional bird and explain how he became a gatherer rather than a hunter. The Corn Mother in the Underworld had two earthly counterparts who became the mothers of mankind; one is a Pueblo and the other the mother of foreigners, which can mean either Navajos or whites, depending on the teller and the time. The Pueblo sister is the elder, but she is also shorter, so in one of the contests between the two a device is needed.

This contest is to see on which the Sun, as it rises, will shine first. So the elder sister went to Magpie, who was at that time white, and asked him to go to the East without resting or eating. There it was to shade the Sun with its wings so that the rays would not shine on the alien sister.

> *The bird went as instructed, for it was very strong and skillful. But, while on its way, it got hungry and it passed a place where a puma had killed a deer. Here, although it had been instructed not to rest, it stopped and found a hole in the side of the deer where the intestines were exposed. The bird put its head into the gash to eat, and as it did so it got blood on its back and wings and tail, and it flew on not noticing that it was stained with the blood.*

Magpie did, however, reach the Sun in time and spread his wings on the left of the Sun to cast a shadow in the direction of the foreign sister, so the light first fully illuminated the face of the native mother. She was nonetheless angry with Magpie for disobeying her and being all dirty with blood.

> *So she said to it, "For stopping and eating you will not know from now on how to kill your own meat. You will not be a hunter, you*

will eat what others have killed and left, and most of the time you will eat what is spoiled. Your color also will be spotted from now on, you will not be white as you were at first."[2]

Magpie is still something of a hunter of mammals, but small ones like meadow mice or gophers, and for the most part, magpies live by gathering wastes, whether animal or grain, or by eating insects. While they will go to remote and high elevations, magpies also like human habitations of any kind. Mrs. Bailey noted that, "On our way through the country the Magpies were found commonly not only where there were sheep and goats but also in Indian and adobe villages. . . ."[3]

Around Taos where the birds are common, Magpies have gained a special role as consorts of the Corn Girls. Sometimes Magpie-tail Youth is married to the Corn Sisters, or they may be called Corn Mothers. All of the stories are variations on the Orpheus myth, in which there is a journey into the Underworld. More simply one can think of the myths as related to grain, which as seed rests underground for part of the year and the arises eventually to mature. For the Greeks this was represented by the goddess Demeter and her daughter Kore (or, Persephone).[4]

magpie

MAGPIES

At Taos the Underworld has an entrance through their sacred Blue Lake, which the government has recently returned to them. So even though the myths are closely related to the flight of the Corn Maidens as told at Zuñi, they have a watery rather than an earthy setting. The story called "Magpie and the Corn Mothers" and its variant tell of a visit to the land of the dead and develop the fertility motif, which in the second version includes game as well as corn. Where the Zuñi Corn Maidens flee because of some affront, the flight at Taos is caused by a domestic quarrel.

Magpie was married to both Blue Corn Girl and Yellow Corn Girl. The latter became jealous of Magpie's attention to her sister, so she set out on a journey eastward with the intent of drowning herself in the sacred lake at the bottom of which is the mythical Big House, or home of the dead. Magpie sends Blue Corn Girl after the sister to bring her back; then he follows after the sisters, who were "singing all the way."

> Now Magpie was coming up to them. He was hurrying to catch them, they jumped into the lake. After the water quieted down, a yellow corn ear and a blue corn ear came up on top of the water. Magpie grasped them, and went back home and arrived at Cottonwood and said to himself, "I never will be a human being."[5]

These sisters are givers of themselves, much as Salt Woman is, because the ripe ear of corn must be stripped of its seed and enter the Underworld before it can return to mankind. Why Magpie feels left out will shortly appear. The variant story takes into account the origin of wild turkeys, which is like a myth we have already heard from Laguna. Yellow Corn Girl leads her faithful turkeys along on the fatal pilgrimage.

"I am going to the Mothers and Fathers. I leave you and my child to Blue Corn girl and I am going to the Big House, to the Fathers, never to return," The turkeys are too faithful to desert their mother, so they follow and that is why there are turkeys in those mountains today. Yellow Corn Girl's final words are a request that Blue Corn Girl nurse her little boy; then as she drowns an ear of corn floats up to the surface of the lake.

Blue corn is typical Indian corn, and though there are many other colors, the ears are seldom all yellow. In this story the Corn spirit is transformed into a literal ear of the grain.

> *Blue Corn girl put it to little brother's mouth and he sucked on it and this was his mother nourishing him. Blue Corn girl went back and found Magpie-tail boy sitting by the fire with his head bowed. He said, "I am Magpie-tail boy and we were living here happily and now we hand on everything under water" [to the spirits and the dead who dwell there]. And Blue Corn girl said, "I am Blue Corn girl and now the people have me as a source of nourishment."* [6]

Magpie is very much like a human in that he hunts, gathers wild berries, and will eat cultivated corn, and as a group these birds talk a lot, even using a few words of man's speech. They like to follow around after man whether he is afield or in the village. Despite these similarities his despair is always, "I will never be a human being."

In yet another Taos story Magpie-tail Youth, the husband, rescues Yellow Corn Girl. She is returned to our world in the form of a dead rabbit wrapped in a corn husk. This package is placed under a blanket and sung over until she returns to life. Magpie Boy is given bow and arrows and clothing, and the resurrected wife is given a Hopi robe and moccasins for her use, thus accounting for most of the necessities of civilized life. The attendant spirit then

> *went in the west room and south room and last the east room again and brought different kinds of fruits, huckleberries, chokeberries, green corn, for them to take home and eat. He told them, "Now you take all this, when you get to your home at the cottonwood husk this green corn and throw it outside your house, also the fruit peels, for the people to see and for the witches to see."* [7]

The Taos Indians speak the Tiwa language; another pueblo at Isleta, just below Albuquerque, has the same language. But in time the dialects have become so diverse that few members of either pueblo understand each other. There the village is divided into seven Corn groups and everyone must belong to one. The one called Black Corn is subdivided into Magpies and Poplars,[8] which indicates that myths as well as birds find their way down the cottonwooded banks of the Rio Grande.

Below Taos and north of Santa Fe are a number of Tewa villages in good magpie country, but there the birds are related to the division of peoples rather than to agriculture. One suspects that their chattering speech, which seems to be in some foreign language, is involved, but this is not the basis of recorded stories. The Tewas also had a sacred lake from which they emerged, but it was in southern Colorado. From there they were led southward in migration by T'owa'e, their equivalent of the Little War gods.

> They came to a big river. There was Magpie. He put his tail across the river and on it T'owa'e passed over. The two old ones [Summer chief and Winter chief] came on the other side. Then Magpie's tail turned over in the middle of the river and the people fell down into the water.

Those who fell in became fish, while one group of people was left on the opposite bank of the river.

> They were calling to one another. They threw stones and sticks at one another. Then those who stayed on the other side said, "That is what you need. You are Navaho, Ute, Apache, Kaiowa, Comanche." So when they called their names, they said, "You belong to them." They have their own languages. They could not talk to each other.[9]

The same story is also used to explain divisions of the Pueblo group into two sets, the Summer people and the Winter people. The chief of each division, or moiety as anthropologists like to call it, governs the village for part of the year and then turns leadership over to his counterpart. The dividing line in this story is the Rio Grande, and the pueblo of San Juan on the east side represents one half. On the opposite bank is a ruin, near the first capital of New Mexico under Spanish dominion and not far from the present little town of Chamita.

According to this account the Summer people had settled in what is now the ruin, while the Winter people wandered about the plain to the east of the river in search of their fellows, until they settled down in San Juan. It was agreed that a bridge should be built so that the separated factions could join again. A wizard was put to work, and he made a bridge by laying parrot feathers across from one side and magpie tail feathers from the other. Witches caused this delicate structure to collapse or turn over. Those who were lost became fishes, and that is why Pueblos do not eat fish.[10] Ultimately both groups were united in San Juan, where they still live today.

Also that is why both Summer and Winter people are in the pueblo today. We are not told from which side of the river the parrot feather projected, but the Tewas had a mythic Macaw village on the West bank, and, as we have already seen, these birds relate to the summer Sun. Magpie would then have to be on the East bank representing winter. For the Keres farther down the Rio Grande Magpie does represent winter, and that is consistent with nature because of winter flocking and a southward movement downstream. In the Keresan Battle of the Seasons Magpie is ranked among the birds in the army of Winter.[11]

For the western pueblos of Zuñi and Hopi, Magpies are rain birds, even though no one sees them in the area. They do enjoy wet weather almost as much as young boys do and will be found stalking about in the worst of rain storms, probably because they are eating the insects forced to the surface by a saturated soil. At Zuñi the Rain priests wear the tail feathers of magpies as a badge of their office, and no one else may use the bird's feathers.

For those outside of its immediate range the Magpie's white-on-black may stand for the white Dawn against the black Night, so he is a bird of and from the East direction. Like dawn, major storms in the area also come from the east. On the altar of the Flute society at Hopi is a nicely carved image of this bird, along with other rain birds, and magpie skins were used on the altars of the same society.

At worst Magpie causes divisions of races and groups, but he is never really bellicose; he likes people and is usually willing to join them and chat about the nature of things. There are other birds, however, that are specialized for bloody divisions within mankind, whether these are by raiding parties or in larger engagements—these are the birds of war.

13 BIRDS OF WAR

nuthatches, wrens, woodpeckers, jays, and roadrunners

Some anthropologists have concluded that war as practiced by the American Indians was qualitatively different from modern wars as usually practiced. Pueblo myths and rituals would seem to confirm this view, at least for the pre-Spanish period. In theory war parties would go out on a seasonal basis, after harvest time, or there would be small engagements when one was traveling through the lands of another people. One could almost consider this type of conflict a sport, probably not too dangerous.

That is not the whole story, however. The town of Pecos was on the edge of the plains to the east of Pueblo country, where many villages had been wiped out by Comanches or Apaches. Quarai and other pueblos that faced the saline lakes were completely reduced to ruins in the seventeenth century. Pecos sent one thousand warriors out onto the plains, and only a few messengers came back to explain the disaster and why their prosperous town would soon be a ruin. These border wars were no different from the fire raid on Dresden—there were simply fewer people to be killed and perhaps some chance for flight.

Formal war, with its appropriate ceremonies, is not on that level. It threatens like storm clouds, the sounds of drumming thunder will be heard in the background. But the outcome, like the weather, is always in doubt, and any doubtful issue requires the attention of ritual. This holds also for the ghosts who pass back and forth from the dead to the living, or for witches who are also in a realm between the spirit and the human world. So there will be as much talk of warring on witches and of placating the dead as of war in a literal sense.

The White-breasted Nuthatch comes into this scene only once and on the basis of its habit of spending much time upside down, eating insects on tree trunks. Anything upside down or backward is a war trait, because it is the reverse of normal behavior. At Zuñi the name for Nuthatch is "the one who comes down head first." That idea is related to the Salimobia kachinas who are warriors and seed gatherers for the six directions. There is a double set, so twelve of the most muscular and handsome young men are chosen to impersonate them.

Actually, they are honor guards for the gods. Each wears a nuthatch feather during initiations into kiva societies, and they are the only ones who use these feathers on prayer offerings. Most feathers come from a bundle or box, but these must be fresh. The White-breasted Nuthatch is a bird of the transition zone, so the performers must exert great effort to find and kill the bird with a slingshot. The tail and wing feathers exert a magical effect, helping the Salimobia, who must come down the ladder into the kiva head first.

In the old days the ladders were merely notched poles, so entry was quite an acrobatic feat. Then as though to top the bird, the performer must also leave the kiva by ascending the ladder with his feet upward. One does not acquire such a skill without practice. So the impersonators stay in the kiva for seven nights, trying and testing their skills.[1]

white-breasted nuthatch

Canyon Wrens are specific for war, and Rock Wrens are thought of as crazy flying, which is likely a related concept. Doing things wrong confuses an enemy, but there are other reasons for odd behavior so the Rock Wren may relate directly to mental illness rather than its simulation in war rites. The Canyon Wren has a singular voice that is notable not only for its beauty but for the sheer volume that it can pour forth in a desolate canyon, from whence we get the common name of "bugler" for the bird.

At Acoma the role of Canyon Wren had been best elaborated in mythology. In all pueblos there is a town chief and an outside chief. The outside, or country chief, had the "duty to notify the people by crying out all matters of importance relating to outside." There were many unpredictable events, including possible raids, so Iyatiku appointed two assistants to help.

> *She called the oldest one who was to be next in rank Shuti mut [wren youth]. The other was to be called Shpa'timut [mockingbird youth]. In this order they were to rank. Iatiku named them thus because they were to represent these birds, to make their sound and to bring messages to the people, thus relieving Country Chief.*[2]

Canyon Wren is thereby one of the town criers and also the head War chief.

> *The head war chief (shutimiti) goes to the east edge of the mesa . . . a rock under which the spirit of the elder war twin lives, where he prays to the sun which is about to rise. When he has finished he walks up and down the village streets calling to the people.*[3]

The magic that Canyon Wren imparts to the outside chief, in the role of leader of war parties, as opposed to the simpler duty of crying out information, resides in the song of this bird. Among the rocks it echoes back and forth so it is very hard to tell exactly where the bird really is, and that, of course, is a handy trick for fooling an enemy. The same echo effect takes a different twist at Jemez, where the story is located in an abandoned ruin on a mesa top.

A contest is held between evil people, which probably means that the war is against witches, and the True Believers, who are represented by a pair of brothers. These would be comparable with the War Twins or their earthly representatives. One brother has discovered the meeting place of the evil ones, but the Trues are too few and powerless to accept the challenge for a contest of magic.

The youth sets out in search of advice and meets a wren at the base of a cliff. This wren could immediately read his thoughts, just as it is said of a War chief, "their minds were tucked in his temples," a phrase indicating that he knew what was in the minds of others. Wren first gives the youth water, then presents him with the magic formula by which he can ascend the mountain on top of which the gods live. The formula is a kind of echo-play.

"Then the little bird said: 'Now come and I will lead you. But when we come to the top of the mountain and I say, 'We are at the top,' you must say, 'No, we are down at the bottom of it.'" That formula not only guides the youth to the home of the gods of all directions, but with the bird's assistance it is useful in the final life-or-death struggle with the witches.

When the brothers grasp a cane given them by the gods, one of them says, "We are on top of the mountain," and the other answers, "No we are down in the mountain at the bottom of it."[4] Thunder is then heard and then the dance rattle of the gods, and the evil ones are drowned in a downpour of rain that follows.

At Hopi, Canyon Wren is important enough to be represented by a kachina, Turposkwa. The arms of the dancer are feathered and the mask has a beak. On top of the helmet sits a replica of a wren much as it might look sitting on a nest.[5] On the dancer's back is a "moisture tablet," which leads on to the fact that Canyon Wren also appears on the Flute altar. Although we may think of the song as bugling, it can also be thought of as the notes from a flute, as in the rain-bringing Flute ceremony.

Rock Wrens make out in desolate places by a nervous search for insects among the rocks. They are somewhat the avian equivalent of shrews, always on the go with a bobbing motion of the body; even their flight is jerky. From these habits it has earned the Zuñi name Z'ilisho, from *jalish*, meaning insane. The Rock Wren is never touched, lest one become as crazy as the bird. It is said that witches tie Rock Wren feathers to an old piece of one's clothing and then place it on a bush high up on some cliff. That will make the owner of the clothing insane. Rock Wren's story may be as simple as that, but in conjunction with Canyon Wren and the dizzy flying, crazy, backward elements, it seems likely that this poor-voiced wren was also once a bird of war.

woodpeckers

All members of the family Picidae are persistent drummers, and the fact that drumming and war, or thunder and weather, are connected has not escaped notice in many cultures. The Zuñi name for woodpeckers is *tamtununu*, from *ta* meaning wood and a re-duplication of *tunu* to suggest a booming sound like thunder.[6] The Pueblos have both group names and individual names for many of the species in this family, but the Red-shafted Flicker appears most often.

The point is well taken, because these birds will drum for seemingly no reason at all. They are not storing acorns or digging out grubs from dead trees, but as a matter of courtship they will drum heavily on any limb of resonant timbre or on a tin roof for that matter. Our name for the family is derived from the Latin god Picus, who was turned into a woodpecker by Circe, whose Greek name means a hawk.

She fell in love with him and by magic compelled him toward her, and by her song the heavens became darkened. She asks him to accept the Sun as a father-in-law, and when he refuses Picus is turned into a woodpecker. This story from Ovid seems to focus on the weather and a darkening sky, but Pliny refers to a woodpecker as "known by his cognomen Mars."

The same sun, weather, and war associations for birds of this family are used by the Pueblos, but for war the flicker is singled out above the others. The black-tipped salmon red feathers of the under-wings and tail show to great advantage during the flicker's dipping flight; they are the ones that are most desired as war symbols. At Taos flicker and eagle feathers are placed in the mountains as offerings to Red Bear, the spirit patron of warriors.[7] Red is, of course, the color of blood, so even the eagle feathers are dyed that color when presented to war spirits.

At Acoma "black is associated with the dead and the kachinas, carmine or purple with war"—'blood is red.' "[8] At Zuñi both red and black pigments are offered at the War god shrines, but here there is a neat distinction drawn between the uses of red feathers. Red feathers on prayer-sticks are war offerings, but if they are worn in the hair, they are the badge of a Medicine society member. According to Ladd the Zuñis use the feathers of all woodpeckers on "strong" prayer-sticks, but the tail feathers of the flicker are those most desired. As alternatives primary wing feathers from the Lewis' Woodpecker, or the Downy and Hairy species can be used.

There is a story, part of which was told in the chapter on hummingbirds, which explains the colors of various birds. The blind Earthquake demon sets fire to pitch and thus causes a flow of lava. Various birds try to quench the fire, and the Crow for his efforts becomes black. Another, Kowata the flicker, "went too close to the flames also, and the fire colored his wings and tail red."[9]

War and witches are closely related, because the priests of the societies must constantly make war on these enemies; witches will, of course, fight back. In the Keresan pueblo of Santa Ana it is said that witches are small creatures, eight to twenty inches in height, which suggests from the measurements that these witches have taken the form of owls. The witch there "frequently has the feathers of the 'red woodpecker, k'aowa,' on his head, and perhaps in his hand."[10] This bird is again the flicker.

The Zuñis ate flickers at times, which is surprising, because so few birds were used as game, but it seems that the Tewas may also have used the bird for food. In a story from San Juan, two hunters explain their empty-handedness. Each time they find game some bird or animal talks them out of it. During the hunt,

one of them saw a woodpecker [pfio] *and said to his companion,*

"There is a woodpecker on that tree. I am going to kill it." He had scarcely stopped talking when an owl [mahu] appeared and said, "Leave that bird. Don't shoot it. It belongs to me."

Owl then tells them not to take home any game, including a deer they had killed, and because they thought he might be a witch, their game was abandoned and the hunters returned home empty-handed.[11] Owls, incidentally, not only eat woodpeckers but also use their holes for nesting.

A true woodpecker often bores holes for a purpose and not just to be drumming. He may be looking for grubs or storing acorns, but the amazing thing about this activity is the sheer physical drilling—few other birds can perform such a feat. Sometimes the tree is a Douglas fir, like the one that appears in the emergence myth as told at Santa Ana. This tree was the last of those to grow up through the various underworlds, and it became obvious that an opening would be needed for it to grow out into the daylight world.

So Woodpecker Boy (Shpika Miti) was asked if he would make an opening. "Yes," he said, "if you will make me some prayer-sticks. . . . So Woodpecker Boy flew up to the top of the spruce tree and began to peck at the ceiling. He worked for four days and at the end of that time he had a tiny hole pecked through, a little light came through."[12] Badger was called on to enlarge this entrance to-ward the Sun, so Eagle carried him up while the tree kept growing so that Badger could work. He reports back that in the new world "there are lots of clouds and all kinds of colors."

At Hopi, Flicker seems to be almost entirely related to the Sun, either in its annual journey or its daily trip above the earth. Flicker feathers represent the red Dawn, which is important in the color sequence of sunrise. During the Wuwuchim ceremony the Singers society has a standard to which some twenty flicker feathers are attached. According to Frank Waters, this ceremony represents the dawning of the whole ceremonial year. In the processes of rituals the color phases of any single dawn are repeated.[13]

During the Winter Solstice ceremony for the Sun, Flicker is again important, while the standard indicating that the rites are in

common flicker (red-shafted)

progress is set above each kiva. This pole, which is hung with flicker feathers, is taken down at sunset by one of the priests. During this ceremony prayer-sticks offered to the Sun include flicker feathers, as does an offering called *ki'ksi*, or breath, which is made from a branch to which both hawk and flicker feathers are attached.[14] These offerings are thrust into the rafters of the kiva during the Sun ceremony.

There is also a rain connection at Hopi, because the "water flute" of the Flute ceremony is entirely encased in the plumage of Flicker. On one kiva wall mural, a bird is perched on top of a cloud and lightning symbol, and though it would be hard to identify, Stephen was told that it was a woodpecker. From the Hopi name it is in this instance literally a woodpecker and not a flicker.[15]

It is true that everywhere the War Twins are sons of the Sun, and we will soon see again that scalps are rain makers. Yet it is surprising that the two meanings were so completely detached by the Hopis who, despite calling themselves "the peaceful ones," had war rites in plenty—connected with Bear, Mountain Lion, and Snakes.

jays

Of the three jays important to the Pueblos—Steller's Jay, Scrub Jay, and Piñon Jay—it is the last which relates to war. The Piñon Jay has an alternative name of Blue Crow, and in our bird lists it is placed closer to the crow than to other jays. These birds travel about the country in large flocks, so that their cries, though no more jarring than other jays, are amplified many times. The relation to war parties is their consonance with the war cries of both jays and warriors in their charges about the hills and plains.

Various species of jays engage in "mobbing" other predators, which consists of both vocal and physical attacks to drive the enemy away. Usually the intruder is an owl or a hawk, but sometimes gestures will be made to men; Piñon Jays are most fearless and sometimes flock around within a foot or two of a man, to make their warlike gestures.

The Zuñis have more than one explanation for the use of

Piñon Jay feathers by warriors or War priests. One of them is that the birds travel, chattering in purposeless flight; "therefore Zuñi War chiefs would bury its stick mounted feathers near the enemy to rob them of their wits."[16] Ladd gives another explanation, which is that War priests made prayer-sticks with Piñon Jay feathers before going on a raid, with the idea of convincing the enemy that the Zuñis were as numerous as the large and loud-crying flocks.

Piñon Jays were also able to kill ghosts, a subject on which it would be interesting to have more information, because it suggests that they might kill enemy ghosts and thus eliminate the danger of pursuit. When this story begins, the people were still in the Underworld where they were like smoke, yet lived in fear of the jays.

> The people stared and chattered in greater fright than ever before at seeing the dead seemingly come to life!
>
> "Akaa! kaa!" cried a flock of jays.
>
> "Hear that!" said the villagers. "Hear that, and ask what's the matter. The jays are coming; whoever they light on dies!—Run you two Aii Murder!" And they left off their standing as though chased by demons. On one or two of the hindmost some jays alighted. They fell dead as though struck by lightning.[17]

It would seem that the mobbing of jays can work both ways and that the stragglers from a war party may also be killed, but it is equally possible that the jays were killing the ghosts of the enemy dead who were pursuing returning warriors. One of the fascinating things about myths is that they are seldom precise; only in retelling can various possibilities come to light.

Blue is a directional color for the West, so jays, in particular the Steller's Jay, often stand for that point on the compass. At Hopi the jays along with bluebirds represent the West on the altars of several ceremonies. At Zuñi this bird not only stands for the West, in which case Scrub Jay feathers may be substituted if none of the crested species are available. They also are the badge of priests, who are entitled to wear them in their hair on ceremonial occasions. If they display the Bluejay feather in public, it is a matter for censure or even an occasion for bringing in the Whipping kachinas.[18]

In the same pueblo jay feathers are not only used on strong prayer-sticks, for war and hunting, but they also appear when a house or a field is dedicated, the latter for the stimulation of corn. When it is the fields and corn Cushing specifies the Piñon Jay, which has no aversion to varying its diet with a bit of corn. However, protection and the jay's relation to war symbols would seem to be the motive for placing the feathers around house foundations and new fields.[19]

In the Tewa pueblo of Tesuque, feathers of an unspecified jay are scattered on the ground or under stones in a shrine on a hill to the south. Because these offerings are made as a part of a Game dance, it is thought that they may be for the increase of game.[20] Because one has to guess here, it seems that they may be comparable with the "strong" prayer-sticks of the Zuñis, which are useful for either hunting or war.

roadrunners

Roadrunners, or Chaparral Cocks, which was a much better name for them, are nothing but grounded cuckoos. But they are much more impressive birds. Roadrunners prefer the sagebrush flats where they can live for a long season on a diet of lizards and such. But some of them extend their range up the Rio Grande to northern Santa Fe County, where the elevation is 7,000 feet but still in the sage-juniper-piñon habitat.

This bird has short, rounded wings, which do not take it high in the air, but they are useful for short glides that culminate long runs at very fast speeds. So it is above all a racer. When it is running full tilt, both the head and tail are held parallel with the ground, and the whole bird stretches out as straight as an arrow in flight. It has other stances, many of which have been captured on the designs of Sia pottery. Both the tousled black-tipped crest and the long tail of the bird can be manipulated expressively.

Besides its speed, what most impressed the Pueblos was the arrangement of the toes on the bird's feet. Like other cuckoos they have two toes pointing forward and two pointing backward, which

Steller's jay

ornithologists classify as zygodactyl. Woodpeckers have similar feet, but they do not run on the ground, so the "X" imprint is not visible. Where a few roadrunners have been wandering about, the sand is completely covered with a confusion of X-like tracks going in no particular direction. When this maze is coupled with the bird's strength and speed, it is easy to imagine its roles—and they are various.

To begin with, war parties need to confuse their trails. In a Zuñi ritual the scalp-kickers wear the feathers of this bird in the toes of their moccasins.

> *The quill ends of two feathers of the chaparral cock—one an upper tail feather and the other an under tail feather—have been crossed and placed in line by their brothers in consanguinity between the second and middle toes of the left foot, and the moccasins carefully drawn over. "The feathers give courage, for knowledge and courage come from this bird, who is the keeper of courage."* [21]

The feathers are crossed like the tracks of the bird, and being on the left foot is the opposite of normal, which like anything reversed or backward is a war symbol. War is the reverse of normal life, but, more importantly, reversals confuse the enemy. After the women reach the scene of the Scalp dance, the two scalp-kickers tie similar and larger feather crosses to the left sides of their heads. These are worn for four days.

While the kicking is taking place, the Shi'wanni or Rain priests are standing by in a line, which brings to a crux the relationship between Roadrunner, who plays a large part in both the myths and rites of the Scalp ceremony, and rain making. All of the dead bring rain, when they pass over the villages in cloud form. Most of them will be relatives, but even the enemy dead take this form. "Though in his life the enemy was a worthless lot, now through the Corn priest's rain prayers and seed prayers, he has become a rain person." [22]

In the myths behind the Scalp ceremony the crossed tracks are again foremost. The Little War gods in the course of bellicose adventures killed a Navajo girl, but she refused to remain dead and in fact pursued them. At last in their flight from her they reached Shipa-polima, which is the shrine of the Stone Lions near Cochiti. There members of a Stone Knife or Ant society taught them how to use a flint knife, how to scalp a dead enemy, and how to perform connected rituals. In one version White Bear, which seems to refer to a constellation in the sky, gave them his own knife for the deed.

There was next an explanation.

"We did what you told us to do, we killed her, we laid her with her face to the sky, as you said." The Ant people said, "Now look at the altar. What do you see?" They saw the tracks of Chaparral Cock. Older Brother said, "It looks as if it came in." "No," said Younger Brother, "it is going out." They said these things four times. "Look around back of the altar," said the Ant people. There they found the Chaparral Cock. "How many feathers are on it?" "There are twelve feathers. That will be your count when you kill Navajo, that will be your taboo time."[23]

The Roadrunner feathers indicated are from the tail by means of which the bird steers itself. Sometimes these are ten in number and sometimes twelve, but the multiple of four obviously had more appeal to the Pueblos than the decimal count. In the complex Scalp ceremony the feathers from this bird are used not only in the moccasin toes of one who kicks the scalp, but also inside a pottery drum where the feathers are crossed, and along with them lie two crossed pieces of yucca.

On the fifth day of the ceremony the scalps are taken to a secluded spot on the Zuñi River, a mile or so west of the town. There they are bathed in yucca suds whose foam is indicative of clouds—hence their combination with crossed feathers in the drum.

The scalps are afterward rubbed with kaolin, for rain, and a bit of the scalp is taken into the mouth, that the Zuñis may have brave hearts and that the Gods of War will empower them to destroy the enemy. "Should the victor possess a good heart, the killing of the enemy brings much rain."[24]

Most of the dead are not enemies, but one's own friends and relatives. As ghosts they may be dangerous as well as helpful, so they are invited back to the village only once a year, and now the native rites have been joined with the Christian celebration of All Soul's Day. The Tewa pueblo of Nambe lies on the northern edge of Roadrunner's range and both bird and the deceased are noted on this day. Each family calls on some old man to take food out for the dead, who return to their former village at this time. He is followed by other family members.

> *Before leaving the house each had taken a piece of charcoal and outside had marked on his left sole and on his left palm the cross-like track of the chaparral cock, so that the dead would not make him sick or do him any harm. The chaparral cock has magic.*[25]

His magic consists in confusing the way to the village, because, except for this one day, the dead are not wanted. "Do not remember us. Even when you are moving about, we do not need to hear you. Go away from here."

The Chaparral Cock and the Turkey have two similarities— they are both bound to the earth and to the dead beneath it. An altar for the dead from Cochiti shows tracks of both birds on each side. Father Dumarest's interpretation of the symbolism is

> *that during the great journey from the upper to the middle world the deceased is put by the* chiani *under the protection of the* iareko, *of the lion and bear, of the eagle, of the serpent, of the turkey and chaparral cock.*[26]

There is a transition, either way, between the nether world and this one. Iarriko is a fetish representing the Mother goddess in the Underworld, and the dead descend to her in stages similar to those by which mankind arose from the depths, but the order is reversed. Roadrunner tracks have another reverse meaning at Cochiti. While the dead may pursue or return to haunt people, evil feelings and witches may also haunt the dead on their journey.

In one early account funeral rites at Cochiti consist of placing an ear of blue corn and a club alongside the deceased. Around these tokens a circle of Roadrunner tracks is scratched into the floor of the room. These tracks "constitute a magic circle for the purpose of preventing evil spirits or Brujos from finding out where the soul of the deceased goes and thus protect that soul from their persecutions."[27] Perhaps there may be an inversion of the role of the dead here, with a pretense that it may be the dead rather than the living who are in danger of harm. In either case the enigmatic bird tracks will be a barrier to confuse the unwanted.

For an Indian to be lost on his home territory is quite a serious matter; in ordinary circumstances he would certainly find his way even in distant mountains. So being truly lost brings one near the realm of the dead and calls for a curing rite if one returns. One Tewa society makes a special "road" of chaparral cock tracks when it is about to cure a lost person who has been recovered. The road is made at San Juan, Tesuque, and probably elsewhere, by putting trails of cornmeal in front of the altar. Pieces of crossed yucca are placed on the trail at intervals for the participants to step on.[28]

Everyone thinks of Roadrunner as strong and capable of great endurance. The bird is also brave, because it enjoys taking on a

roadrunner

rattlesnake in a fight, so it figures in a number of curing ceremonies that are devoted to strength. In the Little Fire society rites at Zuñi, medicine water is passed around, then "two characters representing the chaparral cock, each holding an eagle wing feather in each hand, leave the choir and hop and skip birdlike to the altar."[29] The medicine rubbed over the body is in part composed of powdered sunflowers, which helps those using it "to have brave hearts."

Another curing society, the Shuma'kwe, is devoted to the treating of rheumatic troubles and convulsions. The director of the society must be from the Roadrunner clan, which is understandable from the straightness, strength, and swiftness of the bird. These qualities also contribute to racing, particularly at Sia where the bird is much more abundant than at Zuñi or in the Hopi country. Two and a half miles south of Sia is a mountain named after the bird, and a number of races are run around it. Although nothing specific is said, any race can be presumed to either speed the sun back to summer, speed rain clouds toward the village, or both.

At Hopi, where roadrunners are quite rare, it is sun and speed that are acccounted for. War is not mentioned, nor are the dead. In the fall of 1892 Stephen was in a kiva, when a young man had chanced to kill one of these birds.

> *He brought it to the Corner kiva, . . . The bird was carefully*
> *skinned, and the skin and feathers divided among the kiva inmates,*
> *as these feathers are highly prized for the making of prayer feathers*
> *at the winter solstice ceremony. Prayer-feathers of this bird tied to*
> *a horse's tail make him swift and tireless. I note the body here.*
> *Kwa'lakwai says he is to eat it.*[30]

He will eat the bird to become as swift and tireless as it is, and probably to gain its courage and endurance.

14 BIRD OF PURIFICATION
turkey vultures

War is a matter of death or of contact with death. Purification is necessary to bring back into the living world a harmony that has been broken. If all life, from stones to animals to men, has but one breath, hunting also disturbs that unity and again calls for rites of purification. Rites that cleanse are a restoration of normal courses after any breach, so even the natural death of a friend or relative requires a separation of the two realms—the living from the dead and the dead from the living.

Sickness in epidemic proportions may arrive, touching the entire pueblo, and for this evil there will be rites to exorcise the evil causing it. But not all contact with the spirit world is a struggle with evil or death. When one has participated in a ceremony, he has for that time joined with the spirits and has also absorbed their power. Their great power can be dangerous to ordinary people, so after the rites a participant who has played the role of a spirit must be returned to himself, lest the power of the role and the sacred objects handled injure him. In English, "discharming" is the word used for the process of returning from the spirit world to everyday life.

Turkey Vulture can preside over any of these dangerous transitions, because he is a very powerful medicine man, a priest who can dispel evil, break contact with the dead, or merely give a general blessing to the towns of the living. Vultures do walk with ceremonial dignity while they preside over the disposition of carrion, a fact that directly relates them to the dead of either game or human kinds. Both Turkey Buzzard and Mountain Turkey have bald heads, because they lost those feathers when the Sun was raised into the sky. Turkey made the first try; then "the chief told buzzard to try. He is cleverer and stronger than the turkey, and he pushed the sun further up. All his feathers came off, yet he persisted for he is a very powerful medicine man."[1]

The buzzards come with the summer to northern New Mexico and Arizona; by September they have begun a flight to the south and by mid-October are out of the first state and only in the warm south of the other. At Picuris there is a children's story related to the seasonality of the bird. There a hunter's wife was stolen by Giant, but the hunter is able to seize her in turn and flee. Butterflies and woodrats aid the fugitives. Buzzard circles by and asks the Giant what the trouble is.

> *"See if you can make it hot, so that I can catch them wherever they sit down to rest in the shade and take the woman away from him." To this request Buzzard responds, "I do not like very much heat, as I am baldheaded."*

After saying this he flew away, but in a little while did call the heat. The Giant was sweating as he went along the road, but hunter and wife remained quite cool.[2]

At Taos the bird was also regarded as a friend and a vulture should not be killed since he helped to recover slain warriors, while on the other hand, Mrs. Bailey notes that Indians formerly used a great number of vulture feathers in fletching their arrows, so there was no general taboo on killing these birds. The Zuñis never use buzzard feathers on prayer offerings, because buzzards eat dead things. But they are used on masks and to make collars for some kachinas.[3]

At Cochiti the vulture as a purifying agent in times of sickness takes on an objective form as the Buzzard kachina. The Ma'sha-wa kachina does not often dance, but the mask belonging to the Giant Medicine society is important.

When epidemics occur in the pueblo, the war captain, having first con-
sulted the Giant head who, in turn confers with the Shru'tzi head,
brings this ka'tsina from house to house to bless and cleanse the com-
munity. He may appear briefly at masked dances, especially those im-
mediately after or during a time of numerous illnesses.[4]

In the pueblo of Santa Ana, Buzzard Old Man belongs to a group of benevolent spirits called *maiyanyi. Ianyi* is a Keresan word that is often taken to be the equivalent of manna and represents a kind of power and blessing that can be showered down on the village. These spirits include unnamed and formless powers, Catholic saints, some beings from myths, as well as Buzzard Old Man, and their realm extends even to irrigation ditches.[5]

At Hopi the kind of purification that can be called discharming is part of several ceremonies—perhaps all. At the close of the observances the final rite consists of one in which a priest takes a vulture feather, sprinkles it with ashes and, singing his discharming song, flicks the ashes up through the kiva hatchway. The song is addressed to and includes the colors for each of the directions. It goes:

Discharm! Discharm!
From the north
Yellow buzzard, with the wing.

Voth notes that the Hopis believe that each society and its paraphernalia have a particular "charm," which can be injurious to members.

The charm of the Snake fraternity is a swelling which may occur on
any part of the body. . . . Through this discharming rite . . . such
charm is supposed to be removed from the participants, so that after
that they may again mingle with impunity with nonparticipants and
in every-day life.[6]

Ashes are the end of a fire, so at the end of a ceremony, which may be thought of as a blazing episode when compared with normal life, they are scattered by means of a buzzard feather to cool the potent influence.

Should any nonmember come down with a malady similar to the charm of a given society, the head of the group to which the particular symptom pertains is called in to sing his discharming song over the patient. Turkey Buzzard relates in two other ways to the idea of healing wounds and restoring life to its normal course. One of these is a matter of correcting the break caused by taking game; the other a break caused by famine.

Vultures do clean up any leavings of animal life that has died either at the hands of a hunter or from natural causes. In this sense these birds literally cleanse and purify the natural world. There is a complicated story about Arrow Youth, who is the patron spirit of hunters. At the conclusion of the account it is noted that some game must be devoted to the vulture.

The chief of Laguna speaks to one of the War Twins:

"Let me make it good," he said. "It is well to do it tomorrow," said the chief of Ceremonies. Then, at night, he made prayer-sticks, pollen, meal, beads and feathers. Then he said, "Here it is, war captain," said he. "Go ahead. Up on the east cliff lives Turkey-Buzzard-Man. Ask him to come up here-abouts to purify here from north to south Laguna."

The War captain goes first to Red-Paint-Place, then takes the offering to Buzzard with the request that he purify the village.

When the War captain returns with the message that Buzzard will come the chief tells him, "'My son, go ahead and hunt deer from here on the north slope westward. Presently Turkey-Buzzard must eat,' said he, 'after he has finished purifying the village in all directions.'" Arrow Youth then made offerings and early in the morning he went hunting and presented his offerings to Mountain Lion, who is the original Hunt chief. He shot a large deer and then another.

"Enough," said he. "This is all I can carry today to-day." After he brought the meat in, Turkey-Buzzard-Man purified here above all around. . . . Then said Turkey-Buzzard-Man, "Enough," said he. "It has come to be good. From now on, you will not feel any fear and peaceful will be the town." [7]

Just how the vulture purifies comes up in the story of Hummingbird and the famine in which it transpired that one thing was lacking in their offerings—which proved to be tobacco. The smoke of tobacco suggests the rain-bringing clouds that will end the drought. The Mother goddess suggests that they go see Old Turkey Buzzard, which they do, and he tells them the beads and pollen and prayer-sticks are not enough. Turkey Buzzard asked for tobacco, which they found; "Then they divided it and one half they took to Old-Turkey-Buzzard."

With this he agreed to purify the town. "Then he smoked to the north, to the west, to the south and to the east. He smoked to his mothers the chiefs." On arriving at the village Buzzard "purified first from the south down; afterwards from the east down; afterwards from the north down; and afterwards from the west down. Then everything could become clear all around; storm clouds, crops and happiness there around was spread. Then was renewed the food." [8]

So with this final benediction, we have followed the birds down from the Sun to the commonplace level of the village streets. With the aid of all the birds, both gods and men have come to agree. Prayer-sticks, pollen and meal, feathers, and beads have been offered, and Turkey Vulture has purified the town. It is without fear; there is peace. As Buzzard Man himself said—"it has come to be good."

PUEBLO BIRD LIST

This is a simplified list for general reader use. The advanced student can find the native names for the birds in the sources listed in Section 2 of the bibliography. Listed here are only the English common name and the Pueblo language in which a name for the bird has been located. When a subspecies occurs, the English name is placed in quotes.

Some native names may have been made up on the spot, but most of them are sound. The early Hopi names were taken down by the eminent naturalist, Edgar Mearns, who had the birds in hand when asking questions. Linguist J.P. Harrington actually affixed native names, presumably Tewa, to bird skins and sent these to the Bureau of American Ethnology. When these were discovered in a warehouse in Washington, D.C., the student who found them concluded from their repugnant condition, "that a balanced life is more important than a life devoted exclusively to scholarship." Nevertheless, his records would be invaluable. The Zuñi names collected by Edmund J. Ladd are excellent, and Leslie White carefully gathered up names from various Keresan pueblos. The occasional names that occur throughout anthropological texts are less certain, but when checked form the basis for relating birds to their roles in ceremonies and myths. There are many additional native names which are not yet attached to specific birds, which would make a splendid project for some student who knows both birds and linguistics.

LOONS

Common Loon—Hopi

GREBES

Eared Grebe—Hopi
Pied-billed Grebe—Keres

HERONS & BITTERNS

Great Blue Heron—Tewa, Keres, Zuñi, Hopi
Green Heron—Hopi
Great Egret—Hopi
Reddish Egret—Hopi
Snowy Egret—Hopi
Black-crowned Night Heron—Hopi
Least Bittern—Hopi

STORKS

Wood Stork—Hopi

IBIS

White-faced Ibis—Hopi

SWANS

Trumpeter Swan—Hopi

GEESE

Canada Goose—Tiwa, Tewa, Keres, Zuñi, Hopi
"Cackling Goose"—Hopi

DUCKS

General name—Tiwa, Tewa, Keres, Zuñi, Hopi
Mallard—Hopi
Gadwall—Hopi
Pintail—Hopi
Green-winged Teal—Hopi
Blue-winged Teal—Hopi
Cinnamon Teal—Hopi
American Widgeon—Hopi
Northern Shoveler—Hopi
Redhead—Hopi
Ring-necked—Hopi
Canvasback—Hopi
Bufflehead—Hopi
Ruddy—Hopi
Hooded Merganser—Hopi
Common Merganser—Hopi
Red-breasted Merganser—Hopi

VULTURES

Turkey Vulture—Tiwa, Tewa, Keres, Zuñi, Hopi

BIRD HAWKS

Goshawk—Keres, Hopi
Sharp-shinned Hawk—Keres, Zuñi, Hopi
Cooper's Hawk—Tewa, Keres, Zuñi, Hopi

BUZZARD HAWKS

Red-tailed Hawk—Tiwa, Tewa, Keres, Zuñi, Hopi
Swainson's Hawk—Keres, Hopi
Zone-tailed Hawk—Hopi
Ferruginous Hawk—Keres
Harris' Hawk—Hopi
Common Black Hawk—Hopi

EAGLES

Golden Eagle—Tiwa, Keres, Zuñi, Hopi
Bald Eagle—Tiwa, Tewa, Keres, Zuñi, Hopi

HARRIERS

Marsh Hawk—Keres, Zuñi, Hopi

OSPREYS

Osprey—Keres

FALCONS

Prairie Falcon—Hopi
Peregrine Falcon—Hopi

Merlin—Zuñi, Hopi
American Kestrel (Sparrow Hawk)—
    Tiwa, Tewa, Keres, Zuñi, Hopi

GROUSE

Blue Grouse—Tewa, Keres

QUAIL

Scaled Quail—Tiwa, Tewa, Keres, Zuñi
Gambel's Quail—Keres, Hopi
Montezuma Quail—Hopi

TURKEY

"Merriam's Turkey"—Tiwa, Tewa,
    Keres, Zuñi, Hopi

CRANES

Sandhill & "Little Brown" Cranes—
    Tiwa, Tewa, Keres, Zuñi, Hopi

RAILS, GALLINULES, & COOTS

Virginia Rail—Hopi
Sora Rail—Hopi
Common Gallinule—Hopi
American Coot—Zuñi, Hopi

PLOVERS

Killdeer—Tewa, Keres, Zuñi, Hopi
Mountain Plover—Hopi

SNIPES, SANDPIPERS, ETC.

Common Snipe—Keres, Hopi
Long-billed Curlew—Keres, Hopi
Spotted Sandpiper—Hopi
Solitary Sandpiper—Hopi
Willet—Hopi
Greater Yellowlegs—Hopi
Lesser Yellowlegs—Hopi
Baird's Sandpiper—Hopi
Least Sandpiper—Hopi

AVOCETS & STILTS

American Avocet—Hopi
Black-necked Stilt—Keres

PHALAROPES

Wilson's Phalarope—Hopi

GULLS & TERNS

Ring-billed Gull—Hopi
Forster's Tern—Hopi
Black Tern—Hopi

PIGEONS & DOVES

Band-tailed Pigeon—Hopi
White-winged Dove—Hopi
Mourning Dove—Tiwa, Tewa, Keres,
    Zuñi, Hopi
Ground Dove—Hopi
Inca Dove—Hopi

MACAWS & PARROTS

Military Macaw & Scarlet Macaw—
    Tiwa, Tewa, Keres, Zuñi, Hopi

CUCKOOS & ROADRUNNERS

Yellow-billed Cuckoo—Hopi
Roadrunner—Tewa, Keres, Zuñi, Hopi

OWLS

General name—Tiwa, Tewa, Keres,
    Towa, Hopi
Barn Owl—Hopi
Screech Owl—Tiwa, Hopi
Great Horned Owl—Zuñi, Hopi
Pygmy Owl—Hopi
Elf Owl—Keres
Burrowing Owl—Tewa, Keres, Zuñi,
    Hopi
Long-eared Owl—Hopi

GOATSUCKERS

Whippoorwill—Keres
Poorwill—Keres, Zuñi, Hopi
Common Nighthawk—Tiwa, Keres,
    Zuñi, Hopi

SWIFTS

White-throated Swift—Keres, Zuñi,
Hopi

HUMMINGBIRDS

General name—Tiwa, Tewa, Keres,
Zuñi, Hopi
Broad-tailed Hummingbird—Tiwa
Rufous Hummingbird—Tiwa, Hopi

KINGFISHERS

Belted Kingfisher—Hopi

WOODPECKERS

General name—Tiwa, Tewa, Keres,
Hopi
Common Flicker (Yellow-shafted
Flicker)—Hopi
Common Flicker (Red-shafted)—
Tiwa, Keres, Zuñi, Hopi
Gila Woodpecker—Hopi
Acorn Woodpecker—Hopi
Lewis' Woodpecker—Zuñi, Hopi
Yellow-bellied Sapsucker—Hopi
Williamson's Sapsucker—Keres, Hopi
Hairy Woodpecker—Tewa, Zuñi
Downy Woodpecker—Zuñi, Hopi
Ladder-backed Woodpecker—Hopi

TYRANT FLYCATCHERS

Cassin's Kingbird—Zuñi, Hopi
Western Kingbird—Hopi
Ash-throated Flycatcher—Keres, Zuñi,
Hopi
Black Phoebe—Keres, Hopi
Say's Phoebe—Keres, Zuñi, Hopi
Hammond's, Dusky, Western, &
Willow Flycatchers—Hopi
Western Wood Pewee—Hopi
Olive-sided Flycatcher—Hopi
Vermillion Flycatcher—Hopi

LARKS

Horned Lark—Tewa, Keres, Zuñi, Hopi

SWALLOWS

General name—Tiwa, Keres
Violet-green Swallow—Keres, Zuñi,
Hopi
Bank Swallow—Hopi
Rough-winged Swallow—Zuñi, Hopi
Barn Swallow—Tewa, Hopi
Cliff Swallow—Keres, Zuñi, Hopi
Purple Martin—Zuñi, Hopi

JAYS, MAGPIES, CROWS, & RAVENS

Steller's Jay—Tiwa, Tewa, Keres, Zuñi,
Hopi
Scrub Jay—Keres, Zuñi, Hopi
Mexican Jay—Hopi
Black-billed Magpie—Tiwa, Tewa,
Keres, Zuñi, Hopi
Common Raven—Zuñi, Hopi
Common Crow—Tewa, Keres, Towa,
Zuñi, Hopi
Piñon Jay—Keres, Zuñi, Hopi
Clark's Nutcracker—Tewa, Keres

TITMICE, ETC.

Mountain Chickadee—Hopi
Plain Titmouse—Keres, Hopi
Bridled Titmouse—Hopi
Virdin & Common Bushtit—Hopi

NUTHATCHES

White-breasted Nuthatch—Zuñi, Hopi
Pygmy Nuthatch—Keres

DIPPERS

Dipper—Tewa

WRENS

House Wren—Hopi
Bewick's Wren—Hopi

Cactus Wren—Hopi
Long-billed Marsh Wren—Hopi
Canyon Wren—Tiwa, Keres, Zuñi, Hopi
Rock Wren—Keres, Zuñi

MOCKINGBIRDS & THRASHERS

Mockingbird—Tiwa, Tewa, Keres, Zuñi, Hopi
Bendire's Thrasher—Hopi
Crissal Thrasher—Hopi
Sage Thrasher—Keres, Zuñi, Hopi

THRUSHES & BLUEBIRDS

American Robin—Tiwa, Keres, Zuñi, Hopi
Hermit & Swainson's Thrush—Hopi
Western Bluebird—Tiwa, Tewa, Keres, Zuñi, Hopi
Mountain Bluebird—Keres, Zuñi, Hopi
Townsend's Solitaire—Zuñi, Hopi

GNATCATCHERS & KINGLETS

Blue-gray Gnatcatcher—Zuñi, Hopi
Black-tailed Gnatcatcher—Zuñi, Hopi
Ruby-crowned Kinglet—Zuñi, Hopi

PIPITS

Water Pipit—Hopi

SILKY FLYCATCHERS

Phainopepla—Hopi

SHRIKES

Loggerhead Shrike—Zuñi, Hopi

VIREOS

General name—Hopi

WOOD WARBLERS

Orange Crowned & Calavaras Warblers—Hopi
Virginia & Luby's Warblers—Hopi
Yellow Warbler—Keres, Zuñi, Hopi

Yellow-rumped Warbler—Hopi
Black-throated Gray Warbler—Hopi
Grace's Warbler—Hopi
MacGillivray's Warbler—Hopi
Common Yellowthroat—Tewa, Hopi
Yellow-breasted Chat—Zuñi, Hopi
Wilson's Warbler—Zuñi, Hopi

WEAVER FINCH

House Sparrow—Keres, Zuñi

MEADOWLARKS, BLACKBIRDS, & ORIOLES

Western Meadowlark—Tewa, Keres, Zuñi, Hopi
Yellow-headed Blackbird—Tewa, Keres, Zuñi, Hopi
Red-winged Blackbird—Tiwa, Keres, Zuñi, Hopi
Northern Oriole—Tewa, Keres, Zuñi, Hopi
Hooded Oriole—Hopi
Brewer's Blackbird—Tiwa, Keres, Zuñi, Hopi
Brown-headed Cowbird—Zuñi, Hopi

TANAGERS

Western Tanager—Keres, Zuñi, Hopi
Hepatic Tanager—Hopi
Summer Tanager—Tiwa, Keres, Hopi

GROSBEAKS, FINCHES, & SPARROWS

Cardinal—Keres, Hopi
Pyrrhuloxia—Keres, Hopi
Black-headed Grosbeak—Keres, Zuñi, Hopi
Blue Grosbeak—Keres, Hopi
Lazuli Bunting—Zuñi, Hopi
Painted Bunting—Zuñi
Dickcissal—Hopi
Purple Finch—Hopi

House Finch—Keres, Zuñi, Hopi
Pine Siskin—Hopi
American Goldfinch—Hopi
Lesser Goldfinch—Keres, Zuñi, Hopi
Red Crossbill—Hopi
Green-tailed Towhee—Zuñi, Hopi
Rufous-sided Towhee—Zuñi, Hopi
Brown & Abert's Towhee—Zuñi, Hopi
Lark Bunting—Hopi
Sparrows (general name)—Tiwa, Zuñi
Savannah Sparrow—Hopi
Grasshopper Sparrow—Zuñi, Hopi
Vesper Sparrow—Zuñi, Hopi
Lark Sparrow—Zuñi, Hopi
Rufous Crowned & Cassin's Sparrow—
    Hopi

Black-throated Sparrow—Hopi
Sage Sparrow—Hopi
Juncos (in general)—Tewa, Keres, Zuñi,
    Hopi
Chipping Sparrow—Hopi
Clay-colored Sparrow—Hopi
Brewer's Sparrow—Tewa, Hopi
Black-chinned Sparrow—Hopi
White-crowned Sparrow—Keres, Zuñi,
    Hopi
Lincoln's Sparrow—Hopi
Song Sparrow—Zuñi, Hopi
McCown's Longspur—Hopi
Chestnut-collared Longspur—Hopi

NOTE: The pueblos belonging to the six language groups are as follows:
1. Tiwa—Taos, Picuris, Sandia, and Isleta
2. Tewa—San Juan, Santa Clara, San Ildefonso, Tesuque, Pojoaque, and Nambé
3. Towa—Jemez
4. Keres—Acoma, Laguna, Sia, Santa Ana, San Felipe, Santo Domingo, and
   Cochiti
5. Zuñi—pueblo of Halona
6. Hopi—for villages see map p. xiv

NOTES

CHAPTER 1

1. Stevenson, "Zuñi," 416.
2. Stephen, *Hopi Journal,* 1305, 11; "Hopi Tales," 62.

CHAPTER 2

1. Vivian and Mathews, *Kin Kletso,* 18, for tabulation of finds; Hargrave, *Mexican Macaws,* 53, table 9.
2. *Ibid.,* 20.
3. Henderson and Harrington, *Ethnozoology of Tewa,* 45.
4. Bourke, *Snake Dance of Moquis,* 49.
5. White, *San Felipe,* 62; Parsons, "Zuñi Names," 173.
6. Ladd, *Zuñi Ethno-ornithology,* 95; Hodge, "Pueblo Indian Clans," 133; Stevenson, "Zuñi," 40; Parsons, "Pueblo Indian Folk-tales," 234; elsewhere she translates *Tanyi* as "parrot," *Tewa Tales,* 39.
7. Parsons, "Isleta," 216.
8. Mearns, "Ornithological Vocabulary"; Stephen, *Hopi Journal,* 1214; Wallis, "Folk Tales from Shumopovi," 23ff.
9. Dorsey and Voth, *Oraibi Soyal,* 28n.
10. Stephen, *Hopi Journal,* 307n, 219.
11. *Ibid.,* 1072. In his glossary of native terms *gya'zro* is translated as "perroquet or macaw."
12. Colton, *Hopi Kachina Dolls,* 64.
13. Lowie, *Notes on Hopi Clans,* 317.
14. Voth, *Traditions of Hopi,* 158.
15. Wallis, "Folk Tales from Shumopovi," 22–28; Parsons, *Tewa Tales,* 242.
16. Fewkes, "Hopi Katcinas," 24.
17. *Ibid.,* for Ahulani, 70, 121; Dorsey and Voth, *Oraibi Soyal,* 13; Tyler, *Pueblo Gods and Myths,* 150–51.
18. Fewkes, *loc. cit.,* 40–44, 97–98.

19. Pepper, *Pueblo Bonito*, 194–95, 375–76.

20. Judd, *Pueblo Bonito*, 263–65. He lists sixteen Green or Military and eight Scarlet Macaws, plus six parrots, but see Hargrave, *Mexican Macaws.*

21. Hargrave, "Bird Bones," 208; McGregor, *Winona*, 258.

22. Judd, *Pueblo Bonito*, 265; for following, Hargrave, *Mexican Macaws*, 5, 9, 52, 53.

23. Vivian and Mathews, *Kin Kletso*, 18.

24. Parsons, *Pueblo Religion*, 991.

25. Beaglehole, *Hopi Economic Life*, 85.

26. Smith, *Kiva Mural Decorations*, 180, 115n; with sources.

27. Bandelier, *Southwestern Journals*, 364; Lange, *Cochiti*, 152.

28. Stevenson, "Sia," 76.

29. Parsons, *Tewa Tales*, 39–43.

30. Parsons, *Pueblo Religion*, 1087n*.

31. Boas, *Keresan Texts*, 17ff.; Benedict, "Eight Stories from Acoma," 59–61. Here children bend branches to the ground and are flung skyward to become "all the different kinds and colors of birds."

32. Boas, *loc. cit.*, 22, 295.

33. Lange, *Cochiti*, 275, 327, 345.

34. White, *Santa Ana*, 344. At Sia a similar pole is used in the dance for the Blessed Virgin. White, *Sia*, 312.

35. White, *New Material from Acoma*, 104.

36. Fewkes, "Hopi Katcinas," 119–20, Pl. 57, which illustrates standard bearer and pole. See also Colton, *Hopi Kachina Dolls*, Kachina 120, for different tableta.

37. Stephen, *Hopi Journal*, 148.

38. *Ibid.*, 1007 for male aspect, 1081 for connection with Mustard clan.

39. *Ibid.*, 1009, Fig. 493 for bird effigies; Hester, *Navajo Migrations*, 116–18 and Fig. 40.

40. Stevenson, *Ethnobotany of Zuñi*, 93.

41. Fewkes, *loc. cit.*, 95; Stephen, *Hopi Journal*, 446. For Mashanta, *ibid.*, 358. Also Colton, *loc. cit.*, kachinas 194, 45.

42. Dumarest, *Notes on Cochiti*, 216.

43. Stevenson, "Zuñi," 419, Pl. 101, where these feathers are deep red at base and green at tip, or yellowish throughout; twenty small red parrot feathers form a collar.

44. White, *Santa Ana*, 81, Fig. 5; White, *Santo Domingo*, 97.

45. For a more reliable account, Kroeber, *Zuñi Kin and Clan*, 93ff.; Eggan, *Western Pueblos*, 198ff. See also Durkheim and Mauss, *Primitive Classification*, 43ff. For Cushing on Macaw clan, "Zuñi Creation Myths," 367ff.; he also has a different view in *Zuñi Breadstuff*, 30.

46. Kroeber, *loc. cit.*, 101; Eggan, *Western Pueblos*, 198–201, 212ff. See Chapter 9, this book.

47. Cushing, *Zuñi Creation Myths*, 385.

48. Titiev, *Old Oraibi*, 137–38 and ref. in 60n; Eggan, *loc. cit.*, 94.

49. Waters, *Book of Hopi*, 54.

50. *Ibid.*, 231–34. See Eggan, *loc. cit.*, 103 for the standard list of clans and the ceremonies they control.

51. Parsons, *Pueblo Religion*, 240.

52. Stephen, *Hopi Journal*, 173; Parsons, *loc. cit.*, 175 for location of Kishyu'ba.
53. Stephen, *loc. cit.*, 215–16.

CHAPTER 3

1. Parsons, *Taos Tales*, 114–15.
2. Stevenson, "Zuñi," 114.
3. Ladd, *Zuñi Ethno-ornithology*.
4. Wheeler Survey, *Explorations*, 427.
5. Monson and Phillips, Checklist, 17; Woodbury and Russell, *Birds of Navajo Country*.
6. Stephen, *Hopi Journal*, 853.
7. *Kwa'hu*—tail feathers; *kwapu'hu*—downy eagle feathers; *kwa'hut kalensa*—primary wing feathers, and so on.
8. Voth, *Traditions of Hopi*, 198, 234.
9. Simmons, *Sun Chief*, 64–65.
10. Stephen, *Hopi Journal*, 540.
11. Buechner, *Pronghorn Antelope in Texas*, 311.
12. Bourke, *Snake Dance of the Moquis*, 27, 252.
13. Dumarest, *Notes on Cochiti*, 194; Lange, *Cochiti*, 133.
14. Bailey, *Birds of New Mexico*, 179.
15. Beaglehole, *Hopi Hunting*, 18–19.
16. *Ibid.*, 20.
17. *Ibid.*, 22.
18. Harrington and Roberts, "Picuris Children's Stories," 319–23.
19. Boas, *Keresan Texts*, 34, 284.
20. Parsons, *Social Organization of Tewa*, 297; Parsons, *Tewa Tales*, 241.
21. Stephen, *Hopi Journal*, 215–16.
22. Stevenson, "Zuñi," 420.
23. White, *Sia*, 307; White, *Santa Ana*, 339.
24. Stephen, "Hopi Tales," 62.
25. Bunzel, "Zuñi Origin Myths," 586.
26. Parsons, *Pueblo Religion*, 8.
27. Stevenson, "Sia," 67.
28. Voth, "Eagle Cult," 109.
29. Beaglehole, *Hopi Hunting*, 21.
30. Bourke, *Snake Dance*, 139.
31. Stephen, *Hopi Journal*, 724.
32. Voth, *Oraibi Powamu*, 76.
33. Tyler, *Pueblo Gods and Myths*, 66ff.
34. Voth, *Traditions of Hopi*, 159–67.

35. Stephen, *Hopi Journal,* 100.
36. Stirling, *Origin Myth of Acoma,* 25.
37. *Ibid.,* 30.
38. Parsons, *Pueblo Religion,* 286. Next quote, Bunzel, "Zuñi Ritual Poetry," 799.
39. *Ibid.,* 784.
40. Stevenson, "Zuñi," 524–25.
41. Lange, *Cochiti,* 328. For Bear as curer, *Pueblo Animals and Myths,* 202ff.
42. White, *New Material from Acoma,* 119, Pl. 12.
43. Parsons, "Isleta," 333.
44. *Ibid.,* 446.
45. Parsons, *Social Organization of Tewa,* 205–206.
46. Roediger, *Ceremonial Costumes,* 194.
47. Fewkes, "Hopi Katcinas," 77, Pl. 15. Colton, *Hopi Kachina Dolls,* Kachina 71.
48. Bunzel, "Zuñi Katcinas," 866–67. See Parsons, "Zuñi Tales," 49–51 for companion myth on offerings to eagles.
49. Stevenson, "Zuñi," 524; Parsons, *Notes on Zuñi,* Part 1, 224.
50. Bunzel, *loc. cit.,* 1068.
51. *Ibid.,* 169; Parsons, *Pueblo Religion,* 1105–1106.
52. Ellis, "Patterns of Aggression," pieces together the evidence for this set of associations.
53. Voth, "Eagle Cult," 107. Turkey feathers with white tips on dark ground were also used; Eggan, *Western Pueblos,* 84.
54. Dorsey and Voth, *Oraibi Soyal,* 46.
55. Bunzel, "Zuñi Katcinas," 864.
56. Parsons, *Taos,* 102.
57. Goldrank, *Cochiti,* 39.
58. Ellis, "Patterns of Aggression"; Ellis, *Basic Jemez Patterns.*
59. Stephen, *Hopi Journal,* 307n.
60. Beaglehole and Beaglehole, *Hopi of Second Mesa,* 21, 24.
61. Cushing, "Zuñi Creation Myths," 418.
62. Stevenson, "Zuñi," Pl. 108; Cushing, *Zuñi Fetishes,* Pls. 10, 11.
63. Parsons, *Scalp Ceremonial of Zuñi,* 31.
64. Bunzel, *Zuñi Texts,* 133.
65. Stevenson, "Zuñi," 21.
66. Stephen, *Hopi Journal,* 1012, Fig. 499.
67. Stephen, "Hopi Tales," 14; next quotes, 15, 17.
68. Stevenson, "Sia," 38.
69. Stirling, *Origin Myth of Acoma,* 77–78.
70. Sebag, "La Geste de Kasewat"; also *Marxisme et Structuralisme,* 187.
71. White, *New Material from Acoma,* 176.
72. *Ibid.,* 172–78; Boas, *Keresan Texts,* 111–18.
73. Espinosa, "Pueblo Indian Folk Tales," 80–82.
74. Benedict, *Zuñi Mythology,* Vol. 2, 91–98; Parsons, "Zuñi Tales," 246.

CHAPTER 4

1. Ladd, *Zuñi Ethno-ornithology,* 90.
2. Figures from Ligon, *Merriam's Wild Turkey,* 30.
3. Personal communication from New Mexico Department of Game and Fish.
4. Ladd, *Zuñi Ethno-ornithology,* 92.
5. Parsons, *Pueblo Religion,* 22.
6. Lange, *Cochiti,* 132; Lange, "Notes on Use of Turkeys," 204ff.
7. Reed, "Turkeys in Southwestern Archaeology," 195ff.
8. Winship, "Coronado Expedition," 573.
9. Reed, *loc. cit.,* 200.
10. Cushing, *Zuñi Breadstuff,* 604.
11. Parsons, *Pueblo Religion,* 22.
12. White, *Santa Ana,* 281.
13. Lange, *Cochiti,* 112.
14. White, *Sia,* 180.
15. Stephen, *Hopi Journal,* 22, 605.
16. Gunn, *Schat-Chen,* 26.
17. Wormington, *Prehistoric Indians,* 70.
18. Judd, *Pueblo Bonito,* 66.
19. Reed, *loc. cit.,* 197.
20. Winship, *loc. cit.,* 573.
21. Wormington, *loc. cit.,* 55.
22. Boas, *Keresan Texts,* 177–80.
23. Parsons, *Pueblo Religion,* 241.
24. Voth, *Traditions of Hopi,* 199–201.
25. Parsons, *Taos Tales,* 95.
26. White, *San Felipe,* 37.
27. Parsons, *Tewa Tales,* 52–57.
28. Schorger, *Wild Turkey,* 29.
29. Voth, *Oraibi Marau,* 29–30.
30. Parsons, *Pueblo Religion,* 290–91.
31. White, *Santa Ana,* 175–76.
32. Dumarest, *Notes on Cochiti,* 172. For difference in names, Tyler, *Pueblo Gods and Myths,* 117ff.
33. Bunzel, "Zuñi Ritual Poetry," 677.
34. Parsons, *Pueblo Religion,* 645.
35. Lange, *Cochiti,* 235 (from Boas).
36. Stephen, *Hopi Journal,* 510.
37. Stirling, *Origin Myth of Acoma,* 105.
38. Bunzel, *loc. cit.,* 644; following quote, 799.
39. Mera, *The Rain-bird,* Pls. 45, 48.
40. Parsons, "Isleta," 291.

CHAPTER 5

1. Stevenson, "Ethnobotany of Zuñi," 89.
2. Ladd, *Zuñi Ethno-ornithology*, 106–108.
3. Stevenson, "Zuñi," 189.
4. *Ibid.*, 176. For account of Rain priests, 163ff.
5. Parsons, "Zuñi Tales," 46. The "little bird" mentioned on the same page is the swift.
6. *Ibid.*, 46.
7. Boas, *Keresan Texts*, 284; Gunn, *Schat-Chen*, 217ff.
8. Boas, *loc. cit.*, 160–61.
9. Espinosa, "Pueblo Indian Folk Tales," 73–74.
10. Parsons, "Isleta," 213.
11. Cushing, "Origin Myth from Oraibi," 168.
12. Wallis, "Folk Tales from Shumopovi," 3.
13. Bailey, *Birds of New Mexico*, 364.
14. Benedict, "Eight Stories from Acoma," 65.
15. Boas, *Keresan Texts*, 10–11.
16. Benedict, *Tales of Cochiti*, 5.
17. Boas, *Keresan Texts*, 12. On native tobacco see Parsons, *Pueblo Religion*, 18; Robbins *et al.*, *Ethnobotany of Tewa*, 103ff.
18. Benedict, *Tales of Cochiti*, 10. On deer and rain, Tyler, *Pueblo Animals and Myths*, 72ff.
19. Stephen, *Hopi Journal*, 1271.
20. Parsons, *Pueblo Religion*, 186n.
21. Bunzel, "Zuñi Origin Myths," 587–88.
22. Parsons, "Isleta," 299–300.
23. Voth, *Traditions of Hopi*, 192.
24. Parsons, *Tewa Tales*, 151–53.
25. Harrington and Roberts, "Picuris Children's Stories," 349–51.
26. Henderson and Harrington, *Ethnozoology of Tewa*, 36.
27. Parsons, *Tewa Tales*, 144.
28. White, *Santa Ana*, 248.
29. Tyler, *Pueblo Gods and Myths*, 142ff.
30. Boas, *Keresan Texts*, 95–96.
31. White, *Santa Ana*, 347–48. In one Hopi-Tewa story (Parsons, *Tewa Tales*, 237–38), Dove husband tells where a spring is:
     Neeanaha napoko
     ewiyu heh ewiyu heh "here is a spring"
32. Parsons, *Notes on Zuñi*, Part 2, 315–16.
33. Ladd, *Zuñi Ethno-ornithology*, 95.
34. Benedict, *Zuñi Mythology*, Vol. 1, 67; Parsons, *Scalp Ceremonial of Zuñi, passim.*
35. Stevenson, "Zuñi," 420.

36. Stephen, *Hopi Journal,* 833.
37. Stephen, "Hopi Tales," 6.
38. Voth, *Traditions of Hopi,* 195.
39. Whiting, *Ethnobotany of Hopi,* 66.

CHAPTER 6

1. Beadle, *Undeveloped West,* 506.
2. Stevenson, "Zuñi," 32–33.
3. *Ibid.,* 71.
4. Cushing, *Zuñi Creation Myths,* 409–10.
5. *Ibid.,* 412.
6. Stevenson, *loc. cit.,* 67; Parsons, *Notes on Zuñi,* Part 1, 161–62.
7. Bunzel, "Zuñi Katsinas," 1021; Parsons, *loc. cit.,* 212.
8. Stephen, *Hopi Journal,* 1278.
9. Fewkes, "Hopi Katcinas," 125.
10. Stephen, *loc. cit.,* 470.
11. *Ibid.,* 477–78.
12. Lange, *Cochiti,* 498.
13. White, *Santa Ana,* 210; song, 220.
14. Stirling, *Origin Myth of Acoma,* 30–31.
15. White, *New Material from Acoma,* 75, 82ff.
16. Parsons, *Social Organization of Tewa,* 238, 247.
17. Benedict, *Tales of Cochiti,* 153–54.
18. Stephen, *loc. cit.,* 1011, Fig. 496.
19. *Ibid.,* Figs. 169–71.
20. *Ibid.,* 308–309, Plate 10, for next, Pl. 11.
21. *Ibid.,* 236, Fig. 145.
22. Monson and Phillips, *Checklist of Birds,* 20. Also Woodbury and Russell, *Birds of Navajo Country.*
23. Parsons, *Tewa Tales,* 145. Henderson and Harrington. *Ethnozoology of Tewa,* 46.
24. White, *Sia,* 240; White, *San Felipe,* 22, Fig. 3.
25. Ladd, *Zuñi Ethno-ornithology,* 94.
26. Bailey, *Birds of New Mexico,* 239.
27. Parsons, *Tewa Tales,* 93–94.
28. Parsons, *Social Organization of Tewa,* 162–63, 332n.
29. Henderson and Harrington, *Ethnozoology of Tewa,* 46.
30. Gunn, *Schat-Chen,* 164.
31. Cushing, "Zuñi Creation Myths," 403.
32. Stevenson, "Zuñi," 40.
33. Ladd, *Zuñi Ethno-ornithology,* 93.
34. Parsons, *Notes on Zuñi,* Part 2, 231.

35. Eggan, *Western Pueblos,* 74.

36. Phillips, *et al., Birds of Arizona,* 30; Woodbury and Russell, *Birds of Navajo Country,* 44.

37. Stephen, *loc. cit.,* 960.

CHAPTER 7

1. For song, Bent, *Life Histories of Flycatchers,* 355. Espinosa, "Pueblo Indian Folk Tales," 64, gives *tetse* as the Tewa name for lark and calls *koi* simply snowbird. *Tse* is Tewa for yellow.

2. Parsons, "Pueblo Indian Folk-tales," 217–18.

3. Parsons, *Tewa Tales,* 140, 3n.

4. Boas, *Keresan Texts,* 34, 284.

5. Dorsey and Voth, *Oraibi Soyal,* Pl. 27 and caption.

6. *Ibid.;* Colton, *Hopi Kachina Dolls,* 51.

7. White, *Santa Ana,* 281.

8. White, "Acoma Indians," 173–74.

9. Sebag, "La Geste de Kasewat," 35.

10. Boas, *Keresan Texts,* 114–15.

11. Parsons, "Isleta," 211.

12. Wallis, "Folk Tales from Shumopovi," 62; Voth, *Traditions of Hopi,* 154.

13. Wallis, *loc. cit.,* 52, 55.

14. Parsons, *Tewa Tales,* 283.

15. Stephen, *Hopi Journal,* 1271.

16. *Ibid.,* 791, Fig. 427.

17. Parsons, *Pueblo Religion,* 275 and 275n. Eggan, *Western Pueblos,* 82.

18. Stevenson, "Zuñi," 180–204.

19. Stephen, *loc. cit.,* 870.

20. *Ibid.,* 56–57.

21. Hermequaftewa, *Hopi Way of Life,* 3.

22. Anonymous, *Hopi Hearings,* 82.

23. Ladd, *Zuñi Ethno-ornithology,* 118.

24. Voth, *Oraibi Powamu,* 83 and 83n.

25. Fewkes and Stephen, "Mamzraru'-ti," 232.

26. Cushing, *Zuñi Folk Tales,* 90–91.

27. Voth, *Traditions of Hopi,* 6.

28. Cushing, *Zuñi Breadstuff,* 163, 634.

29. Voth, *Oraibi Soyal,* 28n.

30. Stephen, *loc. cit.,* 782.

31. Voth, *Brief Miscellaneous Hopi Papers,* Vol. 4, 126.

32. Voth, *Oraibi Powamu,* 78, 78n, 80.

33. Bunzel, "Zuñi Katcinas," 1016.

34. White, *Santo Domingo,* 204.

35. Parsons, "Isleta," 393.

36. Parsons, *Tewa Tales,* 160.

CHAPTER 8

1. Parsons, *Taos Tales,* 5.

2. *Ibid.,* 86.

3. Voth, *Traditions of Hopi,* 13.

4. Parsons, *Scalp Ceremonial of Zuñi,* 36.

5. Stephen, *Hopi Journal,* 307n. Also 470 where Duck kachina sings to Nighthawk.

6. Cushing, *Zuñi Breadstuff,* 161.

7. Fisher, "Birds of Keams Canyon," 35.

8. Jaeger, "Further Observations," Vol. 51, 108; see also, Marshall, *ibid.,* Vol. 57, 129ff.

9. White, *Sia,* 112.

10. Bunzel, "Zuñi Origin Myths," 576–79, 597–99. Last quotes, Parsons, "Zuñi Tales," 44–45.

11. Harrington, "Picuris Children's Stories," 299; Parsons, *Taos Pueblo,* 106.

12. Parsons, *Taos Tales,* 165–66.

13. Parsons, *Tewa Tales,* 84.

14. Benedict, *Zuñi Mythology,* Vol. 1, 99n.

15. Parsons, "Zuñi Tales," 46–47. Benedict, *loc. cit.,* Vol. 2, 221.

16. Lange, *Cochiti,* 489. On nests, Stephen, *loc. cit.,* 277.

17. Cushing, *Zuñi Folk Tales,* 203–14.

18. *Ibid.,* 269–76.

19. Eggan, *Western Pueblos,* 85.

20. Simmons, *Sun Chief,* 63–64.

21. Stephen, *loc. cit.,* 259; Parsons, *Pueblo Religion,* 774, 981.

22. Benedict, *loc. cit.,* Vol. 1, 98. Owl feather by sleepless baby, Parsons, *Pueblo Religion,* 92.

23. Benedict, *loc. cit.,* Vol. 1, 104.

24. Bunzel, *loc. cit.,* 594.

25. Stephen, *loc. cit.,* 1271. Next quote, Dorsey and Voth, *Oraibi Soyal,* 37; Stephen, *loc. cit.,* 78.

26. Roberts, *Village of Great Kivas,* 151–52, Pl. 62b.

27. Stevenson, "Zuñi," 333–39.

28. Parsons, *Pueblo Religion,* 113.

29. White, *San Felipe,* 42.

30. Bandelier, *Southwestern Journals,* 270–71. Lange, *Cochiti,* 458.

31. Dumarest, *Cochiti,* 165.

32. Parsons, "Isleta," 431.

33. Stevenson, *loc. cit.,* 394.

34. Parsons, *Pueblo Religion,* 154.

35. Wallis, "Folk Tales from Shumopovi," 28–30; for Chakwena, *Pueblo Animals and Myths,* 148ff.
36. Parsons, *Tewa Tales,* 262–66.
37. Stevenson, *loc. cit.,* 439.
38. Voth, *loc. cit.,* 235.

CHAPTER 9

1. Newman, *Zuñi Dictionary.*
2. Nequatewa, *Truth of Hopi,* 79–83. For Crow kachina, Colton, *Hopi Kachina Dolls,* 23; Fewkes, "Hopi Katcinas," 68.
3. Parsons, *Pueblo Journal,* 93; Stirling, *Origin Myth of Acoma,* 112.
4. Stevenson, "Zuñi," 135–37.
5. Bunzel, "Zuñi Katcinas," 925–28.
6. Parsons, "Isleta," 248, 284, 393.
7. Cushing, *Zuñi Breadstuff,* 47.
8. Stephen, *Hopi Journal,* 517n. Benedict, "Eight Stories from Acoma," 65.
9. Kroeber, *Zuñi Kin and Clan,* 100; Eggan, *Western Pueblos,* 200.
10. Dozier, *Hopi-Tewa,* 336.
11. Stevenson, *loc. cit.,* 40.
12. Cushing, "Zuñi Creation Myths," 385; Cushing, *loc. cit.,* 189.
13. White, *New Material from Acoma,* 145; Stirling, *loc. cit.,* 82.
14. Goldfrank, *Cochiti,* 62.
15. Wallis, "Folk Tales from Shumopovi," 12.
16. Voth, *Traditions of Hopi,* 156–57.
17. Parsons, *Pueblo Religion,* 136.
18. Bunzel, "Zuñi Origin Myths," 594.
19. Bunzel, "Zuñi Katcinas," 994.
20. Stephen, *loc. cit.,* 95.
21. Ellis, *Basic Jemez Pattern,* 25.

CHAPTER 10

1. Nequatewa, *Truth of Hopi,* 29.
2. Parsons, *Taos Tales,* 58–59.
3. White, *Santa Ana,* 81.
4. Espinosa, "Pueblo Indian Folk Tales," 86.
5. Parsons, "Pueblo Indian Folk-tales," 239.
6. Parsons, *Pueblo Indian Religion,* 92; Ladd, *Zuñi Ethno-ornithology,* 116.
7. Stevenson, "Zuñi," 335.
8. Beaglehole, *Hopi of Second Mesa,* 41–42.

9. White, *New Material from Acoma,* 134–35.

10. Stephen, *Hopi Journal,* 988.

11. Voth, *Traditions of Hopi,* 11.

12. Stephen, "Hopi Tales," 6–7; Nequatewa, *loc. cit.,* 21.

13. Wallis, "Folk Tales from Shumopovi," 3, 4. For a different account, Tyler, *Pueblo Gods and Myths,* Chapter I.

14. *Ibid.,* 7.

15. Voth, *loc. cit.,* 11.

16. Stephen, *loc. cit.,* 7.

17. Nequatewa, *loc. cit.,* 27–29.

18. Wallis, *loc. cit.,* 3–4.

19. *Ibid.,* 58.

CHAPTER 11

1. Beaglehole, *Hopi Hunting,* 16.

2. Stephen, *Hopi Journal,* 100.

3. Parsons, *Taos Tales,* 95–96.

4. Voth, *Oraibi Powamu,* 152–53.

5. Stephen, *loc. cit.,* 18.

6. Simmons, *Sun Chief,* 253.

7. Bunzel, "Zuñi Origin Myths," 555, 587.

8. Stephen, *loc. cit.,* 19.

9. Dorsey and Voth, *Oraibi Soyal,* 31.

10. Parsons, *Pueblo Religion,* 275.

11. Parsons, "Isleta," 262.

12. Lange, *Cochiti,* 308–309.

13. Stevenson, "Sia," 113–14, Pl. 28.

14. White, *Santa Ana,* 130.

15. Hargrave, "Bird Bones," 207; McGregor, *Winona,* 258.

16. Cushing, *Zuñi Breadstuff,* 45.

CHAPTER 12

1. Parsons, "Pueblo Indian Folk-tales," 239.

2. Stirling, *Origin Myth of Acoma,* 11–12.

3. Bailey, *Birds of New Mexico,* 485.

4. For New World; Hultkrantz, *Indian Orpheus Tradition,* 263ff. For Old World, Guthrie, *Orpheus and Greek Religion;* Linforth, *Arts of Orpheus.*

5. Parsons, *Taos Tales,* 20.

6. *Ibid.,* 22.

7. *Ibid.,* 26.

8. Parsons, "Isleta," 270–71.

9. Parsons, *Tewa Tales,* 14.

10. Harrington, *Ethnogeography of the Tewa,* 214.

11. Boas, *Keresan Texts,* 284.

CHAPTER 13

1. Bunzel, "Zuñi Katcinas," 990.

2. Stirling, *Origin Myth from Acoma,* 26.

3. White, *New Material from Acoma,* 47.

4. Lummis, *Pueblo Indian Folk-Stories,* 137–46; Parsons, *Pueblo Religion,* 440n.

5. Fewkes, "Hopi Katcinas," Pl. 17; Colton, *Hopi Kachina Dolls,* Kachina 74. Stephen, *Hopi Journal,* 770, Fig. 410.

6. Newman, *Zuñi Dictionary.*

7. Parsons, *Pueblo of Taos,* 102.

8. Parsons, *Pueblo Religion,* 275.

9. Benedict, "Eight Stories from Acoma," 65.

10. White, *Santa Ana,* 326.

11. Espinosa, "Pueblo Indian Folk Tales," 94–95.

12. White, *loc. cit.,* 88–89.

13. Waters, *Book of Hopi,* 137ff.

14. Stephen, *loc. cit.,* 7, 55, 64, 68, 70.

15. *Ibid.,* 237, Fig. 146; 803, Fig. 437.

16. Parsons, *Pueblo Religion,* 275.

17. Cushing, *Zuñi Folk Tales,* 55.

18. Bunzel, "Zuñi Katcinas," 1000.

19. Ladd, *Zuñi Ethno-ornithology,* 109; Cushing, *Zuñi Breadstuff,* 161.

20. Parsons, *Social Organization of Tewa,* 244.

21. Stevenson, "Zuñi," 584.

22. Bunzel, *Zuñi Texts,* 133.

23. Parsons, *Scalp Ceremonial of Zuñi,* 29, 38.

24. Stevenson, *loc. cit.,* 590.

25. Parsons, *Social Organization of Tewa,* 237.

26. Dumarest, *Notes on Cochiti,* 167, Fig. 18.

27. Lange, *Cochiti,* 416.

28. Parsons, *Social Organization of Tewa,* 253.

29. Stevenson, *loc. cit.,* 562.

30. Stephen, *loc. cit.,* 950.

CHAPTER 14

1. Parsons, *Pueblo Religion,* 241.
2. Harrington, "Picuris Children's Stories," 331.
3. Ladd, *Zuñi Ethno-ornithology,* 84.
4. Lange, *Cochiti,* 476.
5. White, *Santa Ana,* 185.
6. Voth, *Oraibi Oa'qol,* 44.
7. Boas, *Keresan Texts,* 74–76.
8. *Ibid.,* 12–13.

BIBLIOGRAPHY

SECTION 1. WORKS ON BIRDS, THEIR BONES, AND WILDLIFE

Bailey, Florence Merriam. *Among the Birds in the Grand Canyon Country.* Washington D. C., U.S. Department of the Interior, 1939.

———. *The Birds of New Mexico.* Santa Fe, New Mexico Department of Game and Fish, 1928.

Beadle, J. *The Undeveloped West.* Philadelphia, National Publishing Company, 1873.

Bent, A. C. *Life Histories of North American Flycatchers, Larks, Swallows, and Their Allies,* New York, Dover, 1963.

Buechner, H. *Life History, Ecology, and Range Use of the Pronghorn Antelope in Trans-Pecos Texas.* South Bend, University of Notre Dame, 1950.

Eaton, Theodore H., Jr., and G. Smith, *Birds of the Navajo Country.* Berkeley, National Youth Administration, 1937.

Fisher, A. K. "A Partial List of the Birds of Keam Canyon, Arizona," *The Condor,* Vol. 5, No. 2 (1903), 33–36.

Hargrave, L. L. "Bird Bones from Abandoned Indian Dwellings in Arizona and Utah," *The Condor,* Vol. 41 (1939), 206–10.

———. *Mexican Macaws, Comparative Osteology and Survey of Remains From the Southwest.* Anthropological Papers of the University of Arizona, No. 20. Tucson, 1970.

Jaeger, Edmund. "Further Observations on the Hibernation of the Poorwill," *The Condor,* Vol. 51 (1949), 105–109.

Jenks, Randolf. *Ornithology of the Life Zones, Summit of San Francisco Mountains to Bottom of Grand Canyon.* Flagstaff, U.S. Department of the Interior, Technical Bulletin No. 5, 1932.

Lange, C. H. "Notes on the Use of Turkeys by Pueblo Indians," *El Palacio,* Vol. 57 (1950), 204–209.

Ligon, J. Stokeley. *History and Management of Merriam's Wild Turkey.* Santa Fe, New Mexico Department of Game and Fish, 1946.

————. *New Mexico Birds and Where to Find Them.* Albuquerque, University of New Mexico Press, 1961.

————. *Wildlife of New Mexico, Its Conservation and Management.* Santa Fe, New Mexico Departmet of Game and Fish, 1927.

Monson, G., and A. R. Phillips. *A Checklist of the Birds of Arizona.* Tucson, University of Arizona Press, 1964.

Parmalee, P. W. "Additional Noteworthy Records of Birds from Archaeological Sites," *The Wilson Bulletin,* Vol. 79, No. 2 (1967), 155–62.

Phillips, A. R., J. Marshall, and G. Monson. *The Birds of Arizona.* Tucson, University of Arizona Press, 1964.

Reed, Eric K. "Turkeys in Southwestern Archaeology," *El Palacio,* Vol. 58 (1951), 195–205.

Robbins, W. W., J. P. Harrington, and Barbara Freire-Marreco. *Ethnobotany of the Tewa Indians.* Bureau of American Ethnology, Bulletin No. 56. Washington, D.C., 1916.

Schorger, A. W. *The Wild Turkey, Its History and Domestication.* Norman, University of Oklahoma Press, 1966.

Schroeder, A. H. "Birds and Feathers in Documents Relating to Indians of the Southwest," Collected Papers in Honor of Lyndon Lane Hargrave. Papers of the Archaeological Society of New Mexico, Vol. 1, Santa Fe, 1968.

Stevenson, M. C. "Ethnobotany of the Zuñi Indians," *Thirtieth Annual Report.* Washington, D.C., Bureau of American Ethnology, 1915.

Voth, H. R. "Notes on the Eagle Cult of the Hopi," in *Brief Miscellaneous Hopi Papers.* Field Museum of Natural History, Publication 157, Chicago, 1912.

Wetmore, A. "Additional Records of Birds from Cavern Deposits in New Mexico," *The Condor,* Vol. 34 (1932), 141–42.

Wheeler Survey. "Explorations and Surveys West of the One Hundredth Meridian." In Vol. V., *Zoology.* Washington, D.C., 1875.

White, Leslie. "Notes on the Ethnozoology of the Keresan Pueblo Indians." Papers of the Michigan Academy of Sciences, Arts, and Letters, Vol. 31 (1945), 223–43.

Whiting, A. F. *Ethnology of the Hopi.* Flagstaff, Museum of Northern Arizona, Bulletin No. 15, 1950.

Woodbury, A. M., and H. M. Russell, Jr. *Birds of the Navajo Country.* Bulletin of the University of Utah, Biological Series, Vol. 9, No. 1. Salt Lake City, 1945.

SECTION 2. SOURCES FOR PUEBLO NAMES OF BIRDS

(Those who wish to study Pueblo birds further will find native names for many birds in the works listed below.)

Boas, Franz. *Keresan Texts.* Publications of the American Ethnological Society, Vol. 8, New York, 1928.

Bunzel, Ruth. *Zuñi Texts.* Publications of the American Ethnological Society, Vol. 15, New York, 1933.

Fisher, A. K. "Partial List of the Birds of Keams Canyon, Arizona," *The Condor,* Vol. 5, No. 2 (1903), 33–36.

Harrington, J. P. "An Introductory Paper on the Tiwa Language, Dialect of Taos, New Mexico," *American Anthropologist,* n.s., Vol. 12 (1910), 11–48.

————, and H. H. Roberts, "Picuris Children's Stories," *Forty-third Annual Report.* Washington, D.C., Bureau of American Ethnology, 1928, 289–447.

Henderson, J., and J. P. Harrington. *Ethnology of the Tewa Indians.* Washington, D.C., Bureau of American Ethnology, Bulletin No. 56, 1914.

Hodge, F. W. "Pueblo Indian Clans," *American Anthropologist,* Vol. 9 (1896), 133–36.

Ladd, Edmund J. *Zuñi Ethno-ornithology*. Unpublished thesis, University of New Mexico, 1963.

Mearns, Edgar A. "Ornithological Vocabulary of the Moki Indians," *American Anthropologist,* Vol. 9, No. 12 (1896).

Newman, Stanley. *Zuñi Dictionary*. Indiana University Research Center in Anthropology, Folklore, and Linguistics, Publication No. 6, Bloomington, 1958.

Parsons, E. C. See Section 3.

Stephen, A. M. *Hopi Journal*. See especially Glossary, check English bird names in index; a few in "Hopi Tales."

Stevenson, M. C. "The Sia." See Section 3.

⸻. "The Zuñi Indians." See Section 3.

Trager, George L. "An Outline of Taos Grammar." In H. Hoijer, *Linguistic Structures of Native America*. New York, Viking Fund Publications in Anthropology, No. 6, 1946, 184–221.

White, Leslie. See Sections 1 and 3.

SECTION 3. WORKS ON ANTHROPOLOGY, MYTHOLOGY, AND ARCHAEOLOGY

Anonymous. *Hopi Hearings*. Hopi Agency, Keams Canyon, Arizona, U.S. Department of the Interior, Bureau of Indian Affairs, 1955.

Bandelier, Adolf F. *The Southwestern Journals of Adolph F. Bandelier, 1880–1882*. Ed. by C. H. Lange, and C. L. Riley. Albuquerque, Univerity of New Mexico Press, 1966.

Beaglehole, E. *Hopi Hunting and Hunting Ritual*. Yale University Publications in Anthropology, No. 4. New Haven, 1936.

⸻. *Notes on Hopi Economic Life*. Yale University Publications in Anthropology, No. 15. New Haven, 1937.

⸻, and Pearl Beaglehole. *Hopi of the Second Mesa*. Memoirs of the American Anthropological Association, No. 44. Menasha, 1935.

Benedict, Ruth. "Eight Stories from Acoma." *Journal of American Folk-Lore,* Vol. 43, 59–88. New York, American Folk-Lore Society, 1930.

_____. *Tales of the Cochiti Indians.* Bureau of American Ethnology, Bulletin No. 98. Washington, D.C., 1931.

_____. *Zuñi Mythology.* 2 vols. *Columbia University Contributions to Anthropology,* Vol. 21. New York, Columbia University Press, 1935.

Boas, Franz. *Keresan Texts.* Publications of the American Ethnological Society, Vol. 8, Parts 1 and 2. New York, 1928.

Bourke, John. *The Snake Dance of the Moquis of Arizona.* New York, Scribners, 1884.

Bunzel, Ruth. "Zuñi Katcinas," *Forty-seventh Annual Report.* Washington, D.C., Bureau of American Ethnology, 1932.

_____. "Zuñi Origin Myths," *Forty-seventh Annual Report, 1920–30.* Washington, D.C., Bureau of American Ethnology, 1932.

_____. "Zuñi Ritual Poetry," *Forty-seventh Annual Report.* Washington, D.C., Bureau of American Ethnology, 1932.

Colton, Harold. *Hopi Kachina Dolls.* Albuquerque, University of New Mexico Press, 1949.

Cushing, Frank Hamilton. "Origin Myth from Oraibi," *Journal of American Folk-Lore,* Vol. 36. Lancaster and New York, American Folk-Lore Society, 1923.

_____. "Outlines of Zuñi Creation Myths," *Thirteenth Annual Report, 1891–92.* Washington, D.C., Bureau of American Ethnology, 1896.

_____. *Zuñi Breadstuff.* Indian Notes and Monographs, Vol. 8. New York, Museum of the American Indian, Heye Foundation, 1920.

_____. *Zuñi Fetishes.* Flagstaff, Ariz., K C Publications, 1966 (facsimile edition). (Original edition, 1880).

_____. *Zuñi Folk Tales.* New York, Putnam, 1901.

Dorsey, George A., and H. R. Voth. *The Oraibi Soyal Ceremony.* Field Columbian Museum, Publication 55, Anthropological Series, Vol. 3, No. 1. Chicago, 1901.

Dozier, Edward. *The Hopi-Tewa of Arizona.* University of California Publications in American Archaeology and Ethnology, Vol. 44, No. 3. Berkeley, University of California Press, 1954.

Dumarest, Noel. *Notes on Cochiti, New Mexico.* American Anthropological Association Memoirs, Vol. VI, No. 3. Lancaster, 1919.

Durkheim, E., and M. Mauss. *Primitive Classification.* Chicago, University of Chicago Press, 1963.

Eggan, Fred. *Social Organization of the Western Pueblos.* Chicago, University of Chicago Press, 1950.

Ellis, Florence Hawley. *A Reconstruction of the Basic Jemez Pattern of Social Organization, with Comparisons to other Tanoan Social Structures.* University of New Mexico Publications in Anthropology, No. 11. Albuquerque, 1964.

————. "Patterns of Aggressions and the War Cult in Southwestern Pubelos." *Southwestern Journal of Anthropology,* Vol. 7, No. 2, 177–201. Albuquerque, 1951.

Espinosa, Aurelio. "Pueblo Indian Folk Tales," *Journal of American Folk-Lore,* Vol. 49, 69–133. New York, American Folk-Lore Society, 1936.

Fewkes, J. W. "Hopi Katcinas, Drawn by Native Artists," *Twenty-first Annual Report, 1899–1900.* Washington, D.C., Bureau of American Ethnology, 1903.

————, and A. M. Stephen. "The Mamzrau'-ti: A Tusayan Ceremony," *American Anthropologist,* o.s. 5 (1892), 217–45.

Goldfrank, Esther Schiff. *The Social and Ceremonial Organization of Cochiti.* American Anthropological Memoirs, No. 33. Menasha, 1927.

Gunn, John M. *Schat-Chen, History Traditions and Narratives of the Queres Indians of Laguna and Acoma.* Albuquerque, Albright and Anderson, 1917.

Guthrie, W. K. C. *Orpheus and Greek Religion.* London, Methuen, 1952.

Harrington, J. P. "The Ethnogeography of the Tewa Indians," *Twenty-ninth Annual Report, 1907–1908.* Washington, D.C., Bureau of American Ethnology, 1916.

————, and H. H. Roberts, "Picuris Children's Stories with Texts and Songs." *Forty-third Annual Report, 1925–1926.* Washington, D.C., Bureau of American Ethnology, 1928.

Hermequaftewa, Andrew. *The Hopi Way of Life Is the Way of Peace.* Taped by Thomas Noble. Printed, n.p. and n.d.

Hester, J.J. *Early Navajo Migrations and Acculturation in the Southwest.* Museum of New Mexico Papers in Anthropology, No. 6. Santa Fe, 1962.

Hultkrantz, Ake. *The North American Indian Orpheus Tradition.* Ethnological Museum of Sweden Monograph Series, No. 2. Stockholm, 1957.

Judd, Neil. *The Material Culture of Pueblo Bonito.* Smithsonian Miscellaneous Collections, Vol. 124. Washington, D.C., The Smithsonian Institution, 1954.

Kroeber, A. L. *Zuñi Kin and Clan.* Anthropological Papers of the American Museum of Natural History, Vol. 18, Part 2. New York, 1917.

Lange, Charles. *Cochiti, a New Mexico Pueblo, Past and Present.* Austin, University of Texas Press, 1959.

Linforth, I. M. *The Arts of Orpheus.* Berkeley, University of California Press, 1941.

Lowie, R. H. *Notes on Hopi Clans.* Anthropological Papers of the American Museum of Natural History, Vol. 30, Part 6. New York, 1929.

Lummis, Charlies. *Pueblo Indian Folk-Stories.* New York, Century, 1920.

McGregor, John. *Winona and Ridge Ruin.* Museum of Northern Arizona, Bulletin No. 18. Flagstaff, 1941.

Mera, H. P. *The "Rain Bird," a Study in Pueblo Design.* Laboratory of Anthropology Memoirs, Vol. 2. Santa Fe, 1937.

Nequatewa, Edmund. *Truth of a Hopi and Other Clan Stories of Shungopovi.* Museum of Northern Arizona, Bulletin No. 8. Flagstaff, 1947.

Ortiz, Alphonso. *The Tewa World.* Chicago, University of Chicago Press, 1971.

Parsons, E. C. *A Pueblo Indian Journal, 1920–21.* American Anthropological Association Memoirs, Vol. 32. Menasha, 1925.

————. "Isleta, New Mexico," *Forty-seventh Annual Report, 1929–30.* Washington, D.C., Bureau of American Ethnology, 1932.

_____. *Notes on Zuñi.* American Anthropological Association Memoirs, Vol. 4, No. 3, Part 1; No. 4, Part 2. Lancaster, 1917.

_____. "Pueblo Indian Folk-tales, Probably of Spanish Provenience," *Journal of American Folk-Lore,* Vol. 31, 216–56. Lancaster, 1918.

_____. *Pueblo Indian Religion.* 2 vols. Chicago, University of Chicago Press, 1939.

_____. *The Scalp Ceremonial of Zuñi.* American Anthropological Association Memoirs, Vol. 21. Menasha, 1924.

_____. *The Social Organization of the Tewa of New Mexico.* American Anthropological Association Memoirs, Vol. 36. Menasha, 1929.

_____. *Taos Pueblo.* General Studies in Anthropology, No. 2. Menasha, Banta, 1936.

_____. *Taos Tales.* American Folk-Lore Society Memoirs, Vol. 34. New York, 1940.

_____. *Tewa Tales.* American Folk-Lore Society Memoirs, Vol. 19. New York, 1926.

_____. "Zuñi Names and Naming Practices," *Journal of American Folk Lore,* Vol. 36, 171–76. New York, American Folk-Lore Society, 1923.

_____. Zuñi Tales," *Journal of American Folk-Lore,* Vol. 63, 1–58. New York, American Folk-Lore Society, 1930.

Pepper, George. *Pueblo Bonito.* Anthropological Papers of the American Museum of Natural History, Vol. 27. New York, 1920.

Roberts, Frank. *The Village of the Great Kivas on the Zuñi Reservation, New Mexico.* Bureau of American Ethnology Bulletin, No. 111. Washington, D.C., 1932.

Roediger, Virginia. *Ceremonial Costumes of the Pueblo Indians.* Berkeley, University of California Press, 1961.

Sebag, Lucien. "La Geste de Kasewat," *L'Homme,* Vol. 3, No. 2 (1963), 22–76.

_____. *L'invention du monde chez les indiens pueblos.* Paris, Francois Maspero, 1971.

_____. *Marxisme et Structuralisme.* Paris, Payot, 1964, 166ff.

Simmons, L. W. (ed.). *Sun Chief, The Autobiography of a Hopi Indian.* New Haven, Yale University Press, 1950.

Smith, Watson. *Kiva Mural Decorations at Awatovi and Kawaika-á.* Papers of the Peabody Museum of American Archaeology and Ethnology, Vol. 37. Cambridge, Mass., 1952.

Stephen, A. N. *Hopi Journal.* Ed. by E. C. Parsons. 2 vols. Columbia University Contributions to Anthropology, Vol. 23. New York, Columbia University Press, 1936.

————. "Hopi Tales," *Journal of American Folk-Lore,* Vol. 42, 1–72. New York, American Folk-Lore Society, 1929.

Stevenson, M. C. "The Sia." *Eleventh Annual Report, 1889–90.* Washington, D.C., Bureau of American Ethnology, 1894.

————. "The Zuñi Indians," *Twenty-third Annual Report 1901–1902.* Washington, D.C., Bureau of American Ethnology, 1904.

Stirling, Matthew. *Origin Myth of Acoma and Other Records.* Bureau of American Ethnology, Bulletin No. 135, Washington, D.C., 1942.

Titiev, Mischa. *Old Oraibi, A Study of the Hopi Indians of Third Mesa.* Papers of the Peabody Museum of American Archaeology and Ethnology, Vol. 22, No. 1. Cambridge, Mass., 1944.

Tyler, Hamilton A. *Pueblo Gods and Myths.* Norman, University of Oklahoma Press, 1964.

————. *Pueblo Animals and Myths.* Norman, University of Oklahoma Press, 1975.

Vivian, G., and T. W. Mathews. *Kin Kletso, a Pueblo III Community in Chaco Canyon, New Mexico.* Southwestern Monuments Association Technical Series, Vol. 6, Part 1. Globe, Ariz., 1965.

Voth, H. R. *Brief Miscellaneous Hopi Papers.* Field Museum of Natural History, Publication 157, Anthropological Series, Vol. 11, No. 2. Chicago, 1912.

————. *The Oraibi Marau Ceremony.* Field Museum of Natural History, Publication 156, Anthropological Series, Vol. 11, No. 1. Chicago, 1912.

————. *The Oraibi Oa'qol Ceremony.* Field Museum of Natural History, Publication 84, Anthropological Series, Vol. 6, No. 1, Chicago, 1903.

————. *The Oraibi Powamu Ceremony.* Field Museum of Natural History, Publication 61, Anthropological Series, Vol. 2, No. 2. Chicago, 1901.

————. *The Traditions of the Hopi.* Field Museum of Natural History, Publication 96, Anthropological Series, Vol. 8. Chicago, 1905.

Wallis, W. D. "Folk Tales from Shumopovi, Second Mesa," *Journal of American Folk-Lore,* Vol. 49, No. 191–92, 1–68. Lancaster, American Folk-Lore Society, 1936.

Waters, Frank. *Book of the Hopi.* New York, Viking, 1963.

White, Leslie. *New Material from Acoma.* Bureau of American Ethnology, Bulletin No. 136. Washington, D.C., 1943.

————. "The Acoma Indians." *Forty-seventh Annual Report, 1929–1930.* Washington, D.C., Bureau of American Ethnology, 1932.

————. *The Pueblo of Santa Ana, New Mexico.* American Anthropological Association Memoirs, Vol. 60. Menasha, 1942.

————. *The Pueblo of Santo Domingo, New Mexico.* American Anthropological Association Memoirs, Vol. 43, Menasha, 1935.

————. *The Pueblo of San Felipe.* American Anthropological Association Memoirs, Vol. 38. Menasha, 1932.

————. *The Pueblo of Sia, New Mexico.* Bureau of American Ethnology, Bulletin No. 184. Washington, D.C., 1962.

Winship, George Parker. "The Coronado Expedition, 1540–1542." *Fourteenth Annual Report, 1892–1893.* Washington, D.C., Bureau of American Ethnology, 1896.

Wormington, H. M. *Prehistoric Indians of the Southwest.* Denver, Denver Museum of Natural History, 1951.

INDEX

Acoma: 25, 28, 47, 57, 58, 60, 61, 68, 88, 96, 114, 122, 137, 164, 175, 177, 178, 179, 201, 211, 214

Alosaka (holder of seeds): 98

Altar(s): 1, 36, 68, 148, 207; Flute, 212

A'neglakya (Jimson Weed Youth): 93

Arrows: fletching, 42, 57, 226; of lightning, 68, 70

Arrow Youth: 228

A'wonawil'ona (Zuñi high god): 6

Balance: birds of, 173–82

Battle of the Seasons: 34, 50, 87, 96, 133, 136, 178, 206

Bear: 39, 58, 67, 84, 122, 216

Beast gods: 11, 39, 58, 66, 122

Big House (Taos home of dead): 204

Birds, by name:

    American Coot: 131

    American Kestrel (Sparrow Hawk): 193, 198–200

    American Robin: Table 2

    Bald Eagle: 40, 41, 42, 43, 44, 51, 53; same ritual value as Golden, 43

    Band-tailed Pigeon: 105

    Bank Swallow: 93, 97

    Barn Swallow: 93, 96

    Bitterns: 113

    Black-billed Magpie: Table 1, 28, 186, 201–208; for East, 9

    Blackbird: Table 1, 146

Black-headed Grosbeak: 150

Bluebird: Table 2, 55, 133, 138, 140–45, 150

Blue Grouse: 71

Broad-tailed Hummingbird: 99

Brown-headed Cowbird: 145

Burrowing Owl: 157, 160–64

Canada Goose: 114

Canyon Wren: 211–13

Cardinal: Table 2, 156

Cinnamon Teal: 119

Cliff Swallow: 93, 95, 98, 160

Common Black Hawk: 40

Common Crow: Table 1, 11, 106, 173–82, 214

Common Flicker (Red-shafted): Table 1, 168, 213, 215, 216

Common Loon: 113

Common Nighthawk: 153–55

Common Raven: 11, 173–82

Common Snipe: 113, 123ff.

Common Yellowthroat: 149

Cooper's Hawk: 108, 119, 194, 195, 196, 198

Downy Woodpecker: 214

Ducks: 6, 113, 114–22

Eagles: Table 1, Table 2, 3, 6, 11, 39, 118, 147, 160, 182, 188; hunt with bow and arrows, 42, 194; number of captive, 46; houses, 48; and war, 64ff.; monsters, 67ff.

Flycatchers: Table 1, 133, 149; Empidonax, 149

Drums and drumming: 10; and war, 213ff.; and pottery, 221
Dusk: birds of, 153–72
Eagle Boy: 195
Eagle dance: 60ff.
Eagle Man (Hunt chief): 57–58
Earth: birds of, 71–89
Echo: Boy, 184; myth of, 179–80; effect, 212
Emergence: Shrike found exit, 188
Evening Star: 70, 167
Exorcism: 40, 225

Feathers: as signs, 1; in dance, 20; trade in, 21; kinds named, 44; carry message, 83; Owl for sleep, 160; offerings, 45; blown through tube, 150
Fertility: stick, 36; human, 38–39, 142; and lightning, 39–40; and crops, 165; and clowns, 200
Fetishes: 4ff., Table 1, 13, 14, 23, 52, 131; jar for, 169
Fire-Brand Youth: 130
Flint Wing (or Bird): 39, 68ff., 137, 138
Flute players: 17

Germinator: see Muyingwu
Ghosts: 209, 217, 222
Guardians and leaders: 88, 114, 117, 126, 129, 132

Hard Beings Woman (Huruing Wuhti): creates birds, 147
Hawk Man (Kwa'chakwa): 198
Hawk Youth and Maid: 195, 196, 198
Heluta: 102
Horned Water Serpent: 10, 20, 123
Horticulture: bird of, 201–208
Hunt chief: 58, 84; Wildcat Man, 84
Hunting: birds of, 193–200, eagle, 45, 48; bird, 69; and owl, 172; and Shrike, 191–92; and hawks, 193

Ianyi: 122, 227
Iarriko (fetish): 4, Table 1, 31, 222

Infidelity: 23ff.
Insanity: and Rock Wren, 212–13
Isleta: 60, 89, 142, 169; corn groups of, 205–206
Iyatiku (Keresan Corn-Mother): 4, 52, 58, 122, 211

Jemez: 28, 47, 49, 52, 65, 86, 171, 182

Kachina: masks, 1, 37, 43, 158, 175; manas (maids), 20, 136; dances, 34; Crows and Ravens relate to, 173; control weather, 175; whipping, 175, 217–18
Kachinas, by name: Ahul, 37; Ahulani, 20, 37; Anya, 21; Buzzard (Ma'sha-wa), 226; Crow (Tumas), 175; Eagle, 118; Hemis, 136, Hilili, 63, 118; Hotsko (Screech Owl), 166; Killdeer, 126; Kwa'hu (Eagle), 62; Mashanta (Flower), 30; Mongwa (Horned Owl), 166; Owl (at Cochiti), 161; Parrot, 16; Pawik (duck), 119; Qoqlo, 136; Rain Bird, 129; Salab Mongwa, 166; Salimobia, 117, 210; Seeds, 129; Shko'o'ko (Cochiti Owl), 161; Shumaakoli, 86; Soyal Manas, 20; Tsitoto (Flower), 30–31; Tunwap, 175; Turposkwa (Canyon Wren), 212; Upik'aiapona, 150; Wai'yosh (duck), 120
Kasewat: 68ff., 137–38
Keeper of Game: 56, 102, 176
Keresan pole (Kastotsho'ma): 13, 27, 37; meaning of, 28
Kiaklo (Myth bearer): 116–117
Kisa, or Kih'sha (Hawk deity): 57, 192, 194ff.
Knife Wing: 39, 65, 66ff.
Kopishtaiya (Keresan spirits): 26, 100
Ku'pishtaya (lightning makers): 67

Laguna: 25, 114, 129, 130, 180, 204, 228
Lake: Salt, 25; of the Dead, 114–116; Blue, 204
Lightning: 39, 65, 121, 122; sticks, 29; weapon of War Twins, 68; ruler of Beast gods, 84; makers, 94; games to make, 164

Magical power: of birds, 2; of song, 48;

in war, 65–66; in hunt, 194; of wren, 211; of Roadrunner, 222

Magpie-tail Youth: 203ff.

Masau'u (Skeleton Man): 144, 156; call of, 162; patron of fire, 162, 188, 189

Middle Place: 32, 113, 117

Migrations: 178

Mi'li (fetish): 4, 6, Table 1, 32, 52, 109

Miochin (spirit of summer): 96

Mockingbird Youth: 185

Moon: birds of, 153–72

Morning Star: 50, 106

Mother of game: 6, 80, 143

Mountain Lion: 9, 39, 67, 174, 193, 216

Muyingwu, or Muingwu (Germinator): 20, 28, 36, 37, 175, 187; and Snipe, 124

Native Cotton: 4, 53, 120, 148

Night: birds of, 153–72

Oak Man (Medicine chief): 58, 122

Old Oraibi: 20, 35, 46, 104, 181

Olivella Flower: 84; as Summer chief, 24ff.

One Horned god (Shotoknungwa): 124

Origin myth: 68

Owl Boy: 167, 170

Oxuwah: 24, 122, 129

Paiyatemu: 28, 107, 122, 131, 142

Pautiwa (Chief of Council of gods): 117, 131, 167, 176, 182

Pekwin (Sun watcher): 94, 178

Picuris: 47, 105, 106, 127, 158, 226

Poker Boy: 17ff.

Pollen: 146, 149, 150, 229

Prayer feathers: 46; number of birds used, 2

Prayer-sticks: 1, 2ff; types, 3; and turkey feathers, 76; clothes of, 78–79; for stillborn, 103; dove feathers not used, 109; for gods, 229

Puberty: and bluebirds, 141, 142–44

Puga Old Man: 128

Purification: 101; bird of, 225–29

Racing: birds of, 193–200; kick-stick, 102–103, 164–65, 195; for Sun, 196; for rain, 197, 224

Rain: birds of, 91–112

Rainbow: 13, 18, 27, 29, 104, 118

Rain deity (Pavayoykashi): 16, 17

Rain priests: 30, 59, 65, 88, 94, 115; and swallows, 92; and hummingbird, 99; and bluebird, 142; wear magpie feathers as badge, 207

Red Bear (Taos war god): 65, 214

Ritual: pilgrimage, 25; sprinkling, 59, 108; whipping, 60, 166, 217–18; smoking, 99; tobacco, 98, 99, 100, 101–102, 229

Salt: 13, 176, 196–97; expeditions for rain, 25ff.

Salt Woman: 25, 26, 204

Sand Altar Woman (Tuwabontumsi): 188

San Felipe: 83, 107, 124, 168

San Juan: 23, 107, 124, 152, 206, 207, 223

Santa Ana: 27, 52, 75, 107, 121, 137, 185, 200, 214, 215

Santo Domingo: 15, 27, 151

Seeds: 37, 98, 105, 110; gathering, 112; and ducks, 116, 118

Serpent, or snake: 39, 53, 63, 69, 118, 216, 222

Shakak (spirit of winter): 50, 68, 96

Shipap (entrance to Underworld): 101, 102, 109

Shipapolima (home of Beast gods): 221

Shiwanna (Keres rain makers): 50, 136, 151

Shi'wanni (Zuñi Rain priests): 93, 108; defined, 94

Shock-of-Hair Youth: 138

Sia: 23, 52, 68, 101, 124, 126, 151, 200, 224

Sickness: caused by witches, 168, 169; by animals, 170; crow and, 181

Six-Point-Cloud-People: 46, 49

Sky: birds of, 39–70

Snow and ice: 2, 60; bluebird for, 141

Societies: Ant, 221; Antelope, 110; Arrow, 65; Eagle, 65, 122; Eagle Down, 58–59, 61; Fire (at Acoma), 122; Flute, 207; Galaxy, 130; Giant Medicine, 226; Horn, 188; Jemez Eagle Catchers, 47; La'lakontu, 109; Little Fire, 6, 224;